Troubleshooting

Microsoft

Access 2002

 Microsoft Office XP Application

Virginia Andersen and John Pierce

PUBLISHED BY
Microsoft Press
A Division of Microsoft Corporation
One Microsoft Way
Redmond, Washington 98052-6399

Library of Congress Cataloging-in-Publication Data
Andersen, Virginia.
    Troubleshooting Microsoft Access Version 2002 / Virginia Andersen, John Pierce.
        p. cm.
    Includes index.
    ISBN 0-7356-1488-1
    1. Microsoft Access. 2. Database management. I. Pierce, John, 1954- II. Title.

  QA76.9.D3 A6353 2002
  005.75'65--dc21   2001059078

Printed and bound in the United States of America.

1 2 3 4 5 6 7 8 9   QWT   7 6 5 4 3 2

Distributed in Canada by Penguin Books Canada Limited.

A CIP catalogue record for this book is available from the British Library.

Microsoft Press books are available through booksellers and distributors worldwide. For further informa-
tion about international editions, contact your local Microsoft Corporation office or contact Microsoft
Press International directly at fax (425) 936-7329. Visit our Web site at www.microsoft.com/mspress.
Send comments to *mspinput@microsoft.com*.

Acquisitions Editor: Alex Blanton
Project Editor: Judith Bloch

Body Part No. X08-41920

Acknowledgments

It was quite an exciting endeavor to write the first version of this book for the new *Troubleshooting* series. This revision, *Troubleshooting Microsoft Access 2002*, was still a challenge but was made much easier by my friend, John Pierce, who stepped forward to take on the duties of coauthor. I very much appreciate his time, efforts, and insight into the troubleshooting genre. Many thanks also to Acquisitions Editor Alex Blanton and Project Editor Judith Bloch of Microsoft Press, and to the editorial staff at nSight.

Matt Wagner of Waterside Productions deserves a special "thank you" for connecting me to Microsoft Press and making it possible for me to work on these innovative products.

Finally, my patient husband, Jack, and all the cats deserve thanks for putting up with me for all these months. At least sitting in front of a computer for hours each day provided a lap for the cats, and they were never reluctant to take purring advantage.

Virginia Andersen

I'd like to thank Alex Blanton and Lucinda Rowley for letting me get my feet wet as an author. Special thanks to Virginia Andersen for setting a good example as an author and for her good humor and her love of cats and roses. Thanks also to Judith Bloch and the editorial team at nSight for their work producing this book.

John Pierce

Quick contents

Contents

Contents

Contents

Contents

About this book

Troubleshooting Microsoft Access 2002 is designed to help you avoid spending lots of time sifting through information, trying to locate the answer to a problem you've run up against. This book's design presents a fresh way to diagnose and solve problems you might have encountered with a database or some of its tables, forms, reports, or other elements. Even if you know only the basics of how Access stores, analyzes, and presents your data, you'll find it easy to locate solutions and fix problems.

We've written this book with two goals in mind: ease and simplicity. If a creative form that you designed isn't displaying any data, you'll quickly be able to figure out whether the form shows no data because there's a problem with the way you designed it or because there just isn't any data to show.

This book helps you to identify your problem, describes what might be causing the problem, and then leads you through the solution step-by-step so that you can get back to the main work at hand.

How to use this book

We didn't intend for you to read this book from cover to cover; instead, we think you'll refer to it when you run up against a problem.

It's designed so that you can jump in, quickly diagnose your problem, and then get the information you need to fix that problem—whether you've just begun to learn about databases and database management programs or whether you are knowledgeable enough to get right to the source of the problem. The problems you're most likely to experience are grouped into chapters that are listed alphabetically; the chapter titles are kept simple so you know at a glance what kinds of topics each chapter covers. Each chapter is broken into two specific elements: the flowchart and the solutions.

Flowcharts

The first thing you'll see when you go to a chapter is a dynamic, easy-to-follow flowchart. The flowchart starts by asking you a broad question, and then it leads you through simple yes-or-no questions to help you pinpoint your problem. If the solution to your problem involves just a handful of steps, you'll be given a quick fix right on the flowchart without turning another page. Your problem will be solved and you'll be right back to work.

If your problem requires a little more explanation and a few more steps, you'll reach a statement of the problem along with the page number on which you can find the solution. And if your problem isn't shown on the flowchart, you'll find a list of related chapters in which your problem might be addressed.

Solution spreads

After the flowchart helps you find the right page, you'll turn to a solution spread. This is where the real troubleshooting takes place. At the top of the solution you'll find the "Source of the problem" section that contains information describing what probably caused the problem. The "How to fix it" section contains clear step-by-step instructions showing how to correct the problem. Each solution contains plenty of illustrations that show you what you should be seeing as you move through the steps. Although each solution is designed to minimize your reading and get you back to work quickly, you will also find some tips and sidebars that contain related material you might find interesting and helpful.

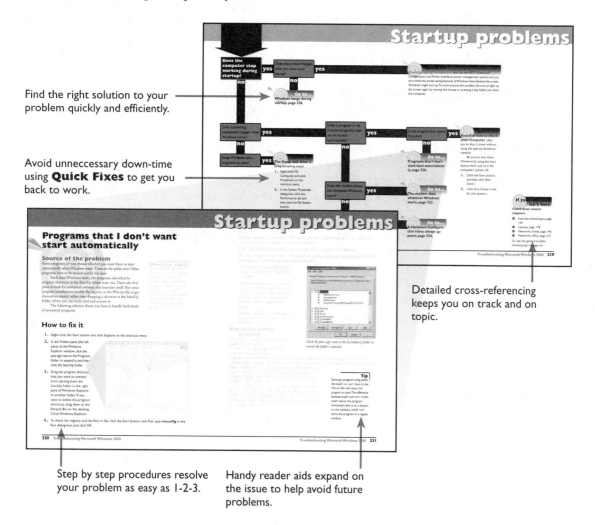

Find the right solution to your problem quickly and efficiently.

Avoid unnecessary down-time using **Quick Fixes** to get you back to work.

Detailed cross-referencing keeps you on track and on topic.

Step by step procedures resolve your problem as easy as 1-2-3.

Handy reader aids expand on the issue to help avoid future problems.

Troubleshooting tips

To troubleshoot, as defined by the *Microsoft Computer Dictionary*, is to "isolate the source of a problem in a program, computer system, or network and remedy it." But how do you go about isolating the source of the problem in the first place? The source often isn't readily apparent; it might be a symptom masquerading as the source, or it might reveal itself to be something other than what you initially thought.

How to troubleshoot

The easiest way to isolate a problem is to stand back and take a look at what you're trying to do at the moment. (I'm trying to extract data from a table with a query, for example, or I'm trying to design a report that will display subtotals.) After you identify the task you're trying to accomplish, narrow the scope of the problem. (I can't enter the right criteria in the query design grid; I can't get the calculation to work.) Write down a description of what you tried to do, how you went about it, and what happened, specifically. For example, you heard a beep, you saw an error message, or you just got the wrong results. If necessary, reconstruct the steps you took that caused the problem in the first place.

Once you understand the problem you're trying to correct, turn to the chapter that deals with the task you're having trouble with, such as "Queries, selection criteria." Then you can follow the path in the flowchart to the right solution—either a quick fix right on the flowchart or a reference to a more detailed solution later in the chapter.

Take it slow

Many of us get frustrated when clicking buttons doesn't solve our problem, so we just click more of them. Doing so won't solve your problem, and it usually compounds the problem exponentially until you have a really snarled-up mess. Then all you can do is give a big sigh and start all over.

A far better strategy is to move slowly, one step at a time, to determine the cause of the problem. You can sort of sneak up on a solution. Keep track of what you do and keep looking around for an escape route. Try not to get boxed into a corner with no way out but Ctrl+Alt+Delete. Once you emerge from the tunnel into the light of a solution, jot down the path you took for future reference.

This might help guarantee you'll never have that problem again—Murphy is alive and well!

When making changes to the tables, forms, and other parts of your database, it's always a good idea to work with copies first. When the changes or the new designs prove to be all right, you can rename these objects to replace the original ones. If the changes don't work, at least you have the unspoiled originals to start working with again.

Let Access help

Access doesn't exactly hold your hand as you trek through the jungle of creating and using a database, but it isn't far from your side. Most of the error messages you see (and we've seen a lot of them) include a Help button. You can click the Help button to see a brief description of the error and what you might have done to bring it on.

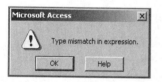

Access also makes its presence known as a generous helper by providing the What's This? button in a lot of the dialog boxes. If you're not sure whether you've set an option or property correctly, click the What's This? button (the question mark in the top right corner) and then click the item in question.

You'll see a description of the item, often with advice about your choices.

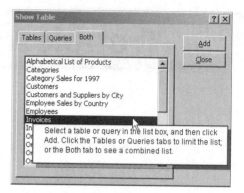

If quick information isn't enough to help you determine what's wrong, you can always resort to the complete online Help topic relating to the activity that's giving you trouble. You can use the Contents tab to browse through topics, or you can search for a topic using the Index tab or the Answer Wizard.

Make sure the database isn't read-only

It's hard to make important changes to the design of a form or report with your hands tied behind your back. If you open the database as read-only, you can't add or edit data and you can't make any changes in the design of forms, queries, reports, or tables. If you selected the Read-Only option in the Open dialog box, close the database and reopen it using the plain old Open button.

If you're still stuck

We have endeavored to anticipate common problems you're likely to run into when using Access, but obviously the list can't be exhaustive. There's even a chance that our solutions won't solve your particular problem. If you run into a dead end, you can turn to Microsoft product support or to other resources, such as the following:

- *http://www.microsoft.com/office*, the Microsoft Office product Web site

- *http://search.support.microsoft.com/kb*, the Microsoft searchable Knowledge Base

- *http://www.microsoft.com/office/access/*, the Microsoft Access product Web site

- *http://www.zdnet.com/zdhelp/*, a popular technology Web site with helpful tips

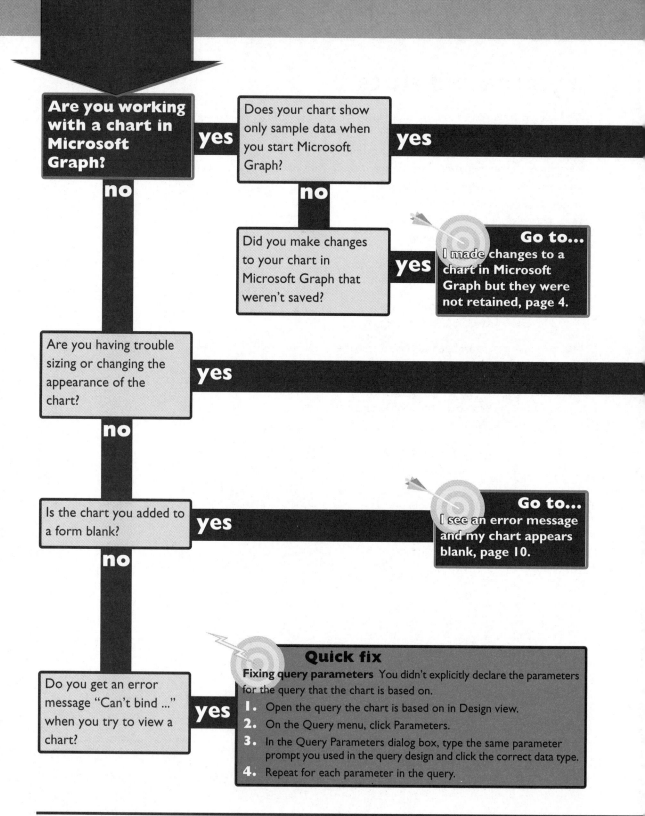

Are you working with a chart in Microsoft Graph?

yes → Does your chart show only sample data when you start Microsoft Graph?

yes →

no ↓

Did you make changes to your chart in Microsoft Graph that weren't saved?

yes →

Go to...
I made changes to a chart in Microsoft Graph but they were not retained, page 4.

no ↓

Are you having trouble sizing or changing the appearance of the chart?

yes →

no ↓

Is the chart you added to a form blank?

yes →

Go to...
I see an error message and my chart appears blank, page 10.

no ↓

Do you get an error message "Can't bind ..." when you try to view a chart?

yes →

Quick fix

Fixing query parameters You didn't explicitly declare the parameters for the query that the chart is based on.

1. Open the query the chart is based on in Design view.
2. On the Query menu, click Parameters.
3. In the Query Parameters dialog box, type the same parameter prompt you used in the query design and click the correct data type.
4. Repeat for each parameter in the query.

Charts and graphs

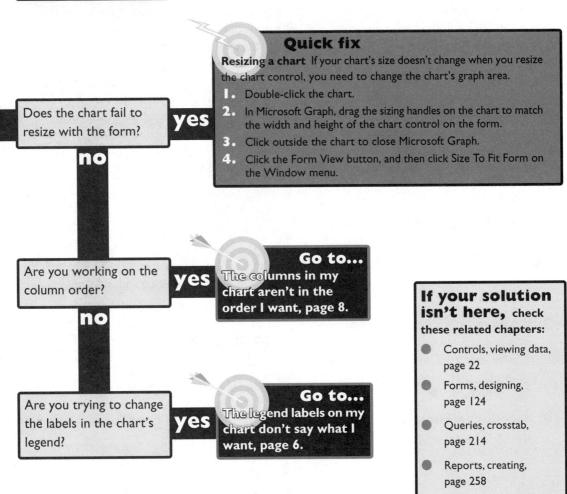

Quick fix

Fixing sample data
Microsoft Access replaces the sample data with your real data the first time you view the chart in the form or report. Open the form or report in Form view or Print Preview.

Quick fix

Resizing a chart If your chart's size doesn't change when you resize the chart control, you need to change the chart's graph area.
1. Double-click the chart.
2. In Microsoft Graph, drag the sizing handles on the chart to match the width and height of the chart control on the form.
3. Click outside the chart to close Microsoft Graph.
4. Click the Form View button, and then click Size To Fit Form on the Window menu.

Does the chart fail to resize with the form? **yes**

no

Are you working on the column order? **yes**

Go to...
The columns in my chart aren't in the order I want, page 8.

no

Are you trying to change the labels in the chart's legend? **yes**

Go to...
The legend labels on my chart don't say what I want, page 6.

If your solution isn't here, check these related chapters:
- Controls, viewing data, page 22
- Forms, designing, page 124
- Queries, crosstab, page 214
- Reports, creating, page 258

Or see the general troubleshooting tips on page xv.

I made changes to a chart in Microsoft Graph, but they were not retained

Source of the problem

You've worked hard making a chart look the way you want it to. You finish it and save it, but when you view it again, the rascal has kept some of your settings and ignored others. Chances are that without realizing it, you have set conflicting properties or values in the underlying record source, in the chart's properties, or in Microsoft Graph. The information shown in your chart comes from all three places, and information in one place may take priority over information in another.

Microsoft Access recomputes and redraws a chart every time you preview or print it, so changes you make in one of these three places might be overwritten by properties or values you set in another. You can use Microsoft Graph to make changes to the appearance of the graph and to change the colors and formatting of the labels, titles, and legend. These sorts of changes will be retained. However, if you tried to change the x-axis labels by editing the datasheet in Microsoft Graph, for example, or if you tried to update the names of the legend labels or any of the chart's data, the values in the query or tables the chart is based on will overwrite your changes.

The following steps show you how to make the changes to your chart stick.

How to fix it

1. If you made changes to a chart in Microsoft Graph that were overwritten by the underlying data or values, you need to return to the query or table the chart is based on and make your changes there.

2. If the form or report containing the chart isn't open, switch to the database window, select the form or report that includes the chart, and then click the Design button. ▶

3. Right-click the chart and then click Properties on the shortcut menu.

Charts and graphs

4. In the Row Source property box, identify the query or table the chart is based on. ▶

5. Close the form or report.

6. In the database window, select the underlying table or query and then click the Open button.

7. Make the changes to the data or to the field names that need to be updated in your chart. ▶

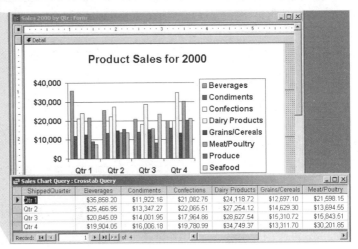

The nature of chart priorities

You can make changes to your chart in three places—or levels— depending on the information you want to change. The settings you make in the higher levels take precedence over settings you make in the lower levels.

● **Top level** The top level is the underlying data, which can be a table, a query, or a structured query language (SQL) statement created by the Chart Wizard. The data overrides changes made at lower levels, if a conflict arises.

● **Middle level** The middle level is the Row Source property for the chart, where the chart's title or labels, for example, can be changed. Changes to the underlying data overwrite changes made at this level, except when the Row Source property contains a calculated field that includes formatting characters. This formatting supercedes the formatting of the underlying data.

● **Low level** The lowest level is the graph in Microsoft Graph. Only changes to the chart's appearance will be retained at this level. Data underlying the graph overwrites changes made to the chart.

The legend labels on my chart don't say what I want

Source of the problem

The Chart Wizard creates the labels in a chart's legend from field values in the underlying data. The labels may not be informative, because the wizard copies the values from the fields used in the data series shown in the chart. For example, if you are tallying up sales of various categories of products during the four calendar quarters, the categories are part of a series. The quarters appear on the chart's x-axis, and the sales totals become the values shown on the y-axis. Only a number might identify the categories. Often, that's not very helpful.

Charts that are based on a query show the query column headings as legend labels. In a chart based on a query that totals the values in a field—for example sales of individual product categories by quarter or year—the legend label for the resulting aggregate field would read SumOf<*field name*>. That doesn't look very professional. In cases like this, the Row Source property of the chart is an SQL statement that constructs the data for the chart. You can modify the SQL statement to make the labels more useful.

The following steps show you how to modify the legend list in your charts.

How to fix it

1. In the database window, select the query the chart is based on and click Design.

2. Find the name of the field that has values you want to display differently in the chart.

3. Replace the field name with an expression that includes the text you want to display in the legend list beside the value from the field. ▶

For example, for a legend that shows only the category ID number, you could replace the CategoryID field name by typing the expression **"Cat "& [CategoryID]**. Be sure to enclose any text you add in double quotation marks and include a space that will appear between the text and the CategoryID field value.

4. View the chart again in Form view to confirm that the label is correct.

To change the legend text when you are working with a chart that displays SumOf *<fieldname>*, edit the SQL statement by following these steps:

1. In the database window, select the form or report containing the chart and open it in Design view.

2. Right-click the chart and then click Properties on the shortcut menu.

3. At the right of the Row Source property box, click the Build (…) button.

4. In the query design window, click SQL View in the View menu.

5. Edit each of the AS clauses in the SQL statement to remove the SumOf prefix. You can also revise the text between the brackets of the AS clause to read as you want your legend list to appear. ▶

6. Save and close the SQL statement window.

7. Switch to Form view to see the new text in the legend. ▶

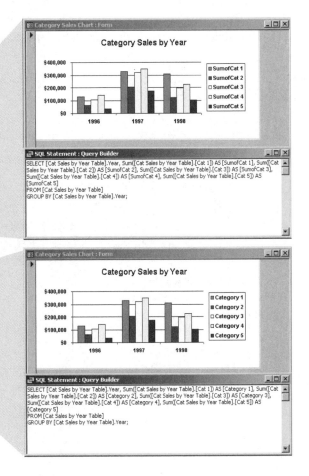

The columns in my chart aren't in the order I want

Source of the problem

The order of the columns in a chart is determined by the order of the fields in the table or query that the chart is based on. To change the order of the columns in a chart, you need to modify the order in which the fields are sorted in the table or query. Suppose you create a bar chart to compare the number of customers by country. Let's say you want to point out which countries had the largest number of customers rather than list countries alphabetically. To do this, you need to tell Access how to sort the values for the number of customers.

You do this by rearranging the field columns and specifying the sort order in the query design grid. If you used the Chart Wizard to create the chart, the query will be in the form of an SQL statement when you access it. But you can still work in the query design grid by selecting the Query Design instead of SQL View in the query builder window.

The following steps show you how to arrange the columns in a chart in the order you want.

How to fix it

1. In the database window, select the form containing the chart and click the Design button.

2. Right-click the chart and then click Properties on the shortcut menu.

3. At the right of the Row Source property box, click Build (...) to open the query design grid.

4. Change the sort order for the field by which the chart columns are arranged. In the example illustrated in the figure, you might want to rearrange the columns in the bar chart so that the countries are listed on the chart's x-axis in descending order of number of customers. To do this, you set the Sort cell to Descending in the Count1: Count(*) field. ▶

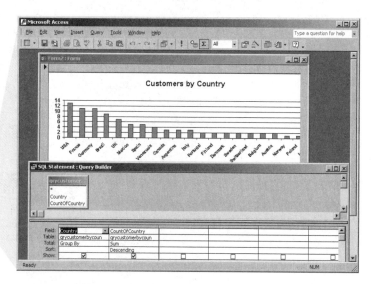

5. If you want to sort on more than one field, arrange the fields in the query design grid with the field you want to sort by first at the left and the other fields to the right in order of precedence.

6. Close the query builder window and display the chart in Form view to review the column order.

Just a few chart definitions

The *Category axis* (the x-axis) is the horizontal line at the bottom of the chart that tells you what category of data the chart displays. The *Value axis* (the y-axis) is the vertical line that shows the values in the chart data. A *series* is a group of related data values from one field in the record source. For example, in the Quarterly Orders by Product chart shown, each product's sales volume represents one of a series of values that are grouped by quarter. The *legend* is the color-coded list of members of the data series. The *labels* are derived from the data in the query or table the chart is based on.

Several features in a chart are provided by and can be customized in Microsoft Graph. Chart titles are optional. They can be placed at the top of the chart and next to each axis. *Gridlines* are horizontal or vertical lines that appear across the chart at the tick marks, which are the short lines that appear on the axes at evenly spaced intervals.

A chart's *scale* is the range of values in the chart and the increments that are marked on the Value axis with tick marks. For example, this chart has a range of values from $0 to $40,000 marked with $10,000 increments. ▶

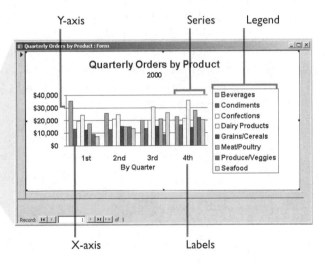

Y-axis   Series   Legend

X-axis   Labels

I see an error message and my chart appears blank

Source of the problem

You went to all that work to create a chart showing how dramatically your company's sales have skyrocketed. Now you open the form or report containing the chart and see that your work of art is completely blank.

The most likely cause of this unsettling problem is that the chart's Row Source property isn't valid. The Row Source property tells Access which query or table it should use to get the data to display in the chart. You might have changed the name of the underlying query or table or deleted it altogether. When Access can't find the data you told it to use in the chart, it just shrugs, displays a couple of error messages and shows you nothing. The chart looks right in the Design view, but it displays incorrectly when you view the real thing. ▶

The problem of blank charts might also occur if you are working with a record-bound chart. A *record-bound* chart is one that is linked to a specific field in a record. In this case, the field linking the chart and the form that includes the chart might be specified incorrectly. For example,

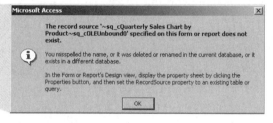

if your chart shows sales performance for several regions separately, the chart would be bound to the Region field. But if you choose Product as the field linking the chart and the form, there will be no match, and you might even be prompted to enter a parameter value. The table or query the chart is based on must contain the field you are using to link the form and the chart. You designate this field in the Link Child Fields and Link Master Fields properties. These properties usually show the same field name, especially if you used the Chart Wizard to create the chart.

The following steps show you how to solve these problems.

How to fix it

To make sure the chart's Row Source property is correct, follow these steps:

1. In the database window, select the form or report that includes the chart and then click the Design button.

2. Right-click the chart control and then click Properties. On the Data tab, check the name entered in the Row Source property box and make sure it shows a valid table or query name. If the name isn't valid, you'll need to correct it. ▶

3. If you have renamed the query or table the chart is based on, choose the new name from the list in the Row Source property box. If the query or table was deleted, you'll need to re-create the chart and base it on a query or table that's still part of your database.

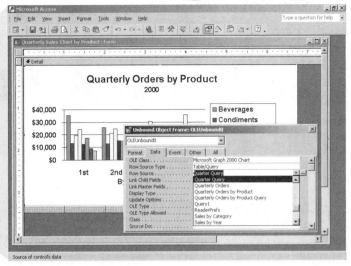

4. Switch to Form view or click Print Preview (if you are working with a chart in a report) and see whether the chart now displays the information you expected.

If you're working with a record-bound chart, open the form or report in Design view and follow these steps:

1. Right-click the chart control and then click Properties.

2. In the Link Master Fields property box, check to be sure the field name matches the Link Child Fields. Enter the matching field name if it does not. ▶

3. Switch to Form view or click Print Preview (if you are working with a chart in a report) to see that the chart now displays the information you expected.

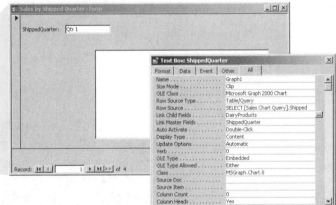

Tip

You can link more than one set of fields. Separate the field names in the property box with semicolons (;). The fields don't have to have the same names, but they must contain the same type of data. In the Link Child Fields property box, make sure the field name selected is included in the table or query that the chart is based on.

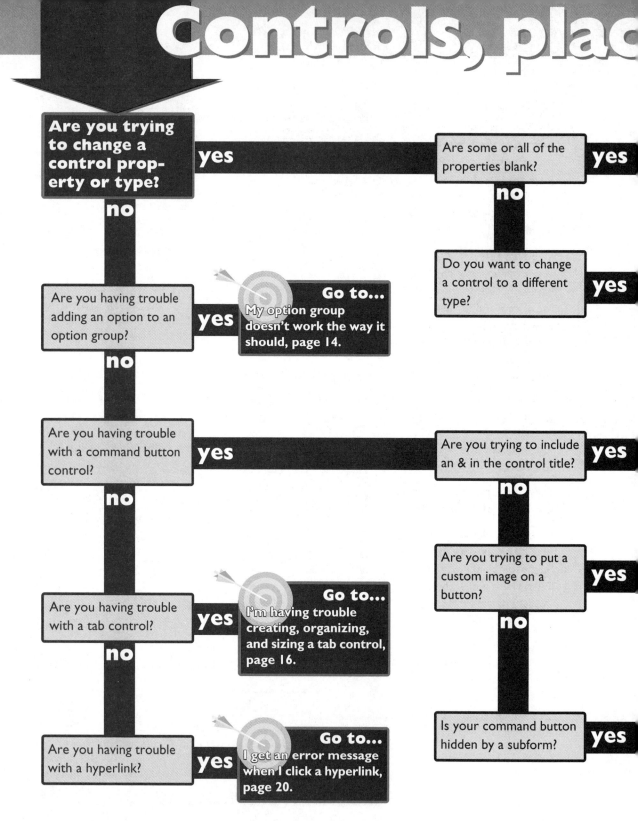

Are you trying to change a control property or type?

yes → **Are some or all of the properties blank?** **yes**

no ↓

no ↓ → **Do you want to change a control to a different type?** **yes**

Are you having trouble adding an option to an option group? **yes** → **Go to...** My option group doesn't work the way it should, page 14.

no ↓

Are you having trouble with a command button control? **yes** → **Are you trying to include an & in the control title?** **yes**

no ↓

no ↓ → **Are you trying to put a custom image on a button?** **yes**

Are you having trouble with a tab control? **yes** → **Go to...** I'm having trouble creating, organizing, and sizing a tab control, page 16.

no ↓

no ↓ → **Is your command button hidden by a subform?** **yes**

Are you having trouble with a hyperlink? **yes** → **Go to...** I get an error message when I click a hyperlink, page 20.

ing and formatting

Quick fix

Changing properties in more than one control If the controls aren't the same type, only the properties that the controls have in common show up.

1. Hold down Shift and deselect the non-matching control(s).
2. If you see no properties, you are in Edit mode. Press Esc to leave Edit mode and display the properties boxes.

Quick fix

Changing the type of control

1. Open the form or report in Design view, and then click the control.
2. On the Format menu, point to Change To.
3. Click the control type from the list of those available.

Quick fix

Adding an & to a command button title Using a single ampersand character in a control's title creates an access key for the command button. You need to use two.

1. Open the form in Design view.
2. Right-click the control, and then click Properties.
3. In the Caption property box on the Format tab, type the title you want using two ampersands: Jack && Jill.

Go to...

I can't make an image fit on a command button, page 18.

Quick fix

Revealing a hidden command button You can't put a subform on top of a command button.

1. Open the form in Design view.
2. Move the subform control aside until you can see the command button.
3. Drag the command button out of the way of the subform.
4. Return the subform control to its original position.

If your solution isn't here, check these related chapters:

- Forms, designing, page 124
- Reports, creating, page 258

Or see the general trouble-shooting tips on page xv.

My option group doesn't work the way it should

Source of the problem

It's always great to be offered a choice, whether it's how well done you want your steak cooked or what movie you want to see. But what if you don't get your way? What if you set up a group of options in Microsoft Access, and when you make a selection, Access runs off to left field and gives you something entirely different? For example, the handy option group can display a set of mutually exclusive choices. This option group control is actually a frame that contains the list of options, which can be anything from a list of friends' names to a list of forms you want to work on next. When a user selects one of the options, it becomes the value of the option group.

If you are trying to add a new option to a group you created with the Option Group Wizard, and the new option doesn't work in Form view, you probably placed it too close to the option group border. Access then considers the new check box, option button, or toggle button a separate control rather than one of the options in the group—even if it does overlap the option group.

The following solution shows how to solve this problem.

How to fix it

1. In the database window, select the form that contains the option group and then click the Design button.

2. Delete the option button, check box, or toggle button that doesn't work.

3. In the Form Design Toolbox, click the icon for the control you are using for the options (check boxes, option buttons, or toggle buttons) and move the mouse pointer over the option group control on the form.

4. When the option group is highlighted, click the mouse to place the control in the group box. ▶

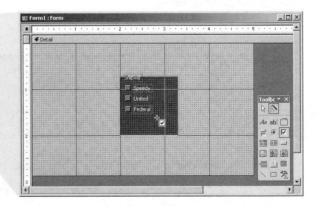

5. Use the commands on the Format menu to align the new option with the others in the group.

6. Change the label to show the name of the new option.

7. Save your changes to the form.

A different approach to options

What if you need to create a group of options that are not mutually exclusive? If you have several yes-or-no options that are related to the same type of information but belong to separate fields, you can create a faux option group. For example, you might want to find out what kinds of books your customers like to read, but you don't want to limit them to only one choice. You can add a box to a form and place option controls in it. Then you can format the box to make it look like an option group created by the Option Group Wizard. To do this, follow these steps:

1. In Form Design view, add the independent options (check boxes, option buttons, or toggle buttons) to the form and arrange them in a group.

2. Right-click the first option control and then click Properties on the shortcut menu.

3. On the Data tab, set the Control Source property for that option to the corresponding field in the table the form is based on. Repeat steps 2 and 3 for the other controls in the group.

4. In the toolbox, click the Rectangle tool and draw a rectangle around the group of option controls. ▶

5. Right-click the rectangle, and then click Properties on the shortcut menu.

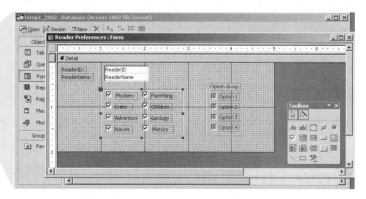

6. Set the properties of the rectangle to resemble a real option group as follows: set Back Style to Transparent, Back Color to White, Border Style to Solid, Border Color to Black, and Border Width to Hairline.

7. Add a label control to the form, placing it so that it overlaps the upper border of the group frame. Type a name for the group of options, and then press Enter.

8. Right-click the label and then click Properties on the shortcut menu.

9. Change the label's Back Style property to Normal and the Back Color property to Light Gray. ▶

Tip

To set the colors for the Back Color and Border Color properties, click the Build button (...) beside the property box and then select the color from the color palette.

I'm having trouble creating, organizing, and sizing a tab control

Source of the problem

It seems that the more helpful a feature can be the trickier it is to use. The professional-looking tab control is a shining example of this well-founded theory. Tab controls are great for grouping related information on a form that needs to display a lot of data. With tab controls, you have a lot of lee-way with respect to the number of tabs to include, the size of the tab control itself, and the appearance of the tabs at the top of the pages. This flexibility is great, but it can cause frustrating problems, because too much data on a single screen can be confusing.

If you are having trouble adding another page to the tab control or changing the order of the pages, you might not be selecting the right control on the form. If you're having trouble resizing the tab control to make room for another control (a command button, for example) or for other information on the form, one of the tabs probably contains controls that are getting in the way. Displaying a large collection of tab pages also can be tricky, especially if you want to see all the tabs at once instead of just one row of them.

The following solutions show you how to deal with these problems.

How to fix it

1. In the database window, select the form with the tab control and then click the Design button.

2. To add another page, right-click anywhere in the tab control and choose Insert Page from the shortcut menu. ▶

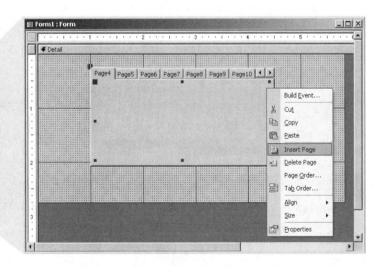

3. To see all the tabs at once, select the tab control (not one of the tab pages), click the Properties button, and set the Multi Row property to Yes. Doing this takes up more vertical space on the form, but it causes all tab captions to be displayed. ▶

Making a tab control the right size can take some work, especially when you've added command buttons and other controls to it. You need to take their size and location into account when resizing the entire set of tab pages.

1. To resize a tab control, look at each tab page and move or reduce the size of controls that exceed the page width you want to achieve.

2. If you want to specify the height or width of the tabs on the tab control, set the Tab Fixed Height or the Tab Fixed Width properties. The default setting (0) sizes the tab widths to fit the contents of the particular tab. ▶

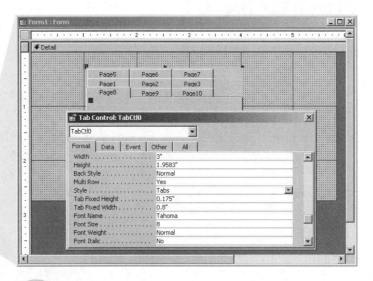

Tip

As you add pages, the widths of the tabs are reduced. When the number of tabs exceeds the width of the control, the tabs created first aren't displayed, so scroll bars are added so you can view all the tabs.

Tip

To open the property sheet for the tab control, double-click one edge of the control. To open the property sheet for a specific page, double-click the page's tab.

I can't make an image fit on a command button

Source of the problem

You have a picture of your favorite mountain resort or one of your firstborn that you want to use on a command button on a form. You add it to the button, but it just doesn't look right. Not only that, Access won't let you resize or position the picture while you're working on the form.

If you don't use one of the images provided by Access, you can get into trouble. And depending on the way you add an image to a button, you can encounter different problems. When you use the Picture Builder to add a picture to a button, the button is automatically resized to fit the image. Another possibility is simply to type the name of the picture file in the Picture property of the command button; in this case the image is cropped to fit the size of the command button you draw.

The following instructions show you exactly how to get your image to fit.

How to fix it

1. Regardless of how you added the picture to the command button, the first step is to open the form in the Design view. To do this, select the form in the database window and then click the Design button. ▶

2. Double-click the command button control to open the Properties dialog box.

3. In the Picture property box in the Format tab, remove the file name.

4. Look at the Width and Height

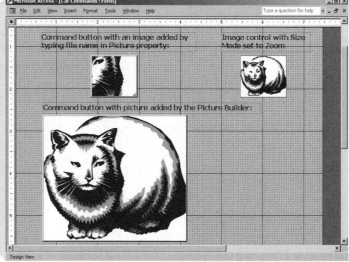

properties of the button and make note of the measurements. This will help you resize the picture to fit.

5. Open the picture file in your image program (such as Microsoft Paint, the program that comes with Microsoft Windows), and resize the image to fit the dimensions of the button. Also, you can crop the picture in the graphics program so that the important part of the image will be centered on the button.

6. Return to the form in Design view, and reenter the name of the picture file in the Picture property box.

7. Switch to Form view to check the picture and to make sure it fits on the command button.

Pictures for every occasion

The Access Picture Builder provides more than 220 images for almost any type of command button you can dream up. Note that the Command Button Wizard uses a lot of them as default images. For example, if you create a button with the wizard that prints the current form, the button will show a picture of a printer.

To start the Picture Builder, open the form you're working with in Design view and then double-click the command button. Then click the Build button next to the Picture property box, and select a picture from the Available Picture list.

These are just a few of the Picture Builder offerings. ▶

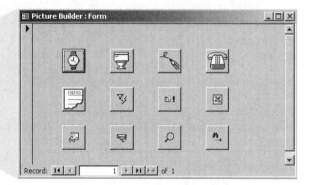

> **Tip**
>
> If you use a custom image on a command button, it's a good idea to add a control tip to explain what the button does.

I get an error message when I click a hyperlink

Source of the problem

You expect the high-tech hyperlink to jump to the destination you set it to. But, like your favorite pet Labrador retriever, it doesn't always obey your command.

If you get an error message when you click a hyperlink and can't reach your destination, several reasons may account for this. ▶

- The destination may have been renamed or deleted. There's no real cure unless you can find out the new name.

- The destination may have been moved to another location and the link is broken.

- The destination may just be busy (assuming you have appropriate access to it).

- The destination is on your company network, but you don't have access to it, or the server is down.

The following solution describes cures for these problems.

How to fix it

1. If the destination has been renamed or you want to link to a new location, find out the name of the destination. If the hyperlink is on your company's intranet, check with your administrator to be sure that you have access to the destination and that the network is operating.

2. Open the form in Design view and then right-click the control that includes the hyperlink.

3. On the shortcut menu, point to Hyperlink and then click Edit Hyperlink. ▶

4. Enter the correct hyperlink address.

5. Click OK in the Edit Hyperlink dialog box, switch to Form view and check the hyperlink to be sure that it works.

Tip

If the unresponsive hyperlink is on the Internet, wait a while and try again.

Hyperlinks to everywhere

The ability to add hyperlinks to a table or form opens up a whole new world for you, the Access user. A hyperlink can jump to a lot of different places and objects:

- A location in another file on your hard disk

- A site on the World Wide Web

- A location on your local area network

- Another database object

- A location in another Microsoft Office document such as a bookmark in Microsoft Word, a named range in Microsoft Excel, or a presentation in Microsoft PowerPoint

Hyperlinks that you place in a table by adding a field and specifying the Hyperlink data type jump to a different location within each record. For example, in a table containing information about popular CDs, you could create a hyperlink field to jump to a sound clip from the CD.

You can assign a hyperlink to a button on a form that jumps to another location. If the hyperlink connects to a document that was created in another application, that application starts automatically.

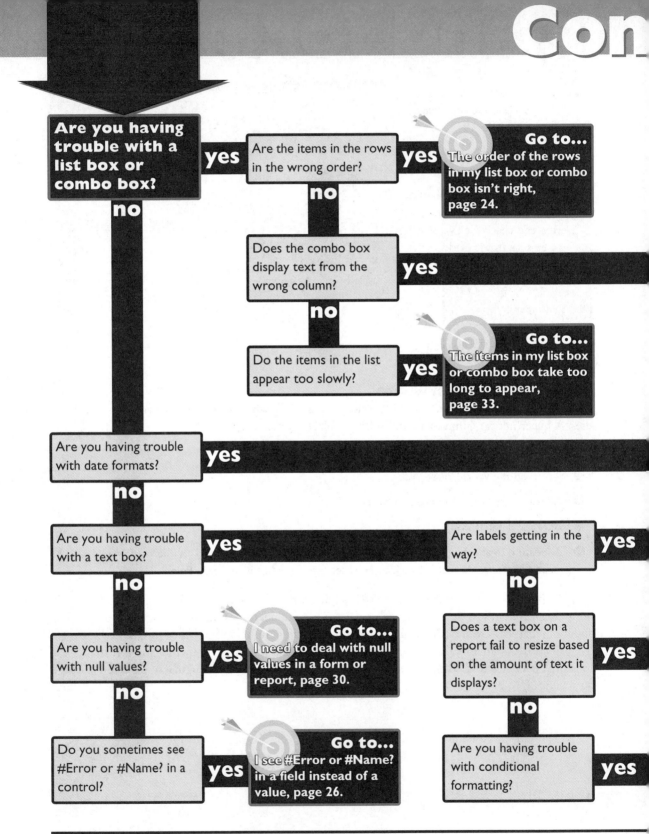

Con

Are you having trouble with a list box or combo box? **yes** → Are the items in the rows in the wrong order? **yes** → **Go to...** The order of the rows in my list box or combo box isn't right, page 24.

no

Does the combo box display text from the wrong column? **yes**

no

Do the items in the list appear too slowly? **yes** → **Go to...** The items in my list box or combo box take too long to appear, page 33.

Are you having trouble with date formats? **yes**

no

Are you having trouble with a text box? **yes**

Are labels getting in the way? **yes**

no

no

Are you having trouble with null values? **yes** → **Go to...** I need to deal with null values in a form or report, page 30.

Does a text box on a report fail to resize based on the amount of text it displays? **yes**

no

Do you sometimes see #Error or #Name? in a control? **yes** → **Go to...** I see #Error or #Name? in a field instead of a value, page 26.

Are you having trouble with conditional formatting? **yes**

Quick fix

Column widths The width of the column you want to see is set to 0.

1. With the form open in Design view, right-click the combo box control and then click Properties.

2. In the Column Widths property box on the Format tab, enter the width (in inches) of each column from left to right, separated by semi-colons.

3. Set the width of any columns you don't want to see to 0.

Quick fix

Fixing date formats You might have applied the Format function to the result of the Month function. The Format function needs a date serial number or a date expression to do its calculation, not an integer, which is what the Month function provides.

1. Open the form or report you are working with in Design view.

2. Right-click the control in which you used the Format function and then click Properties on the shortcut menu.

3. In the Control Source property box, delete the Month function and enter an expression that uses only the Format function. For example, **=Format ([datefield], "mmmm")**.

4. Save the form or report, and then switch to Form view or Print preview to see the results.

Go to...

The text box control labels are in the way, page 32.

Quick fix

Automatically resizing text boxes You need to set the Can Shrink and Can Grow properties.

1. Open the report in Design view.

2. Right click the text box control and then click Properties.

3. On the Format tab, set the Can Shrink and Can Grow properties to Yes.

Go to...

I don't get the right results with conditional formatting, page 28.

If your solution isn't here, check these related chapters:

- Data, setting field properties, page 42
- Expressions, page 98

Or see the general troubleshooting tips on page xv.

The order of the rows in my list box or combo box isn't right

Source of the problem

Nature has a way of putting what you want in the last place you look for it. Similarly, it's lousy when the option you choose most often is the last one on a list. It is helpful for a list box or combo box to display the options in an order you specify, so you don't have to scroll to find the item you want. To change the order of the items in a list box or combo box, you need to sort the records in the list. If you used one of the clever Microsoft Access wizards to build the list or combo box, the items may not be arranged in the order you want. To reorder the items, you can use the Query Builder.

The following solution shows you how.

How to fix it

1. In the database window, select the form that contains the list box or combo box and then click the Design button.

2. Right-click the list box or combo box control whose values you want to rearrange, and then click Properties on the shortcut menu.

3. Click in the Row Source property box, and then click the Build button (…).

4. In the Query Builder, find the field the list is sorted by and change the setting from Ascending to Descending or from Descending to Ascending. ▶

5. Close the Query Builder window and click Yes in the message box asking whether you want to save the changes.

6. Click the Form View button. Open the list box or combo box and check the new order of the rows.

If this set of steps doesn't put the rows in the order you want, you can create and save a new query to use as the row source for the list box or combo box as follows:

1. In the database window, click Queries and then click New. In the New Query dialog box, select Design view and then click OK.

2. In the Show Table dialog box, select the table that contains the fields you are working with in the list box or combo box, click Add and then click Close. ▶

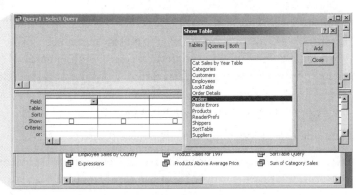

3. Drag the field you want in the first column of the list box or combo box to the first column in the query grid.

4. Set the sort order you want for this field, Ascending or Descending. ▶

5. Drag the second field you want in the list to the query grid.

6. Save and name the query.

7. Open the form with the list box or combo box in Design view.

8. Right-click the list box or combo box and then click Properties on the shortcut menu.

9. In the Row Source property box, select the name of the query you just created.

10. Check the Bound Column property box and be sure the correct column number appears. This is the column whose values are bound to the field named in the Control Source property.

11. Click the Format tab. In the Column Widths property, enter a value for the width of the first column and adjust the Column Count column so it shows the number of columns in the list box or combo box.

> **Tip**
>
> A combo box has two confusing properties: Row Source and Control Source. *Row Source* indicates where the list of options displayed in the drop-down list comes from. *Control Source* tells the combo box where to store the selected or entered data.

I see #Error or #Name? in a field instead of a value

Source of the problem

It's really frustrating to view data in a form you've worked hard on only to see a text box or a list box display #Error or #Name? where you expected to see a value. Several situations can cause this unwelcome event, and there are several corresponding cures. If the control is bound to a field, the #Name? error usually occurs when the control can't find the field that contains the data you want it to display. If the data displayed in the control comes from an expression, one or more of the following could be the source of your trouble:

- The expression in the Control Source property box might not have an equal sign in front of it.

- The expression containing the names of fields or controls might have spaces in them, and you might not have enclosed these names with square brackets.

- The expression might include the name of the control itself, creating a circular reference that Access can't resolve.

The following steps solve these problems.

How to fix it

1. In the database window, select the table or query the form is based on and click the Design button. Review the fields in the table or query and make sure that the field you're having trouble with is still included. If the field isn't in the table or query, it's best to delete the text box that refers to the field from the form.

2. If the field is still there, close the table or query window and then select the form in the database window.

3. Click the Design button to open the form in Design view.

4. Right-click the troublesome control and then click Properties on the shortcut menu.

5. In the Control Source property box, check the spelling of the field and correct it if necessary.

If you are using an expression in the Control Source property, check that the expression is correct.

1. Be sure you've included an equal sign if you typed the expression yourself. The expression you see here won't work. ▶

2. Check the field or control names used in the expression. If a field or control name used in the expression contains a space, enclose the name in square brackets.

3. Check to ensure that matching pairs of quotation marks (single or double) enclose text and other literal values in an expression. You might see an error message if you leave out one of a pair of quotation marks or brackets.

4. Make sure you haven't used the name of the control in the expression. For example, in the figure shown here, the Control Source property for the BestBet field control includes the control's name, =[Field1]+[Field2]+[BestBet]. Including the name creates a circular reference. ▶

5. To fix a circular reference, right-click the control, click Properties on the shortcut menu, and then change the name of the control in the Name property box.

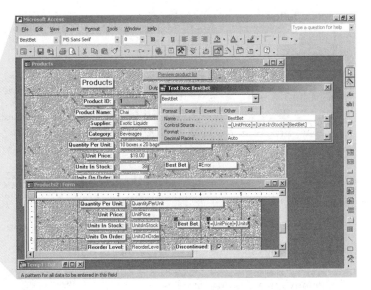

Tip

If you have to change the name of a control, make sure you change the name everywhere it occurs.

I don't get the right results with conditional formatting

Source of the problem

The conditional formatting feature introduced in Access 2002 is helpful. This feature lets you emphasize values in a text box or combo box with a different appearance when the values meet the conditions you've specified. For example, if one of your sales reps exceeds her goal for the quarter, you can automatically highlight the new threshold on future reports. But to make this work, you have to get everything right. A condition can be as simple as matching a single value or something more complex, such as an expression comparing values. If you don't get the results you expect, one of these problems might be the culprit:

- You might have set an interval in your expression that includes (or does not include) the values at the limits of the interval.

- You might have set multiple conditions that conflict with or override one another.

- You might have referred incorrectly to another control in a formula.

  The following solution shows how to correct each of these problems.

How to fix it

1. In the database window, select the form or report that includes the control to which you've applied (or want to apply) conditional formatting.

2. Click the Design button.

3. In the Design view window, select the control and then click Conditional Formatting in the Format menu.

4. In the Conditional Formatting dialog box, review the conditions set for that control.

5. If you want to include the values at the beginning and end of a range in the conditions you are trying to define, use the *Between...And* operator. ▶

6. If you want to set upper and lower limits without including the values at the beginning and end of the range, combine the *Greater Than* and *Less Than* operators in two conditions.

7. If more than one condition evaluates to true for the same field value, change the sequence of the conditions and put the one you want to prevail as the first condition. ▶

Using conditional formatting to manage controls

Did you know that you can use conditional formatting to deactivate a control under specific conditions? For example, if an order is to be shipped COD to a trusted customer, you can make the controls that contain credit card information inactive when COD is selected from the combo box. The credit information fields will no longer be in the tab order, which can save time during data entry. To use conditional formatting to make a text box or combo box inactive, open the Conditional Formatting dialog box (see step 3 in the preceding "How to fix it" section), enter the condition and then click the Enabled button at the far right of the condition box.

Tip

You can use the *Less Than Or Equal To* operator to include the upper limit or the *Greater Than Or Equal To* operator to include the lower limit.

Tip

If you typed an expression such as [Price]<[Cost] as the formatting criterion, you may have misspelled the control reference. Make sure the control names are correct and enclosed in brackets if they include a space. It's safest to get in the habit of using brackets around field names even if they don't include a space.

I need to deal with null values in a form or report

Source of the problem

When you don't know the value that goes in a field, you can just leave it blank, right? That works on paper, but in Access, blank—or null—values can generate unexpected results. You can get into real trouble, for example, if a field with blank values is used in a formula or another expression. Think about what happens when you divide a number by a field that is blank. You won't get the results you need.

If the work you need to do with a field prohibits the use of blank values, you can set the field's Required property to Yes when you add the field to a table. If blank fields are a problem in a form or report, but values of zero are okay, here's the way to solve your problem.

How to fix it

1. In the database window, select the form or report and then click the Design button.

2. In the toolbox, click the Text Box tool. Click in the form to add a new text box to the form or report. ▶

3. Click the Properties button in the toolbar.

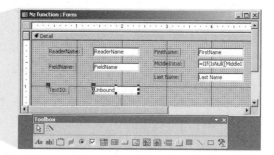

4. In the Control Source property for the text box, enter the expression =Nz([FieldName]), where FieldName is the name of the field that contains the null values giving you problems. The Nz function changes blank values to 0 (for a number field) or to a zero-length string (for a text field).

5. If you want to display some informative text (such as *Need info*) in a blank field, use the expression =Nz([FieldName], "Need info"). ▶

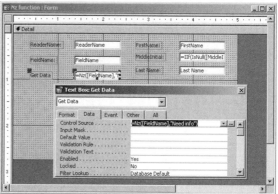

6. Change to Form view to test the expression. ▶

More expressions for dealing with null values

In certain situations, you can use other expressions to handle a field with null values. If you are using the field in an expression that calculates the value of another field, you need to check for blank values before completing the calculation and convert them to zero, which can be used in the expression. To do this, you can combine the Nz function with the Immediate If (IIf) function in an expression such as =IIf(Nz([TotalCost])>100, "High", "Low"). Here, if the TotalCost field is blank, the Nz function changes it to 0, a numeric value that can be compared to 100. If the calculated value of TotalCost is greater than 100, the control displays "High"; if the calculated value is less than or equal to 100, the control displays "Low."

Another way to get around blank values is to use the IIf function with the IsNull function in an expression such as =IIf(IsNull([MiddleInitial]), "NMI", [MiddleInitial]). If the middle initial field is blank, the control displays the text "NMI"; otherwise the middle initial itself is shown. ▶

The text box control labels are in the way

Source of the problem

Every time you add a text box control to your form or report, Access thinks you want to use the label that goes with it. But this is not always what you want, especially if you are pressed for room in the design or if the labels don't really match the values you see in the field.

The following steps show you how to add text boxes without automatically attaching a label.

How to fix it

1. In the database window, select the form or report you're working with and then click the Design button.

2. If the toolbox is not already open, click the Toolbox button on the toolbar.

3. In the toolbox, click the Text Box icon.

4. Click the Properties button on the toolbar. The Default Text Box Properties dialog box appears.

5. In the Properties dialog box, click the Format tab and set the Auto Label and the Add Colon properties to No.

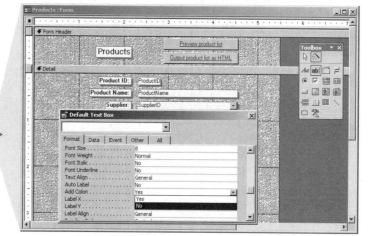

Tip

Changing the settings for the Auto Label and Add Colon properties affects only the form or report you are working on. It doesn't change the default setting for all text boxes.

Tip

If you remove an attached label from a text box control, you can reattach it later. Select the label you want to use, and then click Cut on the Edit menu. Select the control, and then click Paste on the Edit menu.

The items in my list box or combo box take too long to appear

Source of the problem

Sometimes it seems like a list box or combo box takes forever to display its values on the screen. The delay is caused by the time it takes to retrieve information from the database. The following steps solve this problem.

How to fix it

One way to speed up the display of information in the list is to base the list box or combo box on a saved query instead of on the SQL statement created by the List Box or Combo Box Wizard. Follow these steps:

1. In the database window, select the form that includes the combo box or list box and then click the Design button.

2. Right-click the combo box or list box and then click Properties on the shortcut menu.

3. Click in the Row Source property box, and then click the Build (...) button at the right.

4. While you're in the Query Builder window, click the Save button.

5. In the Save As dialog box, enter a name for the query and then click OK. ▶

6. Close the Query Builder window and click Yes when asked to save changes to the query design.

7. Save the changes to the form's design.

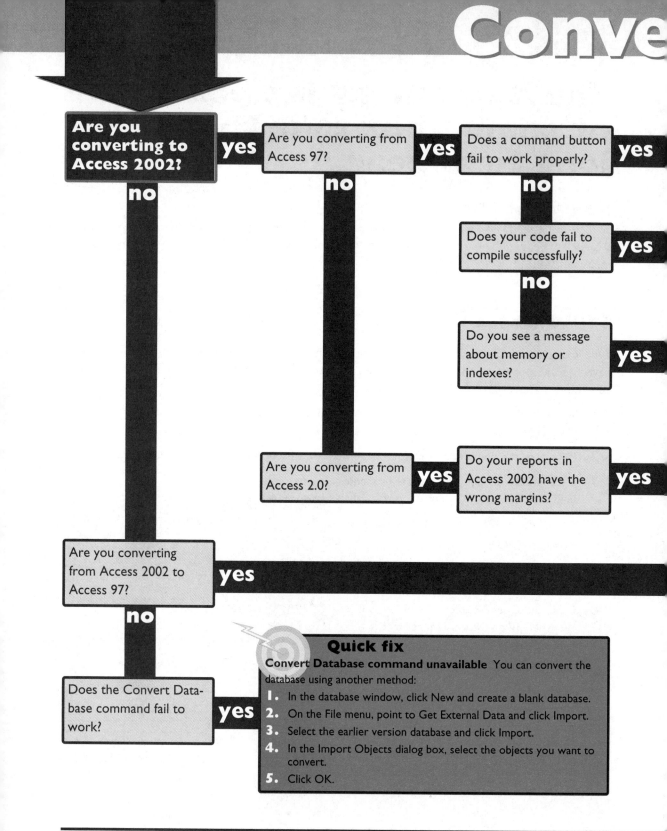

Conve

Are you converting to Access 2002? — yes → **Are you converting from Access 97?** — yes → **Does a command button fail to work properly?** — yes

no ↓ (Are you converting to Access 2002?)

no ↓ (Are you converting from Access 97?)

no ↓ (Does a command button fail to work properly?) → **Does your code fail to compile successfully?** — yes

no ↓ (Does your code fail to compile successfully?) → **Do you see a message about memory or indexes?** — yes

Are you converting from Access 2.0? — yes → **Do your reports in Access 2002 have the wrong margins?** — yes

Are you converting from Access 2002 to Access 97? — yes

no ↓

Does the Convert Database command fail to work? — yes →

Quick fix

Convert Database command unavailable You can convert the database using another method:

1. In the database window, click New and create a blank database.
2. On the File menu, point to Get External Data and click Import.
3. Select the earlier version database and click Import.
4. In the Import Objects dialog box, select the objects you want to convert.
5. Click OK.

Quick fix

Wrong command button
The command button was
created with old Visual Basic
code.

1. After converting the
   database, delete the
   command button from
   the form.
2. Recreate the button
   using the Command
   Button Wizard.

Go to...

My code won't compile,
page 36.

Go to...

I see a message about
being out of memory or
having too many
indexes, page 40.

Quick fix

Wrong report margin
When a report is converted to
Access 2002, the margins are
automatically set to the mini-
mum margin for your default
printer.

1. Open the report in
   Access 2000.
2. On the File menu, click
   Page Setup.
3. Reduce the column width
   and spacing so the total
   width doesn't exceed the
   paper width.

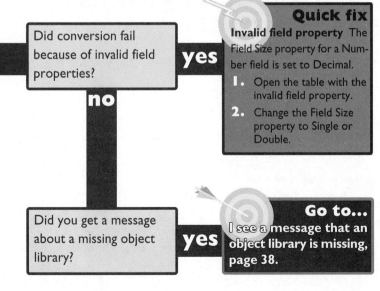

Did conversion fail
because of invalid field
properties?

yes

no

Quick fix

Invalid field property The
Field Size property for a Number field is set to Decimal.

1. Open the table with the
   invalid field property.
2. Change the Field Size
   property to Single or
   Double.

Did you get a message
about a missing object
library?

yes

Go to...

I see a message that an
object library is missing,
page 38.

If your solution isn't here, check these related chapters:

- Data, setting field
  properties, page 42
- Table design, page 290

Or see the general troubleshooting tips on page xv.

My code won't compile

Source of the problem

In this day and age, it sometime seems we've all got to have the latest model cars and the newest type of cellular phone or we just aren't with it.

Well, Microsoft Access is just as fashion-conscious as the rest of us, trying to keep up with the latest trends. Each new version of Access uses the latest version of the Microsoft Visual Basic language and syntax. Although Microsoft works hard to achieve backward compatibility, some changes in the language might cause compilation errors in the code used in your database. These errors can interrupt or stymie database conversion.

When you try to run a database that you've converted to Access 2002 (or if you just run a database in Access 2002 without converting it), you might see an error message without any spe-

cific information about what caused the error. These messages indicate that you'll have to recompile the code in your database and fix each error as it pops up. If you're converting a database from Access 2.0, you may get an error message about syntax errors in the original database. Or you may have used a word to identify a field, control, or database object that is a reserved keyword in a later version of Access. For example, if you used Friend, AddressOf, Decimal, Implements, RaiseEvent, or WithEvents in a program built with Access 2.0, your Visual Basic code won't compile in Access 2002.

Finally, another cause for compilation errors can be the lack of support for older objects, methods, and properties in the newer version of Access you're converting to.

The following steps show you how to solve these problems.

How to fix it

1. To recompile the code in your Access 2002 database, open any of the modules in your database in Design view.

2. On the Debug menu, click Compile <*databasename*>.

3. When an error is detected, the Visual Basic Editor stops the compilation, highlights the offensive statement, and displays a dialog box with a clue about what's wrong with the code. The error message shown here is caused by a duplicate procedure name, Form_Load. ▶

4. Click OK in the message box to close it.

5. Correct the error (in this case, you'd need to give the procedure a unique name), and then click the Continue toolbar button to continue reviewing the code.

6. If you had syntax errors in Access 2.0 code when converting the database, you need to return to the Access 2.0 database, correct the syntax errors, compile all the modules in the 2.0 database, and convert again to Access 2002.

7. If you have used a reserved word as an identifier in an Access 2.0 database, change the identifier so that it doesn't conflict with the Visual Basic reserved keyword. ▶

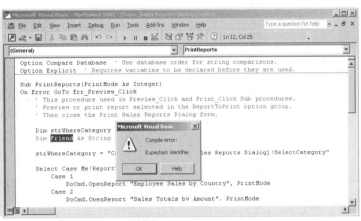

8. To create a cross-reference to another object library, in the Visual Basic Editor window click References on the Tools menu, select the Microsoft DAO 2.5/3.5 Compatibility Library check box, and then click OK. ▶

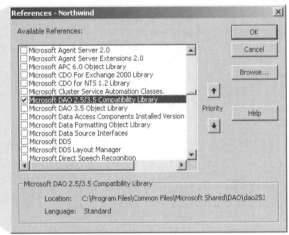

More about references to libraries
If you want to make sure your program uses only the Access 2002 objects, methods, and properties, clear the check box for the 2.5/3.5 Compatibility Library in the References dialog box and then recompile all the modules in the program. The code will no longer rely on the backward compatible library.

I see a message that an object library is missing

Source of the problem

The libraries that Access needs to do its job aren't the same as the public libraries downtown where you did your homework, but at the same time they aren't all that different. Although they don't use the Dewey decimal system to organize everything, the libraries that Access uses are precisely arranged so that Access can find what it needs quickly.

Library files, called dynamic link libraries (or DLLs) by the experts, are essential for running the Visual Basic code that's used to automate and enhance an Access database. Visual Basic can automate almost everything in an Access program. It can, for example, display a single startup screen from which you can open a form, preview a report, or log on to a Web site—anything you want.

Access 2002 (and Access 2000) stores its library files in a directory different from that used in earlier versions of Access. So, for databases converted from earlier versions, you have to give Access a road map to the location of the libraries by setting a reference. The same is true for new databases created in Access 2002 (or 2000) and converted to earlier versions. When you convert an Access 2002 database to Access 97, the required object references often are lost. If they are, you will see a message that at least one of the Access 97 object libraries is missing.

The following steps show you how to restore these references.

How to fix it

1. When you are converting the Access 2002 database to the Access 97 format, click OK when you see the message about missing libraries.

2. Open the database in Access 97.

3. In the database window, select any form or report—the database objects that can include a class module.

4. Click the Code button to open the Visual Basic Editor.

> **Tip**
> You can also open the Visual Basic Editor window by clicking Modules in the database window and then clicking New.

5. On the Tools menu, click References.

6. In the Available References box, clear the check boxes next to the references that are marked MISSING. Clearing the missing references forces Access to look in a different directory for the library files.

7. Select the Microsoft DAO 3.6 Object Library check box. ▶

8. Click OK.

More about backward conversion

Any feature or functionality that is new to Access 2002 obviously will be lost when you convert a database back to Access 97. For example, you will lose all links to data access pages.

Access 2002 uses a slightly different code system for storing characters—the Unicode system instead of the ANSI numbered set of 256 characters. Consequently, some of the characters shown in Access 2002 might not be correctly converted to Access 97. If you're converting a secured database from Access 2002 to Access 97, you must have Open/Run and Open Exclusive permissions set for the database and Read Design permissions set for all the tables, queries, forms, and other objects in the database. After converting the database to Access 97, you need to open it and apply user-level security to restore system security. To set permissions, click Security on the Tools menu and then click User And Group Permissions. Set the options for the database and the database objects in the User And Group Permissions dialog box.

Another conversion gotcha!

Queries built in Access 97 or earlier versions that are based on date criteria can produce the wrong results because of the Y2K compliance built into Access 2002. Dates that you entered in earlier versions of Access using two-digit year values are automatically assigned a four-digit year value in Access 2002. Depending on the value, the century is assumed. The year Access uses to determine which century a date falls in advances by one each year. To remedy this problem, modify the query criteria to specify the full four-digit year value.

I see an error message about being out of memory or having too many indexes

Source of the problem

The version of Visual Basic used by Access 2002 (and Access 2000) is pickier than most previous versions. An Access 2002 database will not accept more than 1000 modules in a database, whereas an Access 97 database can have up to 1024 modules. Additionally, every form and report includes a Has Module property that is set to Yes by default, whether or not any code is attached to it, and each of these blank Yeses counts toward the limit. If you do try to convert a database with more than 1000 modules, Access will display a message saying you are out of memory.

Also, Access 2002 has a limit on the number of indexes you can include with any single table. If you see a message that you have too many indexes, at least one of the tables in your Access 2.0 database exceeds the limit of 32. Access 2.0, for example, automatically indexed all the linking fields involved in a table relationship—both in the primary key field table and in the foreign key table. If you have one table that is involved in a lot of relationships, you can easily exceed the 32-index limit.

The following steps show you how to solve these problems.

How to fix it

1. If you receive an out-of-memory error, open the database you're trying to convert in the earlier version of Access.

2. Delete any unnecessary forms and reports—maybe some of the early trial versions that you abandoned in favor of later ones.

3. Try converting the database again.

If that doesn't work, you can split your application into separate databases and then perform the conversion. Follow these steps:

1. In Access 97, click New Database on the File menu and then create and name a new blank database.

2. On the File menu, click Get External Data and then click Import. In the Import dialog box, navigate to the database you want to convert, and then click Import.

3. In the Import Objects dialog box, use the Select All button to select all the tables and queries in the database you are converting. Also select some of the forms and reports that are related to the same activity. Click OK to import these objects to the new database. ▶

Create a second new blank database, and then follow the steps above to import all the tables and queries to it. Also import the remaining forms and reports and other objects to this database. Then follow these steps:

1. Convert both new databases to Access 2002.

2. In Access 2002, open one of the new databases.

3. On the File menu, click Get External Data and then click Import.

4. Locate the second converted database, and click Import. Select the forms, reports, and other objects in the Import Objects dialog box, and then click OK.

To cure the problem with excessive indexes, follow these steps:

1. Open the Access 2.0 database you're trying to convert.

2. Click the Relationships button, and then look for a table that is involved in several relationships.

3. Delete some relationship lines from that table.

4. In the database window, select one of the tables that is still related to the table you worked with in step 3. Open that table in Design view.

5. In the Field Properties area of the table design window, set the Indexed property for several fields to No. ▶

6. Close the database and convert it again. Repeat the process if your work with the first table doesn't solve the problem.

7. After you successfully convert the Access 2.0 database to Access 2002, establish the relationships and indexes again in the new database.

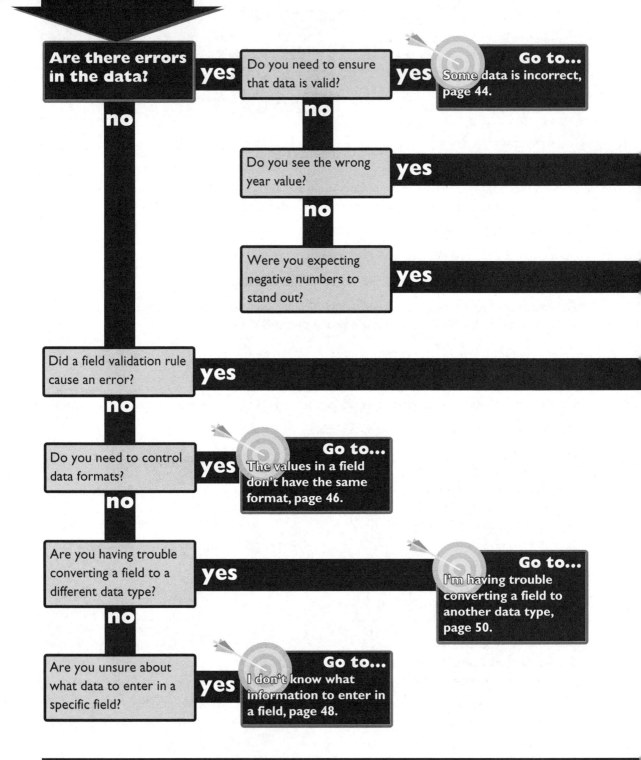

Data, setti

Are there errors in the data? → yes → Do you need to ensure that data is valid? → yes → **Go to...** Some data is incorrect, page 44.

no ↓ (from "Are there errors in the data?")

no ↓ (from "Do you need to ensure that data is valid?")

Do you see the wrong year value? → yes →

no ↓

Were you expecting negative numbers to stand out? → yes →

Did a field validation rule cause an error? → yes →

no ↓

Do you need to control data formats? → yes → **Go to...** The values in a field don't have the same format, page 46.

no ↓

Are you having trouble converting a field to a different data type? → yes → **Go to...** I'm having trouble converting a field to another data type, page 50.

no ↓

Are you unsure about what data to enter in a specific field? → yes → **Go to...** I don't know what information to enter in a field, page 48.

Quick fix

Formatting for four-digit years You need to set the format to show a four-digit year.

1. On the Tools menu, click Options, and then click the General tab.

2. Under Use Four-Digit Year Formatting, choose This Database to limit the date format to the current database or All Databases.

3. If you want the 4-digit year only for a single field, change the field's Format property to mm/dd/yyyy.

Quick fix

Formatting negative numbers You need to create an expression in the field's Format property.

1. Open the table in Design view, and then select the field.

2. In the Format property box, enter the expression #,##0.00[Green]; (#,##0.00)[Red]; "Zero"; "Unknown".

   This expression displays positive numbers in green and negative numbers in red and enclosed in parentheses. (Blank fields display Zero or Unknown.)

Quick fix

Fixing validation rule errors

1. Open the table in Design view.

2. Select the field you set the validation rule for.

3. In the Validation Rule properties box, remove references to other fields in this or another table, controls on a form, or any user-defined functions.

4. Modify the rule so that it applies only to values in this field.

If your solution isn't here, check these related chapters:

- Expressions, page 98
- Relationships, page 248

Or see the general trouble-shooting tips on page xv.

Some data is incorrect

Source of the problem

In spite of what some folks say, those of us who use computers are just as human as anyone else. And because we are human, we make just as many mistakes, especially when entering data. Most of the time, data is entered incorrectly simply because of human error, and that's hard to control. To fix existing errors, you might need to go through your data and sniff out the mistakes. But, luckily, you can train Microsoft Access to diligently prevent future data entry errors from becoming comfortably ensconced in your database. You have two ways to help ensure the accuracy of your data:

● Create a validation rule for individual fields in a table.

● Create a validation rule that applies to a complete record in a table.

A field validation rule applies to the data entered in a single field. The rule limits the data to a range of values or to one of a few specific values. A record validation rule compares values in two separate fields in the same record. For example, you might require the selling price of a product to be greater than the cost to produce it. The record validation rule is enforced when you move to another record and Access tries to save the one you just worked on.

The following steps show how to put these rules to work.

How to fix it

To set a validation rule for a field, follow these steps:

1. In the database window, select the table with the troublesome data and click the Design button.

2. In the Field Name column, select the field you want to apply the rule to, and then click in the Validation Rule property box in the Field Properties area. ▶

3. Enter an expression that will control the value the field can have. For example, if the date in a Date/Time field must not be later than one year from today, type the expression **<Date()+365**. If a number (say the number of units in an order) must fall between 1 and 999, type **>=1 AND <1000**. If you want to limit the data in the field to a short list of values, type the items in that list, enclosing them in double quotation marks and separating them with the *Or* operator—for example, **"Teal" OR "Burgundy" OR "Navy"**.

4. Click in the Validation Text property box, and enter a message that will notify the user when there's something wrong with the value he or she typed in. ▶

5. Save the changes to the table's design.

To set up a record validation rule for a table, follow these steps:

1. In the database window, select the table you want to apply the rule to and click the Design button.

2. In the toolbar, click the Properties button.

3. In the Validation Rule property box, enter the expression for the rule you want to apply—for example, **[Sales Price]>[Unit Cost]**.

4. In the Validation Text property box, enter a message that notifies the user about the rule you've applied. ▶

More about data validation

A field validation rule is enforced when you enter or edit data in that field, whether you're working in a datasheet, a form, or with an append or update query. If the rule is violated, the message entered in the Validation Text property box appears when you move to another field. If you enter a list of values in the Validation Rule property box, Access will insist that the field contain one of those values or leave the field blank.

If you add a validation rule to a field after data has been entered in the field, Access offers to test the existing data against the rule. If you respond No to the offer, you can still run the test later by switching to Table Design view and choosing Test Validation Rules from the Edit menu.

Tip

A table can have only one record validation rule, so if you need more than one criterion, combine them in a single expression with the *And* or *Or* operators.

Tip

If you need help with an expression, click the Build button next to the Validation Rule property box, and the Expression Builder will give you a hand.

The values in a field don't have the same format

Source of the problem

That important report you prepared doesn't look quite right. Yes, the data is right; you checked it. But some people in the office enjoy seeing last names in all caps, and others get a kick out of italics. When there are many people entering and editing data in a database, their personal preferences can give a disorderly appearance to the data. And it's possible that even you occasionally vary the data formats you use. While the data is correct, the motley display is disruptive and can confuse even the most stable of information managers.

The way to fix a haphazard display of data is to set the Format property for a field. By doing this you standardize how the data is displayed and calm any ruffled feathers. Access provides a set of standard formats for Number, Date/Time, and Yes/No fields. You can set custom formats for all types of fields except the OLE Object field type. You add the formatting instructions by using special symbols. Many symbols can be used with all types of fields, while others are used only with certain types of fields.

The following steps show you how to manage the format of your data.

How to fix it

To set the Format property for a text or memo field, follow these steps:

1. In the database window, select the table with the field you want to format and then click the Design button.

2. Select the field in the Field Name column, and then click in the Format property box in the Field Properties area.

3. Using special symbols and placeholders, enter the expression for the format you want to apply to the data. If you enter the formatting instruction >@, Jones will be displayed as JONES. The @ symbol is used to indicate a required character or space. The format setting @@@-@@-@@@@ will display the entry 123456789 as 123-45-6789, perfect for Social Security numbers. ▶

To change the default check box format for a Yes/No field, follow these steps:

1. Open the table in Design view, and select the Yes/No field.

2. In the Field Properties area, click the Lookup tab. From the Display Control list, select Text Box.

3. Click the General tab, and select the format you want in the Format property list. You have a choice of True/False, Yes/No, or On/Off. Save the changes to the table's design. ▶

More about creating custom formats

Here's a table showing some of the symbols you use to set up text and memo field formatting.

Symbol	Effect	Example
@	Indicates a required character or space.	@@@-@@-@@@@ displays the value 123456789 as 123-45-6789. All characters are required.
!	Fills from left to right, forcing values in the field to be left aligned.	Align... ...not Align
"abc"	Displays the characters enclosed in quotation marks.	@;"None" displays the field value, if any, or None if blank.
*	Fills the field with the character that follows.	@*#### displays abc as abc####, with the number of # symbols displayed depending on the width of the field display.
\	Indicates that the character that follows is meant to be a literal instead of a special symbol.	@\! displays the field value Not here as Not here!
[color]	Displays data in color. Available colors are black, blue, green, cyan, red, magenta, yellow, and white.	@[blue] displays the field value in blue.
&	Indicates an optional character or space.	@@@-@@-&&&& displays the value 123456 as 123-45-6. The last four characters are not required.
>	Converts all letters to uppercase.	Tide pool is displayed as TIDE POOL.
<	Converts all letters to lowercase.	TIDE POOL is displayed as tide pool.

I don't know what information to enter in a field

Source of the problem

Although you've tried to identify all the fields in your database with unique and informative names, there still can be some lingering doubt about exactly what data is supposed to go in a field. You need a method of instructing yourself and others about what to enter in a field. One way to get the jump on knowing what data to put in a field is to create an input mask, which serves as a kind of template. Fields that need a specific length (a five-digit ID number, for example) or type of data, or fields that include required characters such as slashes, commas, or hyphens, are good candidates for an input mask. When you move to the field to enter data in it, the input mask is displayed, providing guidance for the data you need to enter.

The following steps show how to curb forgetful data entry habits by using an input mask.

How to fix it

1. In the database window, select the table containing the field you want to work with and then click the Design button.

2. Select the field in the Field Name column. In the Field Properties area, click in the Input Mask property box and then click the Build (...) button at the right. This starts the Input Mask Wizard. ▶

Input Mask Wizard

Which input mask matches how you want data to look?

To see how a selected mask works, use the Try It box.

To change the Input Mask list, click the Edit List button.

Input Mask:	Data Look:
Long Time	1:12:00 PM
Short Date	9/27/1969
Short Time	13:12
Medium Time	01:12 PM
Medium Date	27-Sep-69

Try It: [   ]

[Edit List] [Cancel] [< Back] [Next >] [Finish]

Tip

The wizard works only for text and date/time fields, but you can create an input mask for any type of field. Also, you don't have to use the wizard at all; you can simply enter the appropriate input mask characters in the Input Mask property box. (See the Access online help for more examples.)

3. In the Input Mask Wizard, you'll see some commonly used formats to pick from. Choose the input mask you want.

4. Click in the Try It box to see how the mask will be displayed, and then enter some sample data. ▶

If you want to create a new custom input mask, follow these steps:

1. Start the Input Mask Wizard as described in steps 1 and 2 above.

2. Click the Edit List button.

3. At the bottom of the dialog box, click the new record button in the record navigation bar to display a blank record. ▶

4. For a field that contains coded parts numbers using a format like ABC-1234-56A, for example, type **>LLL-0000-00L** in the Input Mask box. ▶

5. Enter a description of the mask in the Description box, and type an underscore in the Placeholder box.

6. Enter a sample of the data in the Sample Data box.

7. Click Close, and then click Finish in the Input Mask Wizard.

8. Save your changes to the table's design.

9. Open the data entry form and click in the field with the new input mask to see how it looks.

I'm having trouble converting a field to another data type

Source of the problem

No matter how carefully you've defined the fields in your database, the need for information shifts. Someone is always changing something, and you have to go along with it. Your boss asks for a new report that requires date arithmetic, so a text field that contains dates most of the time must now become a Date/Time field. This sounds simple enough, but you have to be explicit with a computer program. Otherwise, it might rebel.

There are several reasons why Access might balk at your conversion:

- You're trying to convert a field to an AutoNumber type.

- The data already in the field is not compatible with the type of field you want to convert to.

- You're tampering with a field that's part of a table relationship.

The following steps show how to solve these problems.

How to fix it

If you see the message shown in the figure, you have tried to convert a field to the Auto Number data type after you've entered one or more records. These steps explain how to add an AutoNumber field:

1. Click OK to dispose of the message.

2. Add a new field to the table, and select AutoNumber from the drop-down list of data types.

3. Save the changes to the table design. As the message indicates, Access will fill in the AutoNumber data on its own.

4. If the field you were trying to convert contains relevant information, leave it as is. If you were just using the field as a primary key field with no other meaning, delete it. The new AutoNumber field will serve that purpose.

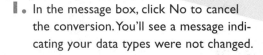

If you see the message shown in this figure, you have tried to convert a field that contains data to a different type of field, but the data in the field doesn't fit the new type. Before the conversion can be successful, you have to revise the incompatible data. The following steps show you how to revise the data: ►

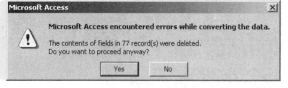

1. In the message box, click No to cancel the conversion. You'll see a message indicating your data types were not changed.

2. Click OK, and then click the View button to switch the table to Datasheet view. If you are asked if you want to save changes to the table, click No.

3. Review the data in the field you are trying to convert, and change the records that aren't compatible with the data type you're converting to.

4. Click the View button again to return the table to Design view.

5. In the table design window, select the new data type for the field and then save the changes to the table design.

If you see the message shown here, you tried to convert the data type of a field that is used in a relationship with a field in another table. To adjust the relationships, do the following: ►

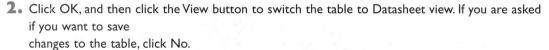

1. Click OK to close the message.

2. In the Tools menu, click Relationships.

3. Right-click the line that runs from the field you're converting to another table or tables, and then click Delete in the short-cut menu.

4. Close the relationships window.

5. With the table open in Design view, select the field you're working with and then select the new data type from the drop-down list.

6. Save the changes to the table.

7. Open the Relationships window and connect the fields in the various tables again.

Tip

You can reestablish the relationships between the fields after converting the data type. Open the Relationships window, and connect the fields in the various tables again. If you need to reestablish the table relationships you deleted, make sure the new data type is compatible with the field formerly related to the field you converted.

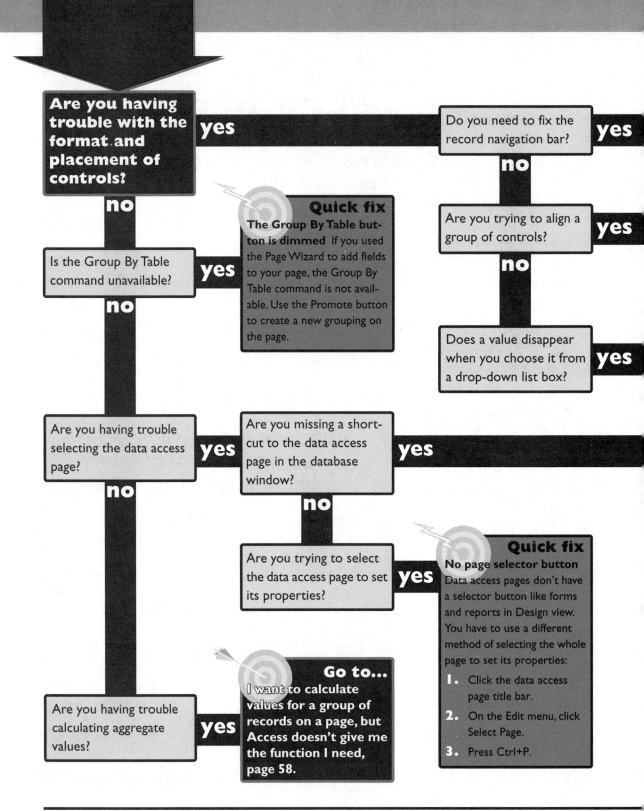

Are you having trouble with the format and placement of controls? **yes**

no

Is the Group By Table command unavailable? **yes**

no

Do you need to fix the record navigation bar? **yes**

no

Are you trying to align a group of controls? **yes**

no

Does a value disappear when you choose it from a drop-down list box? **yes**

Quick fix
The Group By Table button is dimmed If you used the Page Wizard to add fields to your page, the Group By Table command is not available. Use the Promote button to create a new grouping on the page.

Are you having trouble selecting the data access page? **yes**

no

Are you missing a shortcut to the data access page in the database window? **yes**

no

Are you trying to select the data access page to set its properties? **yes**

Quick fix
No page selector button Data access pages don't have a selector button like forms and reports in Design view. You have to use a different method of selecting the whole page to set its properties:
1. Click the data access page title bar.
2. On the Edit menu, click Select Page.
3. Press Ctrl+P.

Are you having trouble calculating aggregate values? **yes**

Go to...
I want to calculate values for a group of records on a page, but Access doesn't give me the function I need, page 58.

Data access pages

Go to...
The record navigation bar doesn't look right, and some buttons are missing, page 56.

Go to...
I'm trying to size and align a group of controls, but I can't select the controls as a group, page 60.

Go to...
The shortcut to my page is missing from the database window, page 54.

Quick fix

Disappearing values
Chances are you specified the wrong column for the data you want stored in the Control Source field for the drop-down list box control.

1. Open the data access page in Design view.
2. Double-click the drop-down list box control.
3. Click the arrow next to the ListBoundField property and then select the name of the foreign key field (the bound column).
4. Switch to Page view and check the results.

If your solution isn't here, check these related chapters:

- Forms, designing, page 124
- Forms, viewing data, page 140
- Reports, creating, page 258
- Reports, previewing and printing, page 268

Or see the general trouble-shooting tips on page xv.

The shortcut to my page is missing from the database window

Source of the problem

You did it. You've joined the crowd on the Internet. Travel arrangements, theater tickets, e-mail to your friends and family. You've even started working with some of your Microsoft Access data on the Web, having created some nice-looking data access pages to display information that lots of people need. Now, when you go to update your page—maybe add a field or two—you open the database but can't find the shortcut to your page. The reason you don't see a shortcut is that you created a stand-alone data access page without having the underlying database open at the time.

If you want a shortcut to your page to appear in the database window, you should have the database open when you create the page. But don't worry. You can still add a shortcut to the database window so that you can open the page from within the database.

The following steps show you how to add a shortcut to your database window.

How to fix it

1. Open the database that serves as the source of the information displayed in your data access page. In the database window, click Pages in the Objects bar.

2. Double-click Edit Web Page That Already Exists.

3. In the Locate Web Page dialog box, find the data access page you created (it should have an .htm extension). You might need to look in a different folder. ▶

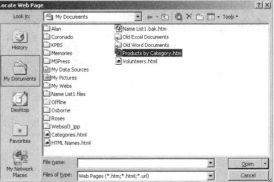

4. Once you locate the file, click Open to open the page in Design view.

5. Add other fields or elements to the data access page as necessary.

Data access pages

6. Save and close the data access page. When you close the page, you'll see a shortcut to it in the database window. ▶

If the page with the missing shortcut was created in Access 2000, you need to take a few extra steps before opening it and setting up the shortcut. When you open the page from the Locate Web Page dialog box, you'll see a message about converting the page. Follow these steps to set up the shortcut. ▶

1. Click Convert in the message box to convert the page to Access 2002. If you decide you'd just rather not work with this page, click Cancel.

2. Access displays a message telling you it's made a backup copy of the original page and shows the location and name of the backup. Copy this information down just in case. ▶

3. Click OK, and the converted data access page appears in Design view where you can make changes as necessary.

4. Make your changes and save the converted page. You'll now see a shortcut to the page in the database window.

The record navigation bar doesn't look right, and some buttons are missing

Source of the problem

The Web guru who works on your database has a mind of her own. She's done a good job creating data access pages and moving your data to the Web, but she doesn't know everything about the way you look at your information. While that's not her fault, she's now gone and removed some of the buttons from the navigation bar that she didn't think you would need. As long as you have permission to make changes to the design of objects in your database, you can easily restore these buttons. And, if you don't like the way the recordset label tells you which record in the bunch you're looking at—for example, "Recordset name 1 of 10" or "Recordset name 1-5 of 25"—you can change that, too.

The following steps show how to change these elements.

How to fix it

To restore the buttons you need to the navigation bar, do the following:

1. In the database window, select the data access page shortcut and then click Design.

2. Right-click the record navigation bar that you want to change and point to Navigation Buttons in the shortcut menu. ▶

3. Select the check box of the button you want returned to the navigation bar.

4. Repeat steps 2 and 3 for each of the buttons you need.

Data access pages

To change the recordset label in the bar, do the following:

1. In the database window, select the data access page shortcut and then click Design.

2. Double-click the recordset label in the record navigation bar.

3. On the property sheet, click the Other tab.

4. Edit the InnerText property to read the way you want. For example, delete Wiz from the label. ▶

More about customizing the record navigation bar

You can also change the image on a button in the navigation bar by selecting the button and changing its Src property to the image file (.gif format) of your choice. With the data access page open in Design view, double-click the button. In the property sheet, click the Other tab and make the change to the Src property. ▶

Tip

If the page shows a record navigation bar in more than one group, you can customize the bars differently.

I want to calculate values for a group of records on a page, but Access doesn't give me the function I need

Source of the problem

You usually group records on a data access page so that you can calculate some aggregate values for the grouped information. You want to add up the total sales, count the number of transactions, or see the average sales for a product. When you drag the field you want to tally to the group header section in the data access design grid, you'll meet the Layout Wizard. This wizard offers you a choice between tabular and columnar layouts and then, with your best interests at heart, also creates the aggregate value, depending on the data type of the detail field. If the field contains numeric or currency data, the Sum function is automatically used. If it is any other data type, Access uses the Count function. If you want to apply a different function to the group of records you're thinking about, you have to do that yourself, without help from the wizard.

The following steps show you how to change to the function you want to use after the wizard has done the hard work for you.

How to fix it

1. In the database window, select your grouped data access page, and then click Design.

2. In the View menu, click Field List.

3. In the Field List, select the field that contains the detail values you want to make calculations on.

4. Drag the field to the group header or footer section where you want the aggregate values to appear. The Layout Wizard appears.

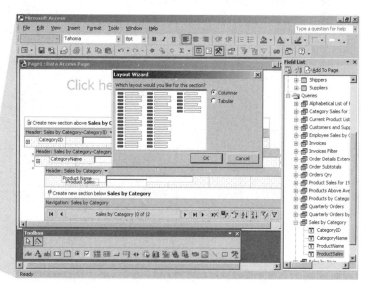

5. Click the layout option you want—Columnar or Tabular—and then click OK. The wizard creates a bound span control in the section. ▶

6. Select the new control and click Properties in the View menu.

7. On the Data tab, choose the aggregate type you want from the Total Type property list. ▼

8. Select the label for the bound span control.

9. On the Other tab, change the Inner Text property for the label to reflect the calculation you've made. For example, **Average sales for this product.** ▶

10. Switch to Page view to see the results. ▶

I'm trying to size and align a group of controls, but I can't select the controls as a group

Source of the problem

You've discovered the great new tool—the data access page—that lets you post Access data on the Internet. Designing a data access page is a lot like designing a form or report. Add the controls you need and set some of their properties so that everything works. Once you've placed the controls in the page grid, you need to clean up the arrangement a little. With forms and reports, all you need to do is hold down the Shift key and select all the controls you want to align or resize alike. When you try to do that to finish the design of a data access page, you find that you can't select multiple controls. What's up?

Well, sometimes it pays to download the latest version of a software product. If Microsoft Internet Explorer 5.5 is on your machine, you won't have this problem. With that version of Internet Explorer, you can select multiple controls on a data access page just like you do on a form or report. If you don't have Internet Explorer 5.5, you can still avoid the long and tedious process of aligning and resizing each control individually because Access provides the Alignment and Sizing toolbar, which has the buttons you need to do the job. This toolbar helps you align and size controls to match one you have already placed in the page.

The following steps show how to use this toolbar to create a neat and tidy data access page.

How to fix it

1. In the database window, select the data access page and then click Design.

2. If you don't see the Alignment and Sizing toolbar, right-click in another toolbar and select it from the list of available toolbars.

3. Select the control you want to use as the pattern for the other controls.

Data access pages

4. In the Alignment and Sizing toolbar, click the button that represents the adjustment you want to make:

- Choose the first button, Align Left, if you want the left edge of the second control to line up with the left edge of the first one you selected.

- Choose the second button, Align Right, if you want the right edge of the second control to line up with the right edge of the first one.

- Choose the third button, Align Top, to align the top edge of the second control to the top edge of the first.

- Choose the fourth button, Align Bottom, to align the bottom edges.

- Choose the fifth button, Size Height, to resize the height of the second control to match the first.

- Choose the sixth button, Size Width, to resize the width of the second control to match the first.

- Choose the last button, Size Height/Width, to resize both the height and width of the second control to match the first.

5. After choosing the adjustment you want to make, select the control you want to adjust.

6. Repeat the steps to align or resize other controls.

Tip

If you want to repeat the same adjustment with more than one control, double-click the button in the Alignment and Sizing toolbar to lock it down. Click the other controls one at a time. When you are finished with that adjustment, click another button in the Alignment and Sizing toolbar or simply press Esc.

One size does *not* fit all

Unfortunately, not all the controls in the data access page can be resized even with the Alignment and Sizing toolbar. You can't change the height of a list box or a drop-down list box (the equivalent of a combo box in a form). The vertical size of these controls is based on the font setting of the data displayed in the control. You can, however, change the number of rows to display, which will affect the overall vertical dimension.

Troubleshooting Microsoft Access 2002 61

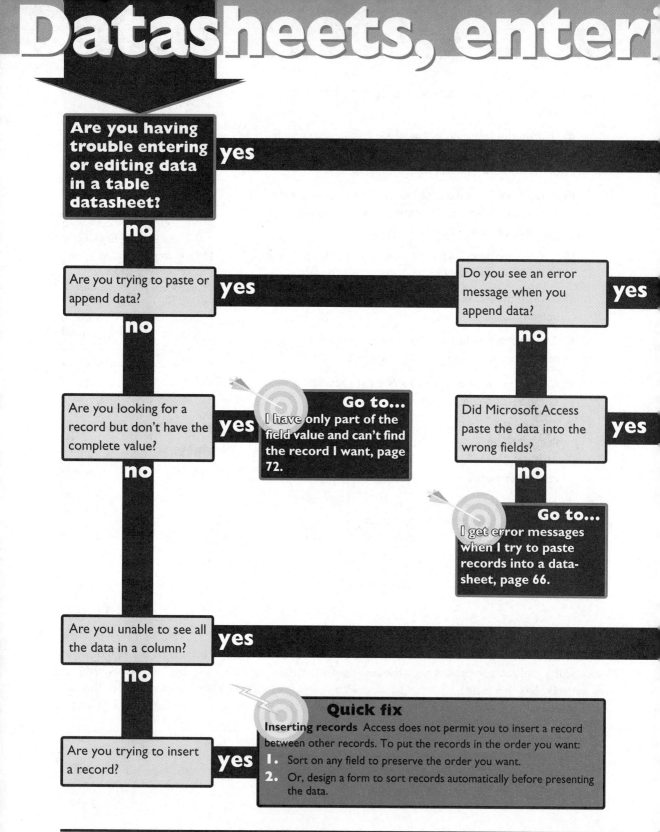

Are you having trouble entering or editing data in a table datasheet?

yes

no

Are you trying to paste or append data?

yes

no

Do you see an error message when you append data?

yes

no

Are you looking for a record but don't have the complete value?

yes

Go to...
I have only part of the field value and can't find the record I want, page 72.

no

Did Microsoft Access paste the data into the wrong fields?

yes

no

Go to...
I get error messages when I try to paste records into a datasheet, page 66.

Are you unable to see all the data in a column?

yes

no

Quick fix
Inserting records Access does not permit you to insert a record between other records. To put the records in the order you want:
1. Sort on any field to preserve the order you want.
2. Or, design a form to sort records automatically before presenting the data.

Are you trying to insert a record?

yes

Does a date field have an input mask?

yes

Go to...
I can't enter dates the way I want in an input mask, page 70.

no

Go to...
I can't enter or edit field data in a datasheet, page 64.

Quick fix

Can't append data You have probably tried to enter a record with the same value in a key field as a record already in the table.

1. Change the value in the existing record or in the record you are adding.
2. Try again.

Quick fix

Wrong field order Access pasted the data in the wrong field because it pastes fields into the datasheet in the same order as they appear in the original (source) record. Reorder the columns in the destination datasheet to match the order in the source (or the other way around).

Quick fix

Resizing columns to see data The field value is too large for the column.

1. Double-click the right edge of the column heading to resize the column.
2. Or, click in the column, click Column Width on the Format menu, and then click Best Fit.

If your solution isn't here, check these related chapters:

- Data, setting field properties, page 42
- Datasheets, viewing data, page 74
- Filtering, page 110
- Queries, selection criteria, page 224

Or see the general troubleshooting tips on page xv.

I can't enter or edit field data in a datasheet

Source of the problem

When all you're trying to do is update the tables in your database with new or revised data, it's a pain to have Microsoft Access say you can't do it. Several simple reasons may explain why you may not be able to edit or enter data in your table datasheet.

- The field you're working with is an AutoNumber data type. You can't edit AutoNumber fields because Access maintains these values automatically.

- You opened the database as read-only. If you did, the New button is dimmed in the database window. Closing the database and opening it normally should solve your problem.

- Another possible reason your value isn't accepted is that you are entering a value that exceeds the field size setting for a field. In a number field, Access might round off the number you enter to the largest value allowed. In a text field, you might be trying to enter too many characters. The default field size for a text field is 50 characters, but the field you're working with might limit you to fewer than 50.

The following steps show you how to solve these problems.

How to fix it

If Access changed a number value you entered or displayed an error message about a value not being valid, follow these steps: ▶

1. Open the table in Design view and then select the field you're having trouble with.

2. In the General tab of the Field Properties area, change the Field Size property to Long Integer. Save the changes to the table design. ▶

3. Switch the table to Datasheet view and enter the value you were trying to enter again.

4. If changing the field size doesn't fix your problem, you might have tried to enter text in a number field. With the table open in Design view, check the field's data type and, if necessary, change it to Text.

If your problem lies with the size of a text field, follow these steps:

1. Open the table in Design view and then select the field you're working with.

2. In the General tab of the Field Properties area, increase the number in the Field Size property to the maximum number of characters you expect to enter. The maximum for a text field is 255 characters. ▶

More about viewing all the columns on your screen

When you are entering or editing data in a datasheet that's too large to view on one screen, keeping track of which record you are working on can be difficult. Keeping one or more of the important columns displayed on the screen while you edit can help orient you. To do this, use the freeze column feature. Select the column or columns you want to remain visible and then click Freeze Columns on the Format menu. As you scroll to other columns, the frozen columns remain visible at the left side of the table. When you are through editing the data, you can unfreeze the columns by clicking Unfreeze All Columns on the Format menu. Unfortunately, Access doesn't put the thawed columns back where they belong, so you will have to drag them to their previous positions.

Tip

If you need more room than 255 characters, you can change the Text data type to Memo, which has a much larger size limit.

Tip

In the Open dialog box, you usually have four options when you click the Open button: Open, Open Read-Only, Open Exclusive, and Open Exclusive Read-Only.

I get error messages when I try to paste records into a datasheet

Source of the problem

Pasting records into a table sounds so easy. Just like fourth grade. Unfortunately, Access is a little pickier than your fourth grade teacher was. If Access can't paste any or all of the data you want to move or copy, you'll see a message describing the problem and maybe even a clue about how to fix it, just like the messages on the homework you got back from your teacher. After explaining the problem, Access displays another message, indicating that it has saved all the records that it couldn't paste in the Paste Errors table. Reviewing the Paste Errors table is a convenient way to troubleshoot your problem.

Access might not be able to paste data for several reasons, including the following:

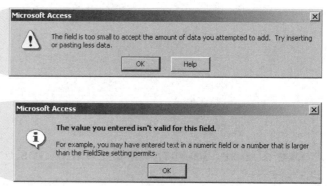

- You tried to paste text with more characters than the field you're pasting it in allows. ▶

- The value you are trying to paste isn't compatible with the type of data the destination field can accept. ▶

- The data you pasted is placed in the wrong columns in the destination datasheet. Access pastes the values in the order they appear in columns of the source datasheet, not by matching field names.

- The source field contains a value that doesn't fit with certain property settings in the destination field, such as a validation rule, an input mask, or a setting in the Limit To List, Required, or AllowZeroLength properties. ▶

- You tried to paste records with more fields than the destination table contains or more than you selected to replace.

● You might find the column names pasted in a record instead of the field values. This can happen if you select the data to paste incorrectly. If you select the whole column of data, you get a delimited string that includes the field name along with the field values. Then, when you paste the selection, the column headings appear in the first record. ▶

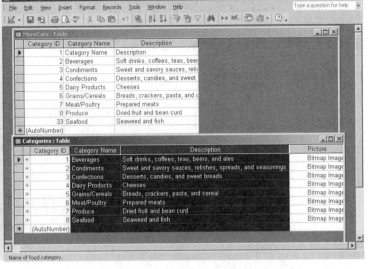

● The value in the primary key field or in a uniquely indexed field might be a duplicate of one already in the destination datasheet. ▶

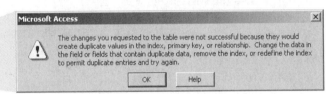

The following steps show you how to solve these sticky pasting problems.

How to fix it

1. In the message box that explains the problem, click OK.

2. Click OK in the message about the Paste Errors table. ▶

I get error messages when I try to paste records into a datasheet

(continued from page 67)

3. In the database window, select the Paste Errors table and then click Open. You might need to correct the errors that caused the paste failure one by one. In this figure, the entries in the Ship Name column are too large for the destination field. ▶

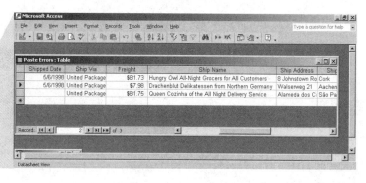

4. Open both the source and the destination tables in Design view.

5. In the General tab of the Field Properties area of the source and destination tables, compare the Field Size property settings of the problem fields. One of the fields might be too small to contain the data you are pasting. For example, text from a field that allows 255 characters won't always fit into a field that allows only 40. Adjust the Field Size property setting in the appropriate table. ▶

Some other data corrections might include the following:

1. Make sure the data types are compatible. For example, you can't paste text into a field with a Number data type.

2. Check the property settings of the destination fields for validation rules, input masks, and other restrictions. The data you are pasting might not follow the rules set up for the field you are pasting the data into.

3. If the problem is that you are pasting records with more fields than the destination table can handle, select fewer fields to paste.

4. After you've modified settings and field types, save any changes you've made to the tables' designs.

5. Select the records in the Paste Errors table and then click the Copy button in the toolbar.

6. In the destination table, select the blank new record row and then click the Paste button.

7. If you receive no more pasting errors, delete the Paste Errors table from the database.

If the column names were pasted into a record along with the field values, delete that record from the destination datasheet.

If the field values show up in the wrong order in the destination datasheet, open the datasheet you are pasting records from and rearrange the columns so that the field names are in the same order as the datasheet you're pasting records into.

If the problem lies in duplicate primary key or unique index values, edit the duplicate values in the source datasheet before trying to paste the records into the destination datasheet.

> **Tip**
>
> Fix the errors and paste the corrected records before you attempt another paste operation. The Paste Errors table holds records only temporarily. The records in the table are overwritten with the next paste failure.

More about pasting problems

You might encounter a few other problems when pasting records from one table to another in Access. One possibility is that the field you are trying to paste into might be in a hidden column. If so, go to the destination table in Datasheet view and click Unhide Columns on the Format menu.

Another problem could be that you did not select a destination for the field or fields you want to paste. Or you might have tried to cut data from or to paste data into a field that is locked or unavailable.

I can't enter dates the way I want in an input mask

Source of the problem

As much as you'd like to think that you can make a process as simple as entering data foolproof, we all know that errors can cunningly sneak into our data through the back door. The input mask, one of the really helpful features of Access, tries to control what and how much data you can enter in a field. However, using the input mask can generate a few problems of its own.

The input mask displays fill-in spaces, often punctuated with special characters such as slashes (/), commas, and periods. An input mask often limits the number of characters you can enter in a field, which can cause problems when you have a longer or shorter value to enter.

Input masks are very particular. If you hear a beep when entering data in a field, the pattern for an input mask may not match the format you're using to enter the data in a field. For example, if you enter a date as 11503 (meaning January 15, 2003), an input mask that requires six characters could display the value 11/50/3 instead of 01/15/03 because you didn't enter the first 0. Neither the month or day can have a value of 50, so this results in an error.

You might also have trouble entering a date in a field with an input mask if the mask conflicts with the display format. For example, dates might be displayed in the format 6-June-2003, while the input mask shows __/__/__. This difference results in your having to enter a value that doesn't look like the values already in the field. You'll hear a beep if you don't fill in all the blanks or if you try to spell out the name of the month that appears in the displayed value.

The following steps show you how to solve these problems with input masks.

How to fix it

If you see an error message that a date value isn't appropriate for the input mask, do the following: ▶

1. Select the entire field entry.

2. Press the Delete key.

3. Enter the date value using the format of the input mask, including the leading zeros.

If the input mask conflicts with the format in which a date field is displayed, take these steps to correct the problem:

1. Open the table in Design view and select the field that is giving you trouble.

2. In the Field Properties area, click in the Input Mask property box and then click the Build button (...).

3. In the Input Mask Wizard dialog box, select the Medium Date mask that matches the setting in the Format property box in the table design. ▶

4. Click Finish and save the table design.

Why is a medium date format better?

To correct the problem with seeing dates in a format that's different from how you're asked to enter them, you could also change the field's Format property to Short Date. However, changing the format to Medium Date is a better solution because it eliminates any ambiguities that can result from the Short Date format. The Medium Date format shows the abbreviated month name instead of all numbers. With the Short Date format, on the other hand, if you enter 08/13/03, Access interprets it as 13-Aug-2003, but if you enter 13/08/03, the date displayed is 03-Aug-2013. If you enter a date in which both of the first two entries are less than 12, Access treats the first entry as the month and the second as the day: 10/08/03 is interpreted as 08-Oct-2003, while 08/10/03 is interpreted as 10-Aug-2003.

Tip

If you have a field whose format needs to conform to a specific pattern—for example, a product code or a catalog number—you might want a special input mask to help with data entry. You can ask the Input Mask Wizard for help in creating one and save it for future use.

I have only part of the field value and can't find the record I want

Source of the problem

It's easy to find everyone listed in your database with the last name of Johnson. But if someone asks you to find all the records that mention cats in a memo field, things get a bit tricky. Or, maybe you need to locate all the businesses on 5th or 6th Avenue because that's where you're heading on your new door-to-door ad campaign. If you know part of a value and that part is at the start of a field, you can simply sort on that field and track down the information you need. But difficulties arise if the part of the value you know is embedded in the field. In these cases, you have to resort to something like the old poker device of wildcards, in this case symbols that take the place of one or more letters or numbers.

If you've already used these special characters in place of real ones, you might have had a problem with the values that turned up. Wildcards are usually used to search text and memo fields, but, if you're careful, you can massage them to search in date and number fields as well.

If you're not finding the right records, you might be using the wrong wildcard. If you are using more than one symbol, you might have placed them in the wrong order. Another problem might be options set in the Find And Replace dialog box.

If you have tried to find data that includes one of the wildcard characters, you might not have found the records you expected. Looking for a wildcard character takes some extra preparation because Access thinks you are using it as a wildcard instead of treating it as the character you want to find. You'll have no problem looking for values that include exclamation points (!) or closing brackets (]), but other symbols need special treatment.

The following steps show you some ways to use wildcards to your advantage.

How to fix it

If you want to find records with a certain value in a field—for example, any order for any product with "tofu" in its name—do the following:

1. Open the table in Datasheet view and click in the column for the field you want to search.

2. On the Edit menu, click Find.

3. In the Find What box, type ***tofu***.

> **Tip**
>
> The asterisk (*) wildcard takes the place of any number of characters and must be used as the first or last character in the Find What box.

4. In the Match box, select Any Part Of Field.

5. Click Find Next. ▶

6. To find additional records with the same partial value, click Find Next again.

If you are looking for addresses on specific streets (in this example, 5th or 6th Avenue), you can mix wildcards with text as follows:

1. Open the table in Datasheet view and click in the column containing the addresses.

2. On the Edit menu, click Find.

3. In the Find What box, type ***[56]th Ave***.

4. In the Match box, select Any Part Of Field. ▶

5. Click Find Next.

If you want to find a value that includes one of the wildcard characters, do the following:

1. Click in the field you want to search, and then click Find on the Edit menu.

2. If you are looking for records that begin with the value *A, for example, type the expression **[*]A*** in the Find What box.

3. In the Match box, select Start Of Field.

4. Click Find Next. ▶

Tip

The pair of square brackets ([ ]) enclose alternative values or a range of values. For example, using [5-9] in the expression would find addresses on 5th, 6th, 7th, 8th, or 9th Avenue.

Datas

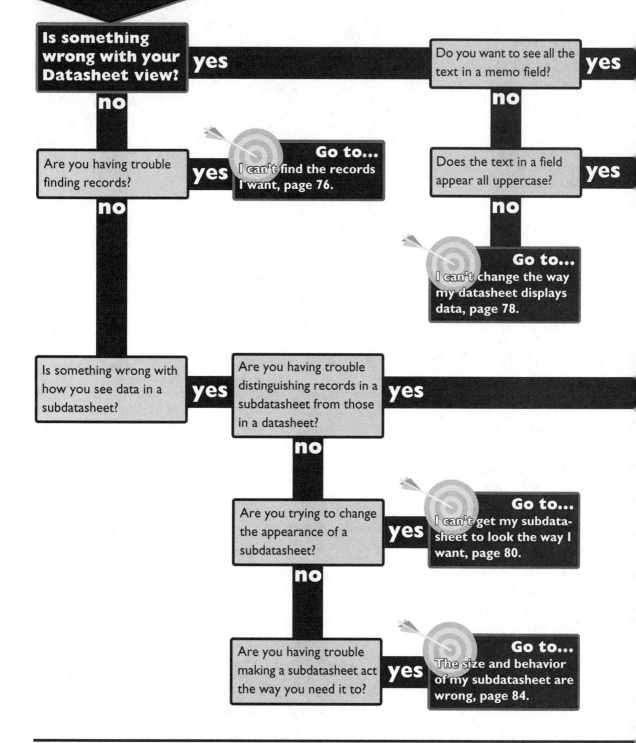

Is something wrong with your Datasheet view? — **yes** → **Do you want to see all the text in a memo field?** — **yes**

no ↓   **no** ↓

Are you having trouble finding records? — **yes** → **Go to...** I can't find the records I want, page 76.

no ↓

Does the text in a field appear all uppercase? — **yes**

no ↓

Go to... I can't change the way my datasheet displays data, page 78.

Is something wrong with how you see data in a subdatasheet? — **yes** → **Are you having trouble distinguishing records in a subdatasheet from those in a datasheet?** — **yes**

no ↓

Are you trying to change the appearance of a subdatasheet? — **yes** → **Go to...** I can't get my subdatasheet to look the way I want, page 80.

no ↓

Are you having trouble making a subdatasheet act the way you need it to? — **yes** → **Go to...** The size and behavior of my subdatasheet are wrong, page 84.

Quick fix

Zooming in on memo fields You can use the keyboard to zoom in on the text in a memo field.

1. Click in the memo field of the record you want to view.
2. Press Shift+F2.

Quick fix

Removing uppercase formatting You need to change a setting in the field's Format property.

1. Open the table in Design view.
2. Select the field.
3. In the Field Properties area, remove the > symbol from the Format property expression.

Quick fix

Formatting subdatasheets

1. Expand the subdatasheet and click in one of the records.
2. On the Format menu, click Datasheets.
3. Change settings for the cell effects, gridline colors, and border styles.
4. Click OK.

If your solution isn't here, check these related chapters:

- Datasheets, entering and editing data, page 62
- Queries, simple select, page 236
- Relationships, page 248

Or see the general troubleshooting tips on page xv.

I can't find the records I want

Source of the problem

Just like car keys, Microsoft Access records seem to run off and hide when you need them the most. Even using the clever search tools Access provides, you still have those days when you can't find a record that you know is there, lurking behind the scenes somewhere. When you use the Find command to locate a record, Access compares the search criteria you specify to the values stored in the field. This approach sounds simple enough, but it can cause a problem when the value is displayed in a form or report in a format that's different from the one in which the value is stored in the database. You usually use the format that a value is displayed in when you enter search criteria. Access, however, searches for data according to the format in which it is stored. There are three reasons that a stored value may not be in the same format as its displayed value:

● The field is a lookup field, which gets its value from another table or from a list of values for specific data. Access stores a reference to the value in the lookup field of the current table, and the lookup field then displays the referenced value. When you use the displayed value to search for a record, you won't find that data in the current table because it is actually stored in the lookup table or the list.

● A date value is stored in a different format. For example, you might display a date as 15-Jan-03, but it is stored as 01/15/03. If you use the displayed format to search for the record, the search fails to find the value.

● You applied an input mask to the field after data had been entered. An input mask formats data to your specifications, so the stored values might be inconsistent and might not meet the criteria of the input mask. If you use the format designated by the input mask to search for a record, you might not find it.

The following steps show you how to solve these problems with finding records.

How to fix it

If the field you are searching in is a lookup field or if you are searching for a date value, follow these steps:

1. In the database window, select the table, query, or form in which you are searching for records. Click the Open button.

2. Click in the field you want to search, and then click Find on the Edit menu.

3. In the Find What box, type the value just the way it is displayed in the field.

4. Select the Search Fields As Formatted check box and then click Find Next. ▶

If the field has an input mask that might be creating conflicts in your search, follow these steps:

1. If the table has only a few existing records, open it in Datasheet view and modify any data in the field that is not formatted in the style designated by the input mask. You can either reenter the data or simply edit it to conform to the input mask.

2. If the table already has numerous records, open it in Design view and then select the field you are searching.

3. In the Field Properties area, in the General tab, remove the input mask from the field. You can then use the Find command to locate the information and add the input mask to the table design again, if you want. ▶

Finding blank fields

There are two types of blank fields. A *null value* means that the value in the field was unknown at data entry time. A *zero-length string* means there is no relevant value for that record. For example, a person without a middle initial could enter a space character or two quotation marks without a space between them in that field to indicate that there is no such thing. This would create a zero-length string. To find records with null values, type **Null** or **Is Null** in the Find What box in the Find And Replace dialog box.

If you need to locate records with zero-length strings, type a pair of quotation marks ("") with no space between them. Be sure to clear the Search Field As Formatted option in the Find And Replace dialog box. Also be sure to select Whole Field in the Match box. ▶

I can't change the way my datasheet displays data

Source of the problem

Although you've probably created some handsome forms for viewing your data, there's no doubt that sometimes you'll just want to look at a simple datasheet. But, as simple as viewing a datasheet might seem, doing so can be problematic. Some of the columns might be missing, or one column might be the wrong width. You might need to change the check box that represents a Yes/No field to something else. If you're missing the subdatasheet of related data, you might have set the table's Subdatasheet Name property to None, which prevents Access from automatically creating subdatasheets from related tables. Or, maybe you have the opposite problem: subdatasheets are always displayed, whether you want them to be or not.

The following steps show you how to solve these datasheet mysteries.

How to fix it

If you are having trouble with columns in your datasheet, follow these steps:

1. In the database window, select the query or table you are working with and then click the Open button.

2. If any columns are missing from the Datasheet view, click Unhide Columns on the Format menu. In the Unhide Columns dialog box, check all of the columns you want to see.

3. Click Close and save your changes to the datasheet layout.

4. If you want to change a column's width to fit the contents of the column, double-click the column divider at the right side of the column.

Tip

Double-clicking a column to change its width only works for data that is already in the column. If you enter a longer value later, the column does not adjust to fit it. You have to adjust the width again.

If you want to change the display of Yes/No values in a datasheet, follow these steps:

1. In the database window, select the table you are working with and then click the Design button.

2. In the Field Name column, select the Yes/No field.

3. In the Field Properties area, click the Lookup tab.

4. In the Display Control property box, change the setting to Text Box. ▶

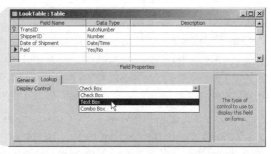

5. Click the General tab and then choose the Format property you want for the Yes/No field. ▶

If you don't see a subdatasheet of related data (or the plus sign) in your main datasheet, follow these steps:

1. In the database window, select the table you're working with and then click the Design button.

2. In the toolbar, click the Properties button.

3. Set the Subdatasheet Name property of the table to Auto. ▶

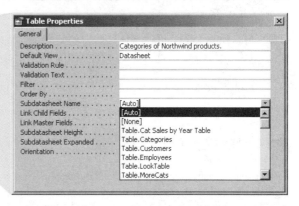

Tip

You can also set the Subdatasheet Name property to the name of any other related table or query in your database.

If you don't want to see the subdatasheet, follow these steps:

1. Open the table or query in Datasheet view.

2. On the Format menu, point to Subdatasheet and then click Remove.

Tip

You can change the default appearance for all datasheet views in your database. On the Tools menu, click Options and then click the Datasheet tab. You can elect to show or hide the horizontal and vertical gridlines and change their color and weight. You can determine how cells will appear. You can also change the font style, weight, and size. Once you set the default datasheet formatting, you can still change individual datasheet views.

I can't get my subdatasheet to look the way I want

Source of the problem

Just because subdatasheets are new on the block, you don't have to go along with whatever they want to show you. You're the boss, and you can coax these helpful views of data to look the way you want. You might have encountered some common problems when viewing data in subdatasheets:

● The subdatasheet always shows the same records from the related table or query instead of showing only the records related to the active record in the datasheet. If this is the case, the Link Child Fields and Link Master Fields properties are probably not set correctly. You can link subdatasheets to a datasheet by the fields that form the relationship between the tables or by any other pair of fields that contain matching data.

● You expanded a few subdatasheets and expected to see them expanded again the next time you opened the table. Access, however, didn't save the view you were using when you closed the table or query datasheet. Unfortunately, when you open a datasheet, it's all or nothing—all subdatasheets expanded or all collapsed. There's no half-and-half.

● You can't find the foreign key field or matching field or fields in the subdatasheet. Access doesn't expect that you want to see duplicate field values when you view a subdatasheet, but you can fix this, at least temporarily.

● You want to eliminate the subdatasheet completely from the Datasheet view. Doing this does not remove the related data from the database.

The following steps show you how to solve these problems.

How to fix it

If you see the same records in the subdatasheet no matter which record is active in the main datasheet, follow these steps:

1. In the database window, select the table or query that contains the subdatasheet and click the Open button.

2. On the Insert menu, click Subdatasheet.

3. In the Insert Subdatasheet dialog box, choose the table or query that contains the data you want to display in the subdatasheet.

4. From the Link Master Fields list, choose a field from the main datasheet that matches a field in the subdatasheet.

5. In the Link Child Fields box, choose the matching field in the subdatasheet. ▶

Tip

If you want to specify more than one matching field between the subdatasheet and main datasheet, enter additional field names in the Link Child Fields and Link Master Fields boxes, separating the field names with semicolons.

Insert Subdatasheet | ? | X

Tables | Queries | Both

OK
Cancel

Cat Sales by Year Table
Categories
Customers
Employees
LookTable
MoreCats
New Products
Order Details
Orders
Orders1
Paste Errors
Products
ReaderPrefs

Link Child Fields: CustomerID

Link Master Fields: Country

CustomerID
CompanyName
ContactName
ContactTitle
Address
City
Region

To change the Subdatasheet Expanded property, follow these steps:

1. Open the table or query containing the subdatasheet in Datasheet view.

2. On the Format menu, click Subdatasheet and then click Expand All or Collapse All. ▶

3. Click Yes when prompted to save the changes to the table's layout if you want to preserve the way the subdatasheet is displayed.

Microsoft Access - [Customers : Table]

File   Edit   View   Insert   Format   Records   Tools   Window   Help   Type a question for help

Font...
Datasheet...
Row Height...
Column Width...
Rename Column
Hide Columns
Unhide Columns...
Freeze Columns
Unfreeze All Columns
Subdatasheet   ▶   Expand All
                     Collapse All
                     Remove

Customer ID		Contact Name	Contact Title	
ALFKI	Alfreds F	Maria Anders	Sales Representative	Obere Str. 57
ANATR	Ana Truj	Ana Trujillo	Owner	Avda. de la Co
ANTON	Antonio	Antonio Moreno	Owner	Mataderos 23
AROUT	Around t	Thomas Hardy	Sales Representative	120 Hanover S
BERGS	Berglund	Christina Berglund	Order Administrator	Berguvsvägen
BLAUS	Blauer S	Hanna Moos	Sales Representative	Forsterstr. 57
BLONP	Blondel	Frédérique Citeaux	Marketing Manager	24, place Kléb
BOLID	Bólido C	Martín Sommer	Owner	C/ Araquil, 67
BONAP	Bon app	Laurence Lebihan	Owner	12, rue des Bo
BOTTM	Bottom-l		Accounting Manager	23 Tsawassen
BSBEV	B's Beverages		Sales Representative	Fauntleroy Circ
CACTU	Cactus Comidas para llevar		Sales Agent	Cerrito 333
CENTC	Centro comercial Moctezuma		Marketing Manager	Sierras de Gra
CHOPS	Chop-suey Chinese	Yang Wang	Owner	Hauptstr. 29
COMMI	Comércio Mineiro	Pedro Afonso	Sales Associate	Av. dos Lusíad
CONSH	Consolidated Holdings	Elizabeth Brown	Sales Representative	Berkeley Gard
DRACD	Drachenblut Delikatessen	Sven Ottlieb	Order Administrator	Walserweg 21
DUMON	Du monde entier	Janine Labrune	Owner	67, rue des Cir
EASTC	Eastern Connection	Ann Devon	Sales Agent	35 King George
ERNSH	Ernst Handel	Roland Mendel	Sales Manager	Kirchgasse 6
FAMIA	Familia Arquibaldo	Aria Cruz	Marketing Assistant	Rua Orós, 92
FISSA	FISSA Fabrica Inter. Salchichas S.A.	Diego Roel	Accounting Manager	C/ Moralzarzal
FOLIG	Folies gourmandes	Martine Rancé	Assistant Sales Agent	184, chaussée
FOLKO	Folk och fä HB	Maria Larsson	Owner	Åkergatan 24
FRANK	Frankenversand	Peter Franken	Marketing Manager	Berliner Platz 4
FRANR	France restauration	Carine Schmitt	Marketing Manager	54, rue Royale

Record: 1 of 91

Unique five-character code based on customer name.

Tip

You can also expand subdatasheets automatically by opening the table or query in Design view and setting the Subdatasheet Expanded property to Yes in the property sheet.

I can't get my subdatasheet to look the way I want

(continued from page 81)

To show the matching fields in the subdatasheet—including those that are hidden—follow these steps:

1. Open the query or table that contains the subdatasheet in Datasheet view.

2. If the subdatasheet is not displayed, click the plus sign to expand it.

3. Click in the subdatasheet.

4. On the Format menu, click Unhide Columns.

5. In the Unhide Columns dialog box, verify that all the columns you want to see are selected. Select any columns that have been hidden that you want to display. ▶

6. In the Unhide Columns dialog box, click Close.

Tip

Access doesn't expect that you want to see duplicate data when you expand a subdatasheet, so the matching field or fields are omitted from the subdatasheet display by default. Using the Unhide Columns command fixes the problem only temporarily. The next time you open the subdatasheet, the columns showing redundant data will be hidden again.

If you want to remove the subdatasheet from the Datasheet view, follow these steps:

1. Open the table or query that contains the subdatasheet in Datasheet view.

2. On the Format menu, click Subdatasheet and then click Remove.

3. If you don't want a datasheet to have a subdatasheet at all, open the table or query in Design view and change the Subdatasheet Name property to None. ▶

More about displaying subdatasheets

Hiding or displaying columns in a subdatasheet has no effect on the underlying data, only on the display of the data.

The fields you use to link a subdatasheet with a datasheet don't have to have the same names, but the fields must contain the same kind of data (for example, both fields must include numbers) and be of a compatible data type and field size. The most commonly used matching fields are the fields that form the relationship between the tables. You can use any fields that you expect to contain the same values. There would be no point in linking a datasheet to a subdatasheet by a field you know will never match.

The size and behavior of my subdatasheet are wrong

Source of the problem

Microsoft had a great idea when it decided to include subdatasheets in Access datasheets. You no longer have to design a form or report in order to see related data. You can now view related data right in the table or query datasheet. But subdatasheets aren't all just fun and games. You might have trouble getting them to behave the way you need. Sometimes you'd rather not see subdatasheets, and sometimes you want to see them all. Sometimes records in a subdatasheet take up a lot of space when they're displayed. Maybe you wish they'd take up less. If you are having trouble making a subdatasheet behave, you have a few options:

- Have the subdatasheets expanded or collapsed when you open the table or query in Datasheet view. Having all the subdatasheets collapsed is the default behavior.

- Limit the number of records that appear when you expand a subdatasheet. The default setting expands each subdatasheet to fit the number of related records it contains. This can often take up a lot of space on your screen.

- Sort the records in a subdatasheet in a different order.

    The following steps show you how to solve problems with subdatasheets.

How to fix it

To change the default setting so that all subdatasheets are expanded when you open the table or query in Datasheet view, follow these steps:

1. In the database window, select the table or query and then click the Design button.

2. On the View menu, click Properties.

3. In the Properties dialog box, set the Subdatasheet Expanded property to Yes. ▶

4. Save the changes to the table or query.

    To set the height of an expanded subdatasheet and limit the number of records displayed in the subdatasheet, follow these steps:

Table Properties

General

Description	Customers' names, addresses, and phone numb
Default View	Datasheet
Validation Rule	
Validation Text	
Filter	
Order By	
Subdatasheet Name	[Auto]
Link Child Fields	
Link Master Fields	
Subdatasheet Height	2"
Subdatasheet Expanded	No
Orientation	Yes
	No

1. In the database window, select the table or query containing the subdata-sheet and then click the Design button.

2. On the View menu, click Properties.

3. In the Properties dialog box, set the Subdatasheet Height property to the height (in inches) you want the subdatasheet to be. ▶

Table Properties	
General	
Description	Customer name, order date, and freight charge
Default View	Datasheet
Validation Rule	
Validation Text	
Filter	
Order By	
Subdatasheet Name	[Auto]
Link Child Fields	
Link Master Fields	
Subdatasheet Height	1"
Subdatasheet Expanded	No
Orientation	Left-to-Right

4. Save the changes to the table or query.

To change the sort order of records in the subdatasheets, do the following:

1. With the table or query open in Datasheet view, click the plus sign beside one of the subdatasheets to expand it.

2. Click in the field you want to sort by and then click the Sort Ascending or Sort Descending button in the toolbar. All the subdatasheets will follow the sort order you select. ▶

More about subdatasheet behavior

Here are some special hints about subdatasheets.

If you want to expand all the subdatasheets only occasionally, point to Subdatasheets on the Format menu and click Expand All. When you close the datasheet, click No when asked if you want to save changes. This way, the property change is not saved, and the next time you open the datasheet the subdatasheets will not be expanded.

If there are more records to display than will fit the height of the subdatasheet, a vertical scroll bar is added to the subdatasheet. If the records in the subdatasheet do not fill the specified height, the subdatasheet shrinks to fit. This way, no display area is wasted.

When you are navigating in a subdatasheet, the navigation buttons at the bottom of the datasheet window refer to records in the active subdatasheet. The navigation buttons help you tell how many records are in a subdatasheet with a specified height display.

You can nest subdatasheets within one another to give an added dimension to viewing related data. Each subdatasheet can have only one subdatasheet nested within it, but you can nest as many as eight levels from the original datasheet.

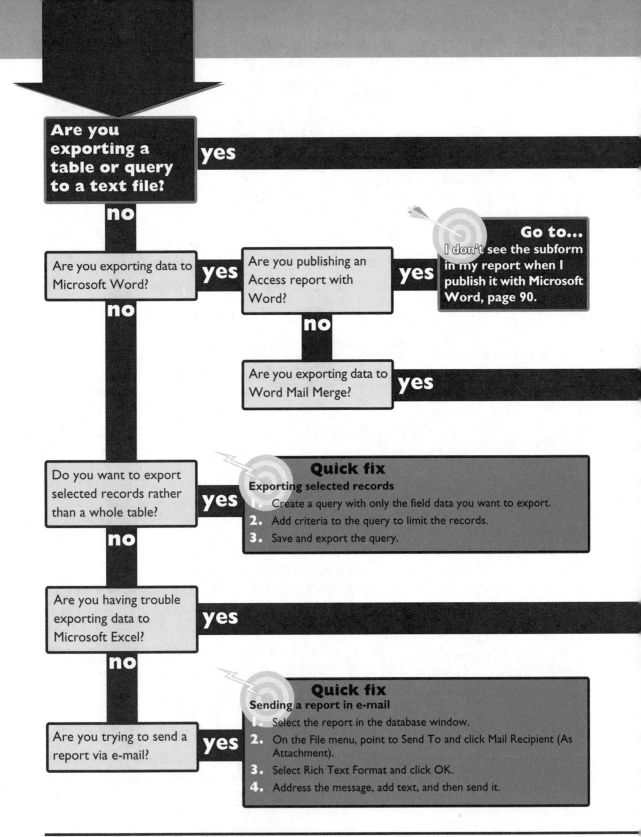

Are you exporting a table or query to a text file? — **yes**

↓ no

Are you exporting data to Microsoft Word? — **yes** → **Are you publishing an Access report with Word?** — **yes** → **Go to...** I don't see the subform in my report when I publish it with Microsoft Word, page 90.

↓ no (from "Are you exporting data to Microsoft Word?")

↓ no (from "Are you publishing an Access report with Word?")

Are you exporting data to Word Mail Merge? — **yes**

Do you want to export selected records rather than a whole table? — **yes** →

Quick fix
Exporting selected records
1. Create a query with only the field data you want to export.
2. Add criteria to the query to limit the records.
3. Save and export the query.

↓ no

Are you having trouble exporting data to Microsoft Excel? — **yes**

↓ no

Are you trying to send a report via e-mail? — **yes** →

Quick fix
Sending a report in e-mail
1. Select the report in the database window.
2. On the File menu, point to Send To and click Mail Recipient (As Attachment).
3. Select Rich Text Format and click OK.
4. Address the message, add text, and then send it.

Exporting

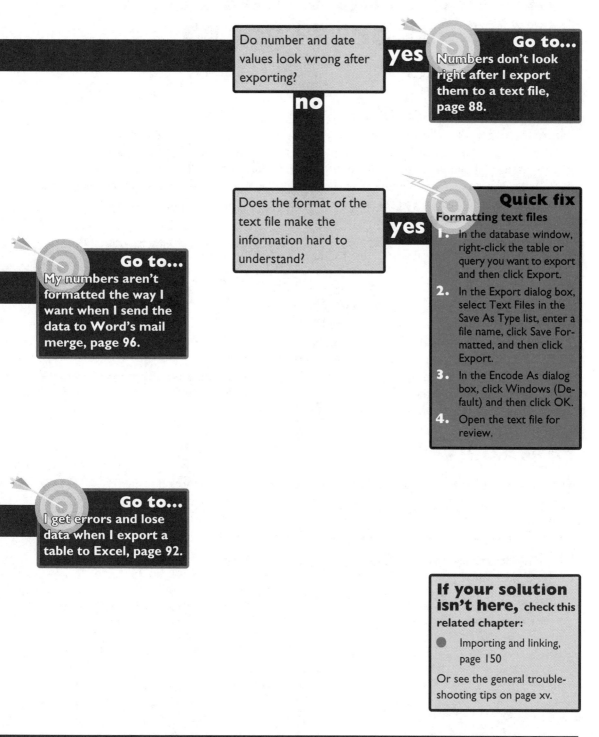

Do number and date values look wrong after exporting? **yes** →

Go to...
Numbers don't look right after I export them to a text file, page 88.

no

Does the format of the text file make the information hard to understand? **yes** →

Quick fix
Formatting text files
1. In the database window, right-click the table or query you want to export and then click Export.
2. In the Export dialog box, select Text Files in the Save As Type list, enter a file name, click Save Formatted, and then click Export.
3. In the Encode As dialog box, click Windows (Default) and then click OK.
4. Open the text file for review.

Go to...
My numbers aren't formatted the way I want when I send the data to Word's mail merge, page 96.

Go to...
I get errors and lose data when I export a table to Excel, page 92.

If your solution isn't here, check this related chapter:
● Importing and linking, page 150

Or see the general trouble-shooting tips on page xv.

Numbers don't look right after I export them to a text file

Source of the problem

Sometimes your work is all by the numbers. One of your key tables has all sorts of number and currency fields, and now, when you try to export the table to a text file, things go crazy. Some of the formatting you defined in the table doesn't carry over to the text file.

One of the problems you might have seen is that the number and currency values align at the left instead of at the right. If you think about this, it makes sense. After all, you converted the numbers to text, and text usually starts on the left. But that doesn't make the number values look any better in the text file. You really need the decimal points, at least, to line up. ▶

Another problem you might have experienced when exporting numbers to a text file is that numbers are truncated to two decimal places. The Export Text Wizard probably thinks that all numbers in your table are currency and that you need only two decimal places.

The following steps show you how to solve these problems with exporting numbers from Microsoft Access to a text file.

How to fix it

If your problem is number alignment or truncated decimal places, do the following:

1. In the database window, click Queries and then click New.

2. In the New Query dialog box, click Design view and then click OK.

3. In the Show Table dialog box, choose the name of the table you want to export, click Add, and then click Close.

4. From the list of field names, drag the fields you want to export to the query design grid, except for any number fields you're having trouble with.

Exporting

5. In the first blank column in the query grid, type an expression to format the number field—for example, **Sales: Format([ItemsSold],"00000.0000")**. Sales is the name that will appear in the column heading when you export the data. ItemsSold is the field name from the table. The Format function defines the format for the value. This expression places five digits before and four digits after the decimal point. ▶

6. Save and close the query.

7. In the database window, select the query you just created and then click Export on the File menu.

8. In the Export Query To dialog box, select Text Files from the Save As Type list and then click Export. This starts the Export Text Wizard.

9. In the Export Text Wizard, select the Fixed-Width option and then click Finish. ▶

10. When you open the text file, you see the numbers with the decimal points lined up. ▶

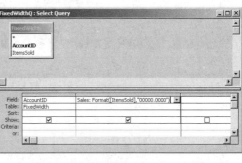

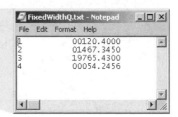

More about exporting dates

Exporting dates to a text file can cause problems, too. When you export a table or query that includes a date field, the value in the text file can include a time format as well as the date. If you don't want to see the time value (and hardly anyone needs the exact time in a typical database), you don't need to show the 0:00:00 that indicates no time value. Once again, a query can save the day.

Follow steps 1 through 4 in the previous solution. In the Field row for the date field you want to format, type an expression such as **Birthdate2: Format([Birthdate],"mm/dd/yy")**. Birthdate2 is the name of the expression, Birthdate is the field name, and the format "mm/dd/yy" displays the date values as 1/15/03, for example, with no time values. Use the Delimited option in the Export Text Wizard dialog box rather than Fixed-Width.

I don't see the subform in my report when I publish it with Microsoft Word

Source of the problem

One of the great things about Microsoft Office is the cooperation among its colleagues. For example, Microsoft Word will turn an Access report into a professional looking document with the Publish It With Microsoft Word Office Links command. Knowing all this, you've spent the last week creating your monthly report in Access, but now, when you call on Word, you see a cryptic message about not being able to process any subforms. The data in the subform looked great in print preview in Access, but Word can't seem to swallow it. ▶

Being brave, you went ahead with the export. The result in Word contained the data from each record in the main report followed by the name of the subform and empty space where the subform records should have been. (Had you clicked No in the message box, the report would still have been exported, but you would again see only the data from the main report and the subform name but less empty space.)

The cause of this problem is that Word can't publish *subforms* in a report, although it can publish *subreports*. Even if you are publishing an Access form with Word, subforms are ignored. In that case, however, you don't get a warning as you do when you publish a report.

The following steps show you how to solve this problem.

Tip

You might need to make some adjustments to the design of the subreport so that it looks its best in Word.

How to fix it

If you see the message about failure to process subforms in your report, do the following:

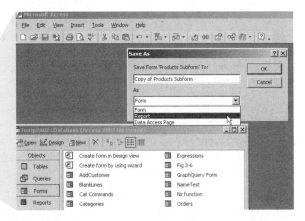

Tip

When you use the Publish It With Microsoft Word Office Links command, you can export tables, queries, forms, and reports. Using the Merge It With Microsoft Word Office Links command, you can export only tables and queries because tables and queries contain the data. Forms and reports are merely designs.

1. In the message box, click No. The report is still exported, but the export takes less time than it does if you click Yes.

2. Close the report in Word and return to Access.

3. In Access, close the report print preview window (if it is open).

4. In the database window, click Forms and then select the subform that's used in your report.

5. On the File menu, click Save As. In the As box in the Save As dialog box, select Report and then click OK. ▶

6. Open the main report in Design view.

7. Select the subform control and then click the Properties button on the toolbar.

8. On the Data tab, in the Source Object property box, select the name of the subform you saved as a report. ▶

9. Save and close the report design.

Now you're ready to export the report again to the Word Publisher:

1. In the database window, select the report.

2. On the Tools menu, point to Office Links and then click Publish It With Microsoft Word.

3. Click Yes to replace the previous report with this new one.

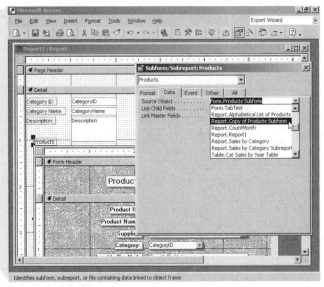

I get errors and lose data when I export a table to Microsoft Excel

Source of the problem

Sending a datasheet from Access to Microsoft Excel seems like a pretty simple job. Both programs look at data in neatly arranged rows and columns, after all. So how come you got errors when you performed the export process, errors like blank dates, pound (#) signs instead of dates, or missing text from a memo field?

A couple of things might have gone wrong, either because of the nature of the data you're exporting or the manner of the export process itself. For example, Excel doesn't recognize dates prior to 1/1/1900. If your data contains a date earlier than that, you might get a Date Out of Range export error and the field will be left blank or filled with pound signs (#). As to missing text, Excel limits its worksheet cells to 255 characters, so any characters over 255 in your memo field might be chopped off, depending on the way you exported the table.

When you export Access data to Excel, you can choose to save the formatting. If you don't select this option, Access creates an Export Errors table and includes a record for each error that occurred in the export. The record describes the type of error and indicates the field in which it occurred as well as the row number. Values of dates earlier than 1/1/1900 are left blank and memo fields exceeding 255 characters are exported intact when you don't select the Save Formatted option. If you do use the Save Formatted option in the Export dialog box, no Export Errors table is created in Access. With this option, cells with ancient date values are filled with pound signs (#), and you lose the excess characters from a lengthy memo field.

The following steps show you how to solve these problems.

How to fix it

If you see an Export Errors table in Access after you have exported a table to Excel, do the following:

1. In the Access database window, select the Export Errors table and then click Open. ▶

⊞ Employees_ExportErrors : Table			_□×
Error	Field	Row
▶ Date Out Of Range	BirthDate	2
Date Out Of Range	HireDate	5
Date Out Of Range	BirthDate	7
∗		

Record: I◀ ◀ | 1 | ▶ ▶I ▶∗ | of 3

2. Print the table, or simply note the location and type of the errors recorded in the table.

Tip

If you exported the table to Excel 95 or earlier, you will also see field truncation errors listed in the Export Errors table if there are any fields with more than 255 characters.

Exporting

3. Start Excel (or switch to Excel if it's already running), and open the Excel workbook that contains the data you exported.

4. Move to the rows indicated in the Export Errors table and correct the data. Most often, you'll be correcting a Date Out Of Range error. If this is the case, click in the blank date field and type the correct date. ▶

Tip

You can prevent the problem of out-of-range dates by adding an input mask to the date field in the Access table. Excel will then accept dates prior to Jan-1-1900.

If the cell contains nothing but pound signs, try the following: ▶

1. Rest the mouse pointer on the cell that contains the pound signs.

2. If you don't see a note, drag the right column divider to widen the column.

3. If you see a note, the date is out of range. Select the cell and type the correct date.

I get errors and lose data when I export a table to Microsoft Excel

(continued from page 93)

To complete truncated memo field text, do the following:

1. In Excel, click in the cell with the missing memo data.

2. Click in the formula bar and complete the memo text. ▶

3. Save the workbook.

More about smart notes

Sometimes, smart notes can bark up the wrong tree.

When you export a datasheet to an Excel worksheet, you will notice that some of the cells contain comment flags. If you select the cell and rest the mouse pointer on the smart tag, you can see the "smart" comment that Excel has to make. In this case, Excel has recognized values in a text cell that contain only numbers. ▶

If you click the smart tag, you can change the format if you need to. We don't need to take the opportunity in this case—postal codes are treated as text.

(continued from page 93)

Tip

If long memos become a common problem, export the data to a text file and then open the text file in Excel. The data in the memo field will not be truncated.

Tip

If you're exporting an Access table or query to an existing Excel file, be careful not to overwrite the data in the spreadsheet. To avoid this, save the exported data to the Microsoft Excel 5-7 or Microsoft Excel 97-2002 format. These formats have a different workbook structure than earlier versions of Excel. The structure includes multiple worksheets, and when you export Access data to one of these formats, the data is placed in the first empty worksheet.

Exporting

My numbers aren't formatted the way I want when I send the data to Word's mail merge

Source of the problem

Microsoft has done a lot to make sharing data between Office programs easy, but sometimes things just don't work out the way you want or expect. When exporting formatted number values to Word for use with Word's mail merge feature, formatting of numbers showing percentages can get lost. Word will listen to and abide by all the data types you can specify in Access, but it ignores the formatting you've set up for the fields in the table's design.

Because only the data is sent to Word, but any special formatting is not, you have to use a different method for getting the formatting across to Word. Luckily, you can create a query and format the results in a way that Word understands. The query converts the percent values into text strings that include the percent sign. Word is perfectly amenable to accepting any type of text string the query wants to send to it, so the formatting stays in place.

The following steps describe how to create a query on which to base the mail merge document.

How to fix it

First of all, create the query that contains the fields you want to use in the mail merge:

1. In the database window, click Query and then click New.

2. In the Show Table dialog box, select the table that contains the data you want to export and then click Add.

3. If you need data from another table, select it and click Add. Click Close after adding the tables you need. ▶

4. In the query design grid, change the field with the percentage formatting to an expression using the Format function. For example, you can type **DiscountPercentage: Format([Discount],"0%")**. Be sure to give the expression a different name from the name of the field itself, or you will create a circular reference with the original field name and cause an error. ▶

5. Save and close the query.

Now merge the new query with Word's mail merge as follows:

1. In the database window, select the query but don't open it.

2. On the Tools menu, click Office Links and then click Merge It With Microsoft Word.

3. In the Microsoft Mail Merge Wizard dialog box, select Create A New Document And Then Link The Data To It. Click OK. ▶

4. In Word, click the Insert Merge Field button on the toolbar and then select the fields one at a time. You can press Enter or Tab to space the fields in the new document. ▶

5. Click the View Merged Data button to see that the formatting has been preserved.

6. Follow the remaining Mail Merge Wizard steps to complete your mail merge list and letter.

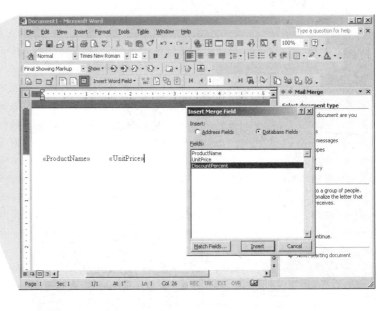

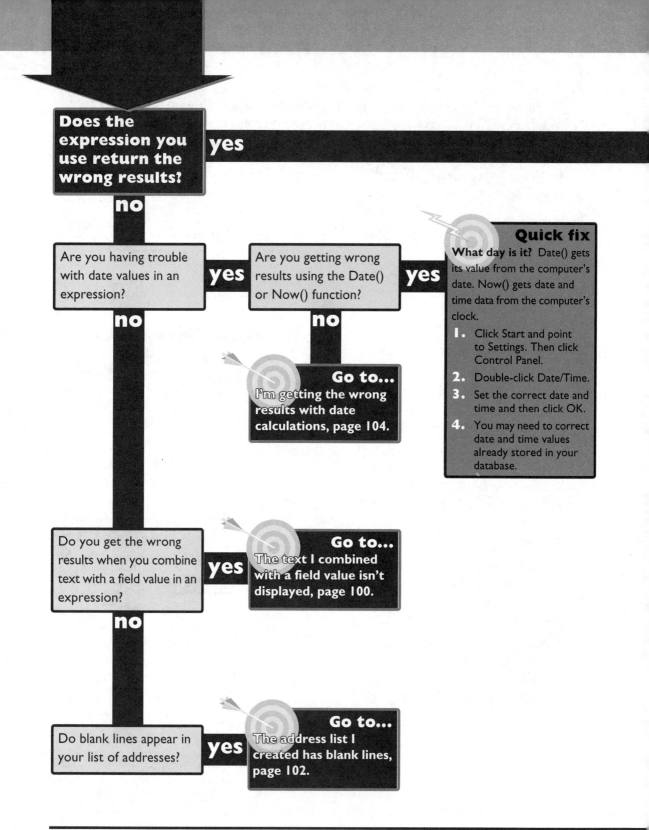

Does the expression you use return the wrong results?

yes

no

Are you having trouble with date values in an expression?

yes

Are you getting wrong results using the Date() or Now() function?

yes

no

no

Go to...
I'm getting the wrong results with date calculations, page 104.

Quick fix
What day is it? Date() gets its value from the computer's date. Now() gets date and time data from the computer's clock.

1. Click Start and point to Settings. Then click Control Panel.
2. Double-click Date/Time.
3. Set the correct date and time and then click OK.
4. You may need to correct date and time values already stored in your database.

Do you get the wrong results when you combine text with a field value in an expression?

yes

Go to...
The text I combined with a field value isn't displayed, page 100.

no

Do blank lines appear in your list of addresses?

yes

Go to...
The address list I created has blank lines, page 102.

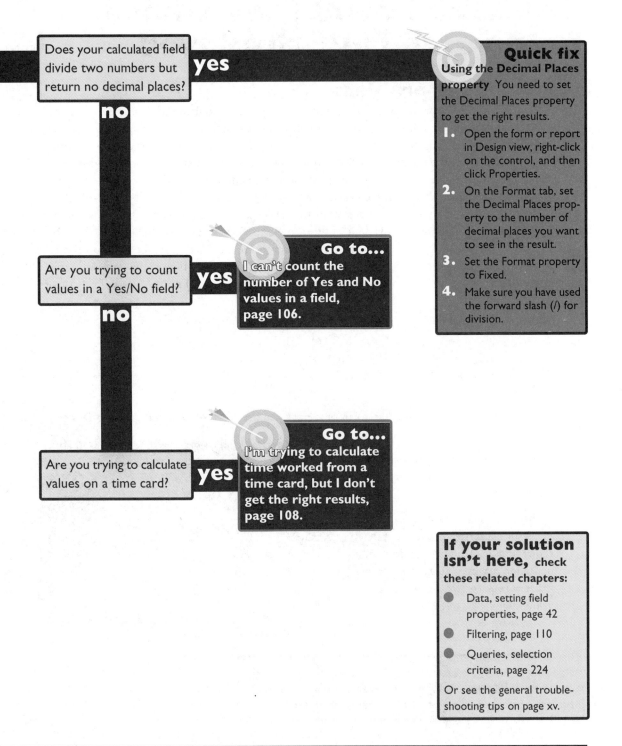

Does your calculated field divide two numbers but return no decimal places?

yes

no

Are you trying to count values in a Yes/No field?

yes

no

Are you trying to calculate values on a time card?

yes

Quick fix

Using the Decimal Places property You need to set the Decimal Places property to get the right results.

1. Open the form or report in Design view, right-click on the control, and then click Properties.
2. On the Format tab, set the Decimal Places property to the number of decimal places you want to see in the result.
3. Set the Format property to Fixed.
4. Make sure you have used the forward slash (/) for division.

Go to...

I can't count the number of Yes and No values in a field, page 106.

Go to...

I'm trying to calculate time worked from a time card, but I don't get the right results, page 108.

If your solution isn't here, check these related chapters:

- Data, setting field properties, page 42
- Filtering, page 110
- Queries, selection criteria, page 224

Or see the general troubleshooting tips on page xv.

The text I combined with a field value isn't displayed

Source of the problem

After listening to all the database gurus and splitting up your information into tiny field-size pieces, now you need to add some text to a field to enhance the information it displays. It sounded simple enough, but when you tried to combine field values with text, somehow it didn't work the way you expected. The problem probably lay in how you marked the text you wanted to display.

Combining field values with text in an expression is called *concatenating*. To combine these elements in an expression, you use the concatenation symbol, the ampersand (&). Microsoft Access interprets *literal values* (such as the text you want to add) exactly as you write them. Strings of characters, numbers, and dates, for example, appear in expressions something like these: "San Diego", 155, or #15-Jan-03#. Notice that strings of characters are enclosed in double quotation marks (the text delimiter), and that dates are enclosed in the pound sign (#), which is the date delimiter. If you used literal values, your error might have occurred because the delimiter you used was incorrect or missing.

The following steps explain how to solve these common problems.

How to fix it

1. In the database window, select the form or report you are working with and click the Design button.

2. Right-click the control you want to add text to and then click Properties on the shortcut menu.

3. In the Control Source property box, make sure you have not left out the required brackets, single or double quotation marks, or date delimiters that are required by the literal value. ▶

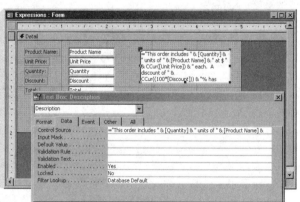

Tip

To see the whole expression, right-click the expression in the Control Source property box and then click Zoom on the shortcut menu.

---

4. Check to make sure the delimiters you used to enclose literal values appear in pairs. ▶

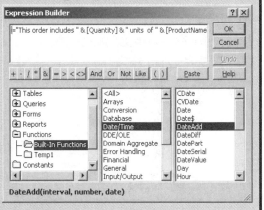

More about using field names in an expression

When you use a field name in an expression, such as when you build a record validation rule or create a calculated field in a form, the field name is the *identifier*. An identifier must comply with certain rules or you'll get unexpected results from your expression. Enclose field names in square brackets (for example, [UnitPrice]) to let Access know that the field name is one you dreamed up, not one of the Access keywords.

If the field in an expression is from a table in the database that's different from the table you're working in, you must also provide a *qualifier* to indicate the name of that table or query. In the expression, separate the qualifier from the identifier with an exclamation mark (the "bang" operator), which tells Access that you thought up the name that follows. For example, Customer![CustomerName] refers to the CustomerName field in the Customer table.

When you use a table name (or the name of another Access object for that matter), you don't have to enclose it in brackets unless it contains a space or a character that has a special meaning to Access, such as an underscore.

If you want more help with expressions

You can use the Expression Builder to help you add functions to an expression. Click the Build (...) button in a property box to start it. ▶

In the lower left pane of the Expression Builder dialog box, you can double-click the plus sign next to Functions to expand the list to include Built-In Functions and the name of the database you're using, if it contains any functions. When you click Built-In Functions, a list of function categories appears in the center pane. Select the category for the function you want, and then select the function you want to use in the rightmost pane and paste it into the expression.

When you click a function name, the syntax you need to enter for the function appears at the bottom of the dialog box, so you can see what additional information you need to add.

The address list I created has blank lines

Source of the problem

You have taken great care to include all possible items in your customer mailing or employee address list. For example, a few customers have a second address line that indicates their building number or office suite, but not all of your customers are so metropolitan. For those without, you got blank lines in the addresses, which doesn't look professional.

You want to leave out the blank lines when you print the complete address list, so you need to combine fields in an expression so that Access will skip the blank fields.

The following steps show you how to skip blank lines in a report.

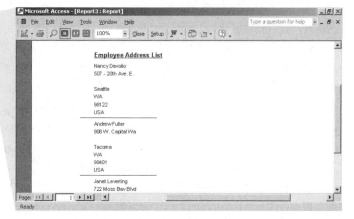

How to fix it

1. Open the report you use to print the address list in Design view.

2. Add a new text box control to the detail section of the report and name it something like Full Address.

3. Right-click in the text box control and then click Properties on the shortcut menu.

4. In the Control Source property box, type an expression such as **IIf(IsNull([Address2]), "",[Address2] & Chr(13) & Chr(10))**. If the Address2 field is blank, this expression returns a zero-length string—in other words, no text. If the field contains data that should be in a separate row (a building or suite number, for example), the expression returns the field value. The field value is followed by a carriage return, created by the *Chr(13)* in the expression, and a line feed, created by *Chr(10)*.

5. You can add more IIf() function statements to the expression to accommodate other fields in the full address. For example, some addresses might include a person's title while others don't. ▶

6. Click Print preview to see the result of your expression.

7. Click the Format tab and set the text box control's Can Grow and Can Shrink properties to Yes so that the control's height ill resize depending on how many lines appear in the address. ▶

> **Tip**
>
> The Can Grow and Can Shrink properties work for controls only in report designs, not in forms.

More about using expressions to handle blank fields

Access provides three handy functions for dealing with blank fields that you can use in expressions in queries or in the Control Source property of a control in a form or report.

The IsNull function answers yes or no to the question "Is the field blank?" For example, the expression IsNull([Address2]) returns Yes if there is no secondary address and No if the field contains a value.

When you combine the IsNull function with the IIf function (IIf stands for Immediate If; you can also think of the IIf function as the test function), you can specify what Access should do if the field is blank. The syntax of the IIf function is IIf(*condition, true, false*). For *condition*, you type the information you want to test; for example, is the MiddleInitial field in an employee's record blank? For *true*, you specify the outcome you want if the condition is true; for *false*, you specify the outcome if the condition is false. With a combination of IIf and IsNull, you can create an expression to control the results of working with blank fields. For example, the expression IIf(IsNull([MiddleInitial]),"NMI",[MiddleInitial]) displays the letters NMI if the MiddleInitial field is blank or the value of the MiddleInitial field if it is not blank. ▶

The third useful function is the Nz function. You use this function to return a specific value if the field is blank. For example, the expression Nz([Address2],"None") returns the value of the Address2 field if the field has a value or the word "None" if the field is blank. You must enclose the text string None in double quotation marks in the expression, but you won't see the quotation marks when None is displayed.

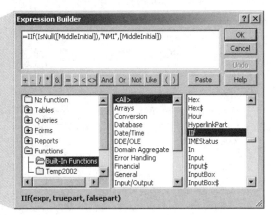

I'm getting the wrong results with date calculations

Source of the problem

It's hard enough to remember the date of your next dental checkup or your mother's birthday. Working with dates and times in an expression can be a real challenge. Dates look so much like simple numbers that Access can confuse the two if you aren't careful. Once confused, Access can give you some bizarre results.

If you included a date in an expression and didn't get the results you expected, you might have forgotten to enclose the date in date delimiter symbols (#). If this is so, Access interprets the date as a number, and you're likely to see an error message that you are trying to divide by zero or see a long decimal number as the result of your expression. When you place a date in an expression in a query, Access automatically adds the delimiters. But when you add a date to an expression in the Control Source property for a text box or a list or combo box in a form, for example, you're on your own.

You might also get into trouble when trying to calculate the span of time between two dates. When you subtract one date from another, the result you see is the number of days between the two. This is not always what you want or expect.

The following steps show you how to overcome these obstacles.

How to fix it

If you get an error message about dividing by zero or see a long decimal number as the result of your expression, do the following:

1. Open the form or report in Design view and then click the control containing the date expression.

2. On the toolbar, click the Properties button and locate the problem date in the Control Source property box. ▶

3. Insert the pound sign delimiter (#) before and after the date.

4. Type the zeros that Access removed from two-digit month, day, or year values. The date is now in the format that Access requires.

5. Save the form or report.

If you are having trouble calculating the time between two dates, do the following:

1. Open the form in Form view or the report in Design view and select the control containing the expression. Notice that the Time With Company field in this example doesn't show the correct data. ▶

2. On the toolbar, click the Properties button and then click in the Control Source property box.

3. Type an expression such as **=DateDiff("yyyy",[FieldName], Date()) & " years"**. This expression calculates the number of years between today's date (which is calculated using the Date() function) and the date in the field you include in FieldName. If you want to see the number of months between the dates, use m rather than yyyy; to see the number of calendar weeks, use ww; and for the number of work weeks use w. Use d for the number of days. ▶

4. Save the form or report.

Tip

If you are calculating the difference in years, keep in mind that the difference is calculated only between the year portion of the two dates. For example, the difference between 8/15/01 and 10/22/1990 will be 11 years even though it is really a couple of months shy of 11 years. This manner of calculation is important if you are calculating ages from date of birth.

I can't count the number of Yes and No values in a field

Source of the problem

Let's say you've kept track of products one by one as they've been approved for distribution. The packaging is ready, the price is set, and now you want to tally up the number of products ready to go in a report for the next stockholders' meeting. It's easy to count Yes votes with a show of hands raised in favor of a proposition, and it's almost as easy to sort ballots in two stacks and count the number of pros and cons. But counting the number of yeses and nos in a field in your Access table isn't quite so simple. When you create your report to summarize this information, you don't get the results you want.

The main source of the problem with counting yes or no values is that you can't use the Sum function with a yes/no field. The Sum function is used only with number and currency fields. You need a way to convert the value in the yes/no field to a number and then add them all up.

The following steps show you how to count these values.

How to fix it

1. In the database window, select the report and then click Design.

2. On the View menu, click Report Header/Footer.

3. In the Toolbox, click the text box icon and then click in the Report Footer section to create an unbound text box in the section. ▶

4. Right-click the text box, click Properties on the shortcut menu and then click the Data tab in the Properties dialog box.

5. In the Control Source property box, type an expression such as **=Sum(IIf([*YesNoField*],1,0))**. For *YesNoField*, substitute the name of the field in your database. The IIf function evaluates to 1 if

the Yes/No field contains Yes or to 0 if the field contains No. The Sum function totals the number of Yeses by adding 1 for each Yes value found in the field. ▶

Text Box: Text6

Text6

Format | Data | Event | Other | All
Control Source . . . . =Sum(IIf([ApprovedForDistribution],1,0))
Input Mask . . . . |
Running Sum . . . . No

6. Repeat step 3 to add another text box control to the Report Footer section. This text box will be used to calculate the total number of No values.

7. In the Control Source property box for this text box, type the expression **=Sum(IIf([*YesNoField*],0,1)).** This expression adds 1 to the total if the IIf function returns 0 because the field contains No.

8. Edit the labels for the text boxes to correspond to the contents of the controls. For example, "Total Approved" and "Total Not Approved." ▶

Text Box: Text11

Text11

Format | Data | Event | Other | All
Control Source . . . . =Sum(IIf([ApprovedForDistribution],0,1))
Input Mask . . . . |
Running Sum . . . . No

9. Save and preview the report. ▶

Approved for Distribution : Report

Outback Lager	☑
Flatemysost	☐
Mozzarella di Giov	☑
Röd Kaviar	☑
Longlife Tofu	☑
Rhönbräu Klosterb	☑
Lakkalikööri	☑
Original Frankfurter	☐

Total Approved: 55   Total Not Approved: 22

Page: 4

Tip

You can also use this technique to count Yes/No values in a group in a report. After you group the report by the field you want to tally, make sure you have set the Group Footer property to Yes in the Sorting And Grouping dialog box. Create an unbound text box control in the group footer section and type the Sum/IIf expression in the Control Source property of the text box.

What about other values?

You're surely not limited to counting yes and no votes. You can count the occurrence of any field value by combining the Sum and IIf functions. For example, say you want to count the number of pet foods offered by your company that are consumed by cats. You could type an expression such as **Sum(IIf([Animal]= "cat",1,0)).** This expression adds one to the total for every record that contains the word "cat" in the Animal field.

I'm trying to calculate time worked from a time card, but I don't get the right results

Source of the problem

Your diligent employees have started using Access to keep careful track of their time on the job. They enter the time they arrive and depart each day plus the amount of time they take for lunch and for well-earned coffee breaks. Then they present you with the details of their activities.

Payday came around, and you had trouble calculating elapsed times. The source of your problem is probably with clock-related entries in the time cards. In addition, you might have had trouble with time and date arithmetic because you had entries both in clock time and elapsed time values.

The following solution shows how to combine arrival and departure times with the elapsed time in minutes to compute total time on the job.

How to fix it

1. Use the Form Wizard to create a form based on the table in which time card entries are stored. Add the fields in which employees record arrival time, departure time, time at lunch, and time on break. Your form would look something like the one shown here. ▶

2. Click the View button on the toolbar to switch the form to Design view.

3. In the Toolbox, click the text box icon and then click in the form to add a text box control.

4. Right-click the text box and then click Properties on the shortcut menu.

5. Click the Data tab. In the Control Source property box, type an expression such as **=([TimeOut]-[TimeIn])*24.** For TimeOut and TimeIn, use the field names from your database. ▶

6. Click the Other tab and change the Name property of the text box to WorkDay.

7. Edit the label for the text box to read something like **Work Day (hrs.)**.

8. Repeat step 3 to add another text box control to the form. You'll use this text box to calculate the total time away from the desk. If the property sheet for the text box is not visible, click Properties on the View menu.

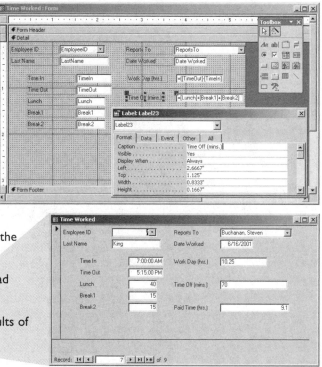

9. In the Control Source property box, type the expression **=[Lunch]+[Break1]+[Break2]**, substituting your field names as required.

10. In the Other tab, change the Name property of the text box to TimeOff.

11. Change the label to read **Time Off (mins.)**. ▶

12. Add a third text box control to the form. In this text box you'll combine the two calculations to come up with the total number of hours at work.

13. In the Control Source property box for this text box, type **=[WorkDay]-([TimeOff]/60).** The lunch and break entries are recorded in minutes so you need to divide the total by 60 to convert the sum to hours.

14. Edit the label for the text box to read **Paid Time (hrs.)**.

15. Switch to Form view to see the results of the calculations. ▶

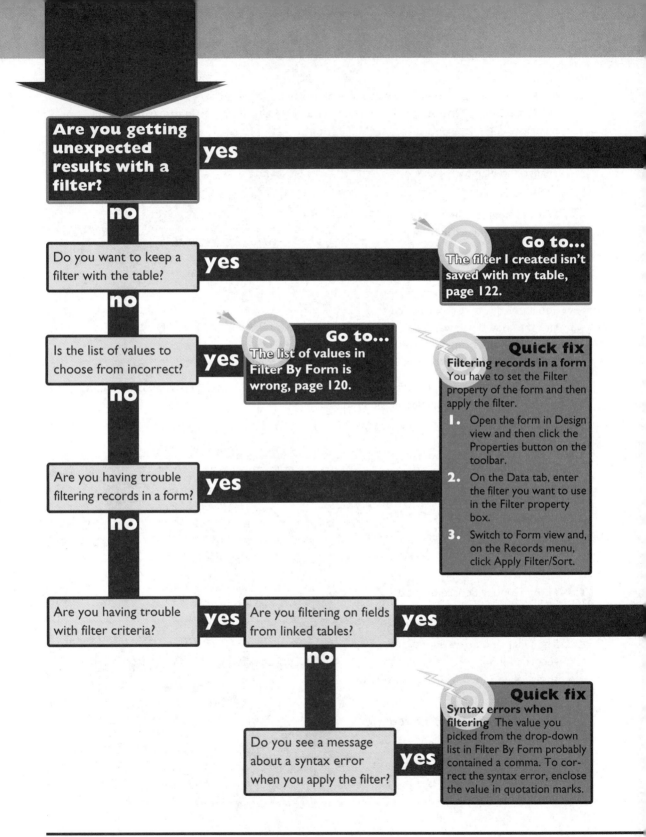

Are you getting unexpected results with a filter?

yes

no

Do you want to keep a filter with the table?

yes

Go to...
The filter I created isn't saved with my table, page 122.

no

Is the list of values to choose from incorrect?

yes

Go to...
The list of values in Filter By Form is wrong, page 120.

no

Quick fix
Filtering records in a form You have to set the Filter property of the form and then apply the filter.

1. Open the form in Design view and then click the Properties button on the toolbar.
2. On the Data tab, enter the filter you want to use in the Filter property box.
3. Switch to Form view and, on the Records menu, click Apply Filter/Sort.

Are you having trouble filtering records in a form?

yes

no

Are you having trouble with filter criteria?

yes

Are you filtering on fields from linked tables?

yes

no

Do you see a message about a syntax error when you apply the filter?

yes

Quick fix
Syntax errors when filtering The value you picked from the drop-down list in Filter By Form probably contained a comma. To correct the syntax error, enclose the value in quotation marks.

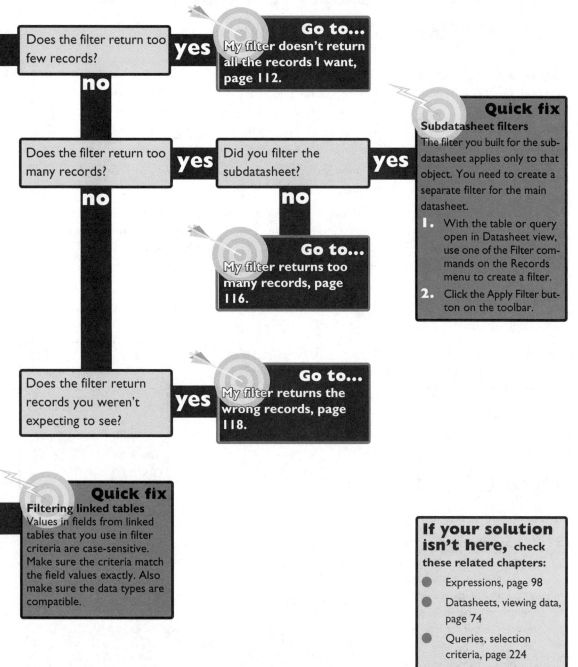

Does the filter return too few records?

yes

Go to...
My filter doesn't return all the records I want, page 112.

no

Quick fix
Subdatasheet filters
The filter you built for the subdatasheet applies only to that object. You need to create a separate filter for the main datasheet.

1. With the table or query open in Datasheet view, use one of the Filter commands on the Records menu to create a filter.

2. Click the Apply Filter button on the toolbar.

Does the filter return too many records?

yes

Did you filter the subdatasheet?

yes

no

Go to...
My filter returns too many records, page 116.

Does the filter return records you weren't expecting to see?

yes

Go to...
My filter returns the wrong records, page 118.

Quick fix
Filtering linked tables
Values in fields from linked tables that you use in filter criteria are case-sensitive. Make sure the criteria match the field values exactly. Also make sure the data types are compatible.

If your solution isn't here, check these related chapters:

- Expressions, page 98
- Datasheets, viewing data, page 74
- Queries, selection criteria, page 224

Or see the general trouble-shooting tips on page xv.

My filter doesn't return all the records I want

Source of the problem

You sent out a fancy questionnaire to your customers and got an impressive response. But when you filtered your database to tally the results, you saw disappointingly few records. Something is wrong here! The source of the problem, as well as the solution, depends on how you filtered the records in the table, query, or form.

- If you used Filter By Form, you might have typed criteria using the *And* operator, which returns fewer records than the *Or* operator.

- If you used Filter By Selection, you might have selected the wrong value. Or, you might be filtering records using a combo box whose values come from a value list instead of from the table itself. When you filter on the value in a combo box, Microsoft Access looks in the first column in the list for matches to the value. If the first column in the list is not the one bound to a field, Access won't find a match.

- If you used the Filter For command, you might have applied more than one filter or the wrong filter criterion.

- If you took advantage of the Advanced Filter/Sort command, you probably specified too many criteria, limiting the number of records returned by the filter.

The following solutions offer ways to resolve these filtering problems.

<table>
<tr><td>

Tip

If you select a value from the Filter By Form list that contains a comma, you must enclose the value in quotation marks. If you select the same value when using Advanced Filter/Sort, Access adds the quotation marks for you.

</td></tr>
</table>

How to fix it

If you used Filter By Form, follow these steps:

1. At the bottom of the Filter By Form window, click the Or tab and add alternative filter criteria. (Typing criteria in the same row of the Look For tab implies the *And* operator—a value has to match "cat" *and* "long hair," limiting the number of records returned.) The additional filter criteria in the Or tab should increase the number of records returned when you apply the filter. ▶

Filtering

2. If step 1 doesn't work, delete any value or expression that might limit the number of records too much. For example, an expression that combines two values with the *And* operator so that both conditions must be met reduces the number of values returned. The expression might be on the Look For tab or in an Or tab in the Filter By Form window. The filter shown in the figure will return only three records from the Northwind sample database Orders table. Removing one of the values from the filter or moving it to the Or tab—it doesn't matter which value you move—increases the number of records returned by the filter to 133. ▶

If you are using Filter By Selection to filter on a value displayed in a combo box that gets its values from a value list, follow these steps:

1. Check to be sure that the value you see is in the first column in the combo box drop-down list. ▶

2. If it is not, you need to change the combo box so that the bound column (the one that contains the values that are stored in the field) appears first. To do that, first open the form in Design view.

3. Double-click the combo box control.

4. On the Data tab, in the Row Source property box, change the value list so that the bound column value is first in each pair in the value list. ▶

5. Change the Bound Column property to 1, the number of the column.

6. If you want to hide the bound column value when you expand the combo box list, type **0** as the first entry in the Column Widths property.

Troubleshooting Microsoft Access 2002 **113**

My filter doesn't return all the records I want

(continued from page 113)

7. To filter on one of the values in the combo box, select the entire value and click the Filter By Selection toolbar button. ▶

If a filter you set up with the Filter For command is already applied to the records, do the following:

1. Remove the filter by clicking the Remove Filter button.

2. Right-click in the datasheet column or form control, type a different value or expression in the Filter For box on the shortcut menu, and press Enter. ▶

3. If that doesn't work, point to the Filter command on the Records menu and click Advanced Filter/Sort.

4. Look at the grid in the Advanced Filter/Sort window. If you have specified more than one expression or value, each one will show up in the grid.

5. Check for incorrect criteria expressions. For example, you might have combined mutually exclusive values with the *And* operator. ▶

If you already used Advanced Filter/Sort to create the filter, follow these steps to change the filtering criteria:

1. On the Records menu, click Filter and then click Advanced Filter/Sort.

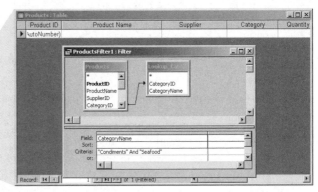

2. Delete some of the criteria you've entered to increase the selection of records returned by the filter.

3. Move some of the criteria to the Or row instead of placing all criteria in the Criteria row, which creates *And* combinations.

4. If that fails to return the number of records you expect, change some expressions from *And* to *Or* in the Criteria row combinations. The filter shown in the figure returns only four records. All records must contain *Davolio, Nancy* in the Employee Name field, but they may have either of the company names. If you move one of the CompanyName criteria to the Or row, the filter returns 13 records. ▶

More about the Filter By Form list

The window that opens when you click the Filter By Form button displays controls that you can use to select or enter values with which to filter the underlying data. Access reads records in the data and finds unique values for each field. It places these values in a combo box or list box for the control. You can then select the value you want to use as a filter from the drop-down list in the filter grid.

Access reads the values in a field to come up with the list of unique values to display in the Filter By Form lists. If there are thousands of records, it can take a while. You can set the Don't Display Lists Where More Than This Number Of Records Read option to a reasonable number. If the recordset contains more records than that, Access doesn't fill the box with the actual field values—only two values: Is Null and Is Not Null. To set this option, click Options on the Tools menu and then click the Edit/Find tab. Then type the maximum number of records you want Access to have to read. ▶

My filter returns too many records

Source of the problem

You tried to find a few good records, and you got snowballed with more than you could handle. You need to figure out how to be pickier without shutting the door completely. When a filter returns too many records, the cause of the problem depends on the type of filter you applied to the table, query, or form.

- If you used Filter By Form, the values or expressions you used weren't the ones needed to return the right set of records.

- If you used Filter By Selection, you probably didn't apply the filter to enough values. With Filter By Selection you can apply a filter to only one value at a time, but you can apply additional filters one after the other to narrow the selection.

- If you used Filter Excluding Selection, you may have selected values in more than one field. Access interprets that action as an instruction to exclude records with the first or the second value, but not records with both values.

- If you used the Filter For command, you didn't repeat the operation on enough values or on values in a different field. You can apply a filter repeatedly to the same or to a different field until you have just the set of records you want.

The following steps show you how to solve these problems.

How to fix it

To fix the problem of too many records if you're using Filter By Form, follow these steps:

1. Open the datasheet you want to filter, point to Filter on the Records menu and then click Filter By Form.

2. In the Look For tab, check the value or expression you've typed to be sure it will select the records you need, or pick a value from the drop-down lists in the grid.

3. Remove one or more of the criteria in the Or tab, or include these values or expressions in the Look For tab so that they are used as *And* criteria.

If you need to further limit the number of records returned by a Filter By Selection operation, you need to select more than one value:

1. Open the datasheet you're trying to filter, select the value you want to filter on first and then click the Filter By Selection button on the toolbar.

2. Select the next value in another field you want to filter on, and then click the Filter By Selection button again. Your second choice filters the records returned by the first filter.

If you're using Filter Excluding Selection, apply the filters separately as follows:

1. Right-click in the first value you want to exclude, and then click Filter Excluding Selection on the shortcut menu. ▶

2. Right-click the second value and repeat step 1.

If filtering by more than one field with Filter Excluding Selection doesn't work, follow these steps:

1. With the datasheet open and filters applied, point to Filter on the Records menu and click Advanced Filter/Sort.

2. Change the *Or* operator in the Criteria row to *And*. ▶

3. Click the Apply Filter button.

If you are working with the Filter For shortcut menu command, do this:

1. Right-click the datasheet in the field you want to filter.

2. In the Filter For box on the shortcut menu, type the value you want to filter on and then press Enter. Notice that you can use wildcards in the filter. ▶

3. Repeat the filter to add another value. Each time you add a value, you further limit the number of records.

My filter returns the wrong records

Source of the problem

If you looked in your database for all the owners of sport utility vehicles and turned up with a list of cat lovers, that would not be helpful at all. Just hope you catch the mistake before sending out your notices of free brake inspections.

One reason for getting wrong results from a filter is that you are using the wrong field or fields in the filter. You might also have typed the wrong value or filter criteria. Another possibility is that you used the wrong operator in the filter expression.

If you are using an expression to filter records and the value starts with the word *is*, that's at least part of your problem. *Is* is a reserved word in Access and can be used only in an expression that compares values with Null or Not Null. If you type **is*** as the filter expression, you get an error message.

The following solution shows you how to solve these problems.

How to fix it

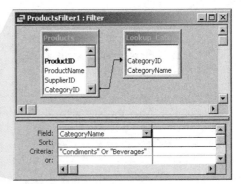

1. If you have typed expressions in the Filter By Form or Advanced Filter/Sort window, make sure you are using the right operator. Deciding when to use *Or* and when to use *And* can be tricky. Use *Or* when you want to include records with either value in the field, such as Condiments or Beverages. ▶

2. Use *And* when you want records that include distinct values in two different fields, such as Condiments (Category) and Exotic Liquids (Company). ▶

3. If your filter uses multiple criteria, make sure you've placed the criteria in the correct row or rows. Putting the criteria in the same row implies the *And* operator. Using separate rows combines the criteria with the *Or* operator.

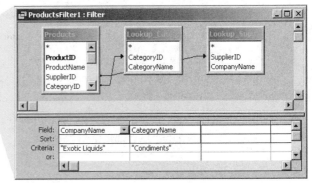

4. If your expression starts with the word *Is* and you typed **Is***, you will see an error message. ▶

5. Click OK in the message box and then respond No to keep the Filter By Form window open.

6. Enclose the part of the expression that includes the word *Is* in quotation marks, including any wildcard character (*) you've added.

Tip

If the records returned by a filter aren't sorted in the order you want, you can rearrange the fields in the Advanced Filter/Sort design grid. Place the field you want to sort by first in the leftmost column, with other fields to the right. For example, sort first by Last Name, and then, for records with the same value for Last Name, sort by First Name.

Which filter to use?

The filtering method you use depends on what you want to do.

If you want to search for records that meet more than one criterion at once, you can use any of the five types of filters: Filter By Selection, Filter By Form, Filter For, Filter Excluding Selection, or Advanced Filter/Sort. They will all apply conditions with the *And* operator.

If you use Filter By Selection, you have to apply each condition separately. The order doesn't matter; all the conditions must be met by the values to be returned by the filter. With the other methods, you can combine all the conditions in one operation.

If you want to combine conditions with the *Or* operator or type criteria expressions, you must use Filter By Form, Filter For, or Advanced Filter/Sort.

If you also want the records sorted in concert with the filtering process, you have only one choice: Advanced Filter/Sort. You can, however, still sort records after they've been returned by the filter. All you have to do is click one of the Sort buttons on the toolbar.

The list of values in Filter By Form is wrong

Source of the problem

Value lists are very helpful—they let you pick the value you need from the list Access displays. That's much easier than having to remember (and spell correctly) the value you want to use to filter dozens or hundreds of records. But sometimes the drop-down list is blank, or worse yet, you see only the ubiquitous Is Null and Is Not Null options to choose from.

In other cases, a value list is so long it seems to take days to find the value you want, even if you have tried to limit the number of unique values in the list. The field is probably a lookup field that doesn't even listen to such limitations. If that's the case, you can change the Row Source property of the field so that it limits the choices in the list.

The following steps demonstrate how to use value lists effectively.

Tip

Another reason you don't see the values you want in the list is that the field you're looking at is a memo field, an OLE Object field, or a hyperlink field. These types of fields can be filtered only for whether they are blank or not, so you can't do much about that.

How to fix it

If the list is blank or you see only the values Is Null or Is Not Null in the list, follow these steps:

1. On the Tools menu, click Options and then click the Edit/Find tab.

2. In the area labeled Show List Of Values In, select the option Local Nonindexed Fields. This option removes the restriction that Access show values only in fields that are indexed.

3. Increase the number in the setting for Don't Display Lists Where More Than This Number Of Records Read.

4. Click OK in the Options dialog box and then try the Filter By Form operation again.

Tip

To find out whether a field is indexed or not, open the table that contains the field in Design view. Select the field in the Field Name row and then check whether the Indexed property for that field is set to Yes or No in the Field Properties area.

If the field you're filtering is a lookup field, follow these steps:

1. In the database window, select the table that includes the field and then click Design.

2. Select the field in the Field Name column and then click the Lookup tab in the Field Properties area.

3. Click the Build (...) button next to the Row Source property box. ▶

4. In the upper pane of the Query Builder window, right-click and select Properties from the shortcut menu.

5. Change the Top Values property from All to the number or percentage of values you want to display in the list. ▶

6. Close the Properties dialog box and then close the Query Builder window. Click Yes to apply the change.

7. Save your changes to the table design.

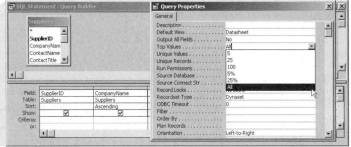

Queries make good filters

Queries are saved as database objects on their own and can be called upon to serve as filters at any time. However, a query has to follow a few requirements to qualify as a filter.

The query must be a simple select query (it can't be an action query or a crosstab query) that's based on the same table or query that underlies the datasheet or form you're filtering. It also can't include fields from any other tables or queries. You can't filter with queries that have records grouped by field values or queries that compute aggregate values such as Sum, Count, Avg, Max, or Min.

The filter I created isn't saved with my table

Source of the problem

Even though you spent hours—or several minutes anyway—creating a filter to isolate the records you wanted, why can't you call it up again at a later date? Only the last filter you built is saved with a table, and only then if you answer "Yes" when asked whether you want to save the changes to the table. When you open the table again, you can reapply that filter.

But the filter you created last week, before you made several changes to the table, is long gone. Microsoft knew this could create a problem and thoughtfully added a way to save the filter as a query. If you save a filter as a query, you can reapply the filter you saved.

The following steps show you how to save your filter as a query.

How to fix it

1. In the database window, select the table with the records you want to filter and then click Open.

2. On the Records menu, click Filter and then click Filter By Form or Advanced Filter/Sort to create the filter you need.

3. Click the Save As Query toolbar button. ▶

4. In the Save As Query dialog box, enter a name for the query and then click OK.

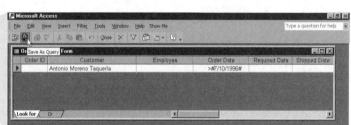

When you want to apply the filter, follow these steps:

1. Select the table in the database window and then click Open.

2. On the Records menu, point to Filter and then click Filter By Form or Advanced Filter/Sort, whichever method you used to create the filter.

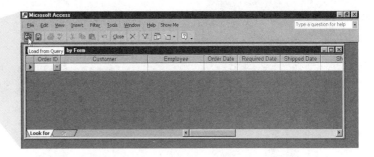

3. Click the Load From Query toolbar button. ▶

4. In the Applicable Filter dialog box, select the query you want to use. ▶

5. Click OK.

6. Click the Apply Filter button. ▶

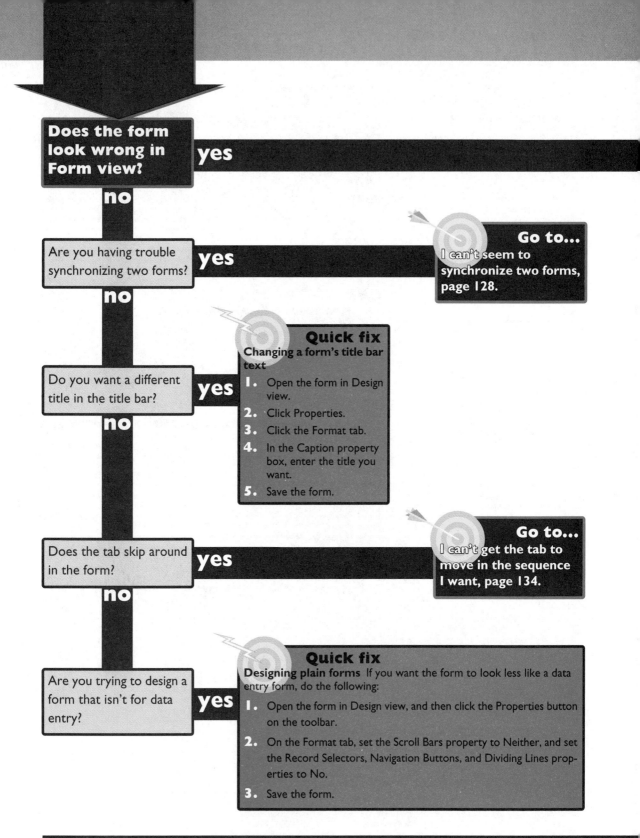

Does the form look wrong in Form view? → **yes**

no

Are you having trouble synchronizing two forms? → **yes**

Go to...
I can't seem to synchronize two forms, page 128.

no

Quick fix
Changing a form's title bar text

Do you want a different title in the title bar? → **yes**

1. Open the form in Design view.
2. Click Properties.
3. Click the Format tab.
4. In the Caption property box, enter the title you want.
5. Save the form.

no

Does the tab skip around in the form? → **yes**

Go to...
I can't get the tab to move in the sequence I want, page 134.

no

Quick fix
Designing plain forms If you want the form to look less like a data entry form, do the following:

Are you trying to design a form that isn't for data entry? → **yes**

1. Open the form in Design view, and then click the Properties button on the toolbar.
2. On the Format tab, set the Scroll Bars property to Neither, and set the Record Selectors, Navigation Buttons, and Dividing Lines properties to No.
3. Save the form.

Forms, designing

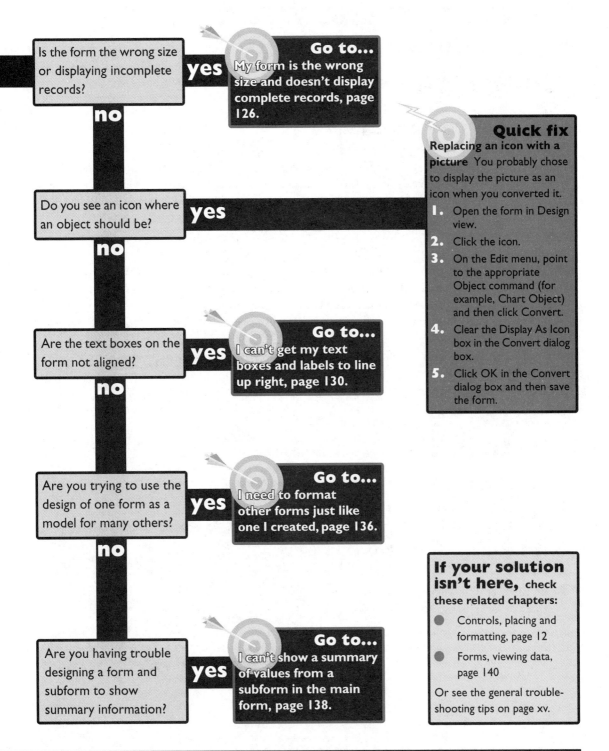

Is the form the wrong size or displaying incomplete records?

yes → **Go to...** My form is the wrong size and doesn't display complete records, page 126.

no

Do you see an icon where an object should be?

yes →

Quick fix
Replacing an icon with a picture You probably chose to display the picture as an icon when you converted it.
1. Open the form in Design view.
2. Click the icon.
3. On the Edit menu, point to the appropriate Object command (for example, Chart Object) and then click Convert.
4. Clear the Display As Icon box in the Convert dialog box.
5. Click OK in the Convert dialog box and then save the form.

no

Are the text boxes on the form not aligned?

yes → **Go to...** I can't get my text boxes and labels to line up right, page 130.

no

Are you trying to use the design of one form as a model for many others?

yes → **Go to...** I need to format other forms just like one I created, page 136.

no

Are you having trouble designing a form and subform to show summary information?

yes → **Go to...** I can't show a summary of values from a subform in the main form, page 138.

If your solution isn't here, check these related chapters:
- Controls, placing and formatting, page 12
- Forms, viewing data, page 140

Or see the general trouble-shooting tips on page xv.

My form is the wrong size and doesn't display complete records

Source of the problem

We usually think of a form as an object fixed in size and appearance, like the IRS Form 1040. Microsoft Access forms, however, can be nonconformists. Sometimes they do whatever they want.

If you're having trouble keeping a form at the size you want (for example, you want it to be the same size when you open it as it was when you saved it), you need to know how a form is related to the form window. A form has its own height and width, and these dimensions don't necessarily match those of the window in which you view the form. (One benefit of these independent dimensions is that the form looks the same when you print it no matter how it looks in the form window.) But you can display the form in the window at the size you want. If a form didn't retain changes you made to its size, you probably resized the window rather than the form.

Problems with a form's size can also be blamed on the form's Auto Resize property, which sizes the form to display a complete record. You might want the form to display complete records when it opens. If you set the Auto Resize property to Yes but the form still shows partial records even though the screen has room for a complete record, you might have switched to Form view from Design view rather than opened the form in Form view from the database window.

The following solutions show you some ways to solve these problems.

How to fix it

If you're trying to resize the form and the form window, do the following:

1. In the database window, select the form and click the Design button.

2. Drag the right border of the form (not the window) to the width you want.

3. Drag the bottom edge of the form so that the form is at the height you want.

4. On the toolbar, click the Properties button.

5. In the Properties dialog box, click the Format tab and set the Auto Resize property of the form to No. ▶

6. Click the View button.

7. If the form window is maximized, click the Restore button on the title bar.

8. In the Window menu, click Size To Fit Form.

9. Save the form.

If a form you've created doesn't resize automatically to display complete records when you open it, do the following:

1. In the database window, select the form and open it in Design view.

2. On the toolbar, click the Properties button and then click the Format tab.

3. Set the Auto Resize property to Yes. ▶

4. Click the View button to switch to Form view.

5. Save and close the form.

Tip

You can close the Properties dialog box to see more of the form in Design view. To open it again, click the Properties button on the toolbar, or right-click on a control and then click Properties.

Tip

The Size To Fit Form command behaves differently depending on the setting of the form's Default View property. If Default view is set to Single Form, the form window is cropped to fit one record. But if a single record is too large for the screen, the window expands to display as much of the record as possible. If the Default View property is set to Continuous Forms, Access crops any partial record showing at the bottom of the screen. If the window can hold only one record, Access expands the form window to display as much of the record as possible.

Warning

If you open a form first in Design view and then switch to Form view, the form window won't resize. When you need to see a form in Form view at the right size, use the Open button in the database window.

I can't seem to synchronize two forms

Source of the problem

You designed a form for data entry or retrieval and kept it as simple as possible, because a form that looks too busy can be distracting. Still, every once in a while you need to have a little more information about the record you see in the form. So you created a separate form to display the related records. Trouble is, you didn't see information in the second form that was related to the record in the first form. The likely cause of this trouble is that the forms are not linked by fields that contain matching data.

The following solution shows you how to fix this problem using a command button to link two forms and synchronize the view of related information.

How to fix it

To link and synchronize the two forms, do the following:

1. Open the main form in Design view.

2. In the toolbox, make sure the Control Wizards button is selected and then click the Command Button tool. ▶

3. Click in the form where you want to place the button. The Command Button Wizard starts.

4. In the Categories box, click Form Operations. In the Actions box, click Open Form. Click Next.

5. Choose the form that shows the data related to the main form. This is the form that the button will open. Click Next.

6. Select the option Open The Form And Find Specific Data To Display and then click Next. ▶

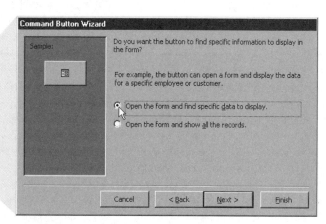

7. In the lists displaying the fields from each form, select the matching fields and then click the <-> button. Click Next. ▶

8. Type text or choose an image to place in the button. Click Finish. The figure shows the Products form linked to the Categories form. You open the synchronized form by clicking the command button labeled Products. ▶

Tip

You don't have to show the linking fields in the main form or the subform, but they do have to be included in the underlying table or query to synchronize the forms.

Synchronizing forms from scratch

You can also use the Form Wizard to create two related forms. In the database window, click Forms and then click New. In the New Form dialog box, select Form Wizard. Click OK. (You don't need to select a table or query from the drop-down list in this step.) From the list of tables and queries, select the one on which you want to base the main form and add the fields you want to include in the form. Then, select the table or query on which you want to base the related form and add the fields you want to include. Click Next.

In the next Form Wizard dialog box, click the Linked Forms option and then click Next. In the next two sections of the Wizard, change the style of the forms and rename the forms if you want. Click Finish. When the main form opens, click the button that opens the linked form.

I can't get my text boxes and labels to line up right

Source of the problem

Some people are perfectionists, and some people aren't. Most of the time you probably don't care that much about precision when you're placing controls in a form. But for a form that has text boxes and labels all over the place, it's important that they are all positioned correctly. Precise placement gives a form a professional appearance and is handy for keeping the data in the form accessible and easy to work with. Several factors are at play if you're having trouble placing and aligning text boxes and their labels in a form.

- If some controls move when you don't expect them to, you might have included more controls than you wanted when you drew a rectangle to select the controls.

- If you are trying to move one or more text box controls to a precise location, the form grid sometimes can get in the way.

- If you are trying to align the labels one way and the text boxes another, you might have selected both controls at once rather than each separately.

- If you're having trouble with the spacing in a group of controls, you might have selected a control outside the row or column you're trying to adjust. Or, you might have turned off the Snap To Grid option, which often results in uneven placement.

The following solutions show you some ways to resolve these problems.

How to fix it

If text boxes move with a group of controls but you don't want them to, do the following:

1. If you selected multiple controls, either by dragging the selection arrow in a ruler or by drawing a rectangle around the controls in Design view, hold down Shift and click the text box or label you don't want to move. ▶

Forms, designing

2. If you just want to move the labels and leave the text boxes alone, hold down Shift and click just the labels. This selects only the labels, which you can then move to where you want them.

Tip

The Align buttons on the Formatting (Form/Report) toolbar apply to the text within the text box and label controls, not to the alignment of the controls themselves.

If you're having trouble moving selected text box controls to a precise location, do this:

1. Click the moving handle on one of the text boxes and drag it to the position you want.

2. Select the other text box controls and hold down Shift while you drag the controls. Doing this keeps the selected text boxes horizontally or vertically aligned when you move them. ▶

3. If you need to move the controls just a short distance, hold down Shift and select the controls and then click one of the arrow keys. The selected controls move in the direction of the arrow one-fourth of a grid unit with each click.

If you're trying to align text box controls to the left and align their attached labels to the right, follow these steps:

1. Hold down the Shift key and select each of the text boxes.

2. On the Format menu, click Align and then click Left. ▶

3. Hold down the Shift key and select each of the labels.

4. On the Format menu, click Align and then click Right.

Tip

Using the arrow keys to move the controls temporarily turns off the Snap To Grid feature.

I can't get my text boxes and labels to line up right

(continued from page 131)

If you're having trouble changing the spacing between selected text boxes, try these steps:

1. Select the column of text boxes, including their labels. If you accidentally include a control that is not part of the column, hold down Shift and click in the control to remove it from the selection.

2. On the Format menu, click Vertical Spacing and then click Make Equal. ▶

3. If you want to add space between the text boxes, click Vertical Spacing on the Format menu and then click Increase. This command keeps the top control in place and increases the space between the remaining controls uniformly by one grid interval.

4. To keep the top control in place and decrease the vertical spacing between the controls, click the Vertical Space command and then click Decrease.

> **Tip**
>
> If you are not satisfied with the size of the grid in the form design window, you can change it by changing the Grid X and Grid Y properties of the form. By default, both the horizontal grid (Grid X) and the vertical grid (Grid Y) are set to 24 dots per inch. (The unit of measure depends on the Regional Settings in Windows Control Panel.)

Putting labels above the text boxes

If you don't want the default labels on the left and level with text boxes, you can change the standard placement of the labels by changing the settings of the Label X and Label Y properties for text box controls. To change the settings, click the Text Box control in the toolbox and then click the Properties button.

The Label X property setting determines the horizontal distance from the label text to the upper-left corner of the text box. A negative Label X places the label text to the left of the text box, and a positive setting places it to the right of the upper-left corner of the text box. The Label Y property setting specifies the vertical distance from the upper-left corner of the text box. A setting of 0 aligns the label horizontally with the text box. A negative Label Y setting places the label above the text box, and a positive setting places it below. Combining a positive setting in the Label X property with a negative setting in the Label Y property places the label above the text box.

I can't get the tab to move in the sequence I want

Source of the problem

You've seen horses in a pasture—nibbling a little grass here, taking a couple of steps and nibbling a few more blades there. It seems that there's no pattern involved in the grazing. You might have found that when you started to enter data in a new form and tabbed from control to control, you also found yourself jumping all around on the screen instead of progressing in a logical manner.

The culprit is probably the tab order—the sequential list of controls that determines the path of the cursor through the maze of controls in the form. The tab order is first determined by the order in which you add the controls to the form. But often, after you create the form, you move controls around and add more controls. Under these circumstances, using the Tab key to move from control to control can give the form the behavior of the grazing horse. It's definitely not taking you where you want to go.

Access offers ways to set the tab order just the way you want. However, be warned that when you change the tab order in a form, the order of the columns in the form's Datasheet view will be changed to match.

Another problem you might have encountered is that you can't get to a control at all by pressing Tab.

The following steps show you how to solve problems with the tab order.

How to fix it

To change the tab order of controls in your form, do the following:

1. Open the form in Design view.

2. On the View menu, click Tab Order.

3. In the Tab Order dialog box, click the selector button beside the name of the control you want to reposition in the tab order. With the item highlighted, drag the control's selector button up or down until it is where you want it. ▶

4. Switch to Form view and press Tab repeatedly to move through the controls and see the results of your changes.

5. Return to Design view and repeat these steps for the other controls until you have the tab order you want.

6. Save the form.

Tip

The Auto Order button in the Tab Order dialog box sets the tab order based on the physical layout of controls in the form—from left to right and from top to bottom. If this is the way you want to move through the controls, click Auto Order and don't move the controls by hand.

Tip

The controls are listed in the Tab Order dialog box by their Name property. If you don't recognize the one you want to move, close the Tab Order dialog box, double-click the control and then look at its Name property.

If a control is skipped in the tab order or if you want to skip it when you tab through the controls in a form, do the following:

1. Open the form in Design view and then click the Properties button on the toolbar.

2. Select the control and click the Other tab in the Properties dialog box.

3. Set the Tab Stop property to Yes to include the control in the tab order; set the Tab Stop property to No to omit the control. ▶

4. Save the form.

About other tab order properties

Controls on forms have a few other tab order properties you might want to set. The Tab Index property is a number indicating the control's position in the tab order. The first control to receive focus when the form opens in Form View has a Tab Index of 0.

The Auto Tab property works with fields that have input masks. When the Auto Tab property is set to Yes, the cursor moves to the next control in the tab order when the last character permitted in the input mask is entered.

I need to format other forms just like one I created

Source of the problem

You spent a lot of time creating a new form with just the right style, colors, font, background, and everything else a great form should have. You presented it to management, and they agreed that all the company forms should have that same look. Now, if you could just remember every style you applied to the groundbreaking form. It seems like reproducing all the attributes for each new form might take forever.

That's where the Access AutoFormat comes in. You may have thought that you were limited to using the 10 AutoFormats for forms that Access comes with, but you can save the custom format you created to use with other forms. All you have to do to apply the look to a new form is call up the custom format you saved.

The following solutions describe the ways you can save and reuse a custom form format.

How to fix it

1. In the database window, select the form you want to use as a model and then click Design.

2. On the Format menu, click AutoFormat.

3. In the AutoFormat dialog box, click the Options button. ▶

4. Check Font, Color, and Border if you want those attributes included in the custom AutoFormat. If you don't want to include one or more of these format attributes, clear the check box for it.

5. In the AutoFormat dialog box, click Customize.

6. In the Customize dialog box, choose Create A New AutoFormat Based On The Form '[*Name of Your Form*]'. ▶

7. In the Customize AutoFormat dialog box, click OK.

8. In the New Style Name dialog box, type the name for your new form style and then click OK. ▶

9. You can see in the AutoFormat dialog box that the name you gave to the new format is added to the list of Form AutoFormats. Click Close to return to the form design. ▶

To apply this custom format to other forms, do the following:

1. Open an existing form or create a new form in Design view.

2. On the Format menu, click AutoFormat.

3. In the AutoFormat dialog box, select the custom format name from the list of Form AutoFormats.

4. Click OK.

Tip

This method of creating a model format works for reports, too.

Tip

You don't have to start a custom format for a form or report from scratch. If you like some aspects of one of the predesigned formats, you can make the changes you want to it and save it as a custom format with a different name.

I can't show a summary of values from a subform in the main form

Source of the problem

You designed a neat form showing customer information and a subform displaying data about the business each customer has brought your way. Adding up customer sales in the subform and showing the total in the subform's footer section posed no problem, but now you want to show the same totals in the main form with the rest of the customer data. Unfortunately, you can't do that directly. You can't include a control in a main form that gets its value by calculating the total of data in a subform.

But don't give up; you can fake it. The following solution shows you how to overcome this limitation and display the total of values from a field in a subform in the main form itself.

How to fix it

First you need to make some changes to the subform:

1. In the database window, select the subform and then click Design.

2. On the toolbar, click the Properties button.

3. Click the Format tab and change the form's Default View property to Continuous Forms. ▶

4. If the subform has no footer section, click Form Header/Footer on the View menu.

5. In the Toolbox, click the Text Box icon and then click in the subform's footer section to add a text box control.

6. Right-click in the text box and then click Properties on the shortcut menu.

7. Click the Data tab. In the Control Source property box, type an expression to calculate the total of the values in the field you want to summarize. For example, type the expression **=Sum([ExtendedPrice])** to summarize the values in the field named ExtendedPrice. ▶

8. Edit the text box's label to identify the data the text box will display.

9. Click the Other tab and type a name for the control (for example, **TotalCustSales**) in the Name property box. ▶

10. Save the changes you've made to the subform's design and then close the subform.

11. Open the main form in Design view.

12. In the Toolbox, click the Text Box icon and then click in the detail section of the main form to add a text box control. ▶

13. Right-click the text box and then click Properties on the shortcut menu.

14. In the Data tab, type an expression in the Control Source property box that refers to the summary control in the subform. The expression would be something like **=[*subform name*].Form!**
[*subform control name*], using the names of the form and control from your database. ▶

15. Click the subform control and, on the Format tab, set its Can Shrink and Can Grow properties to Yes.

16. Save the main form.

17. Open the subform in Design view again.

18. Right-click the text box control you placed in the footer section and then click Properties on the shortcut menu.

19. On the Format tab, set the Visible property to No. ▶

20. Save the subform. When you open the main form again, you'll see the summary value.

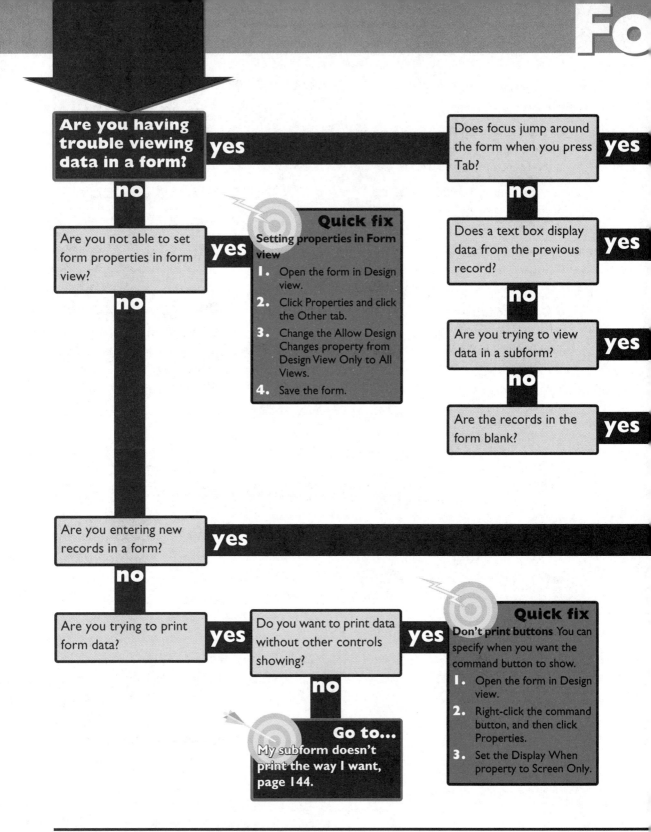

Fo

Are you having trouble viewing data in a form? **yes**

no

Does focus jump around the form when you press Tab? **yes**

no

Are you not able to set form properties in form view? **yes**

no

Quick fix

Setting properties in Form view

1. Open the form in Design view.
2. Click Properties and click the Other tab.
3. Change the Allow Design Changes property from Design View Only to All Views.
4. Save the form.

Does a text box display data from the previous record? **yes**

no

Are you trying to view data in a subform? **yes**

no

Are the records in the form blank? **yes**

Are you entering new records in a form? **yes**

no

Are you trying to print form data? **yes**

Do you want to print data without other controls showing? **yes**

no

Quick fix

Don't print buttons You can specify when you want the command button to show.

1. Open the form in Design view.
2. Right-click the command button, and then click Properties.
3. Set the Display When property to Screen Only.

Go to...

My subform doesn't print the way I want, page 144.

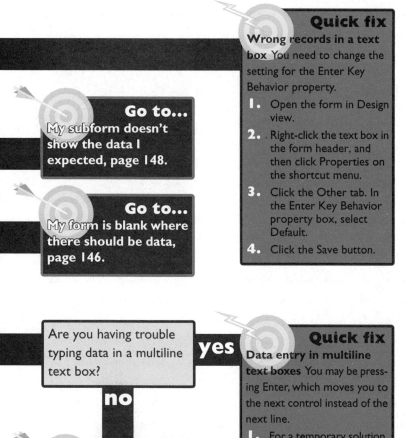

Quick fix

Setting tab order The tab order is determined by the order in which you add controls to the form.

1. Open the form in Design view.
2. Click Tab Order on the View menu.
3. Click the field you want to change in the tab order.
4. Drag the field by the selector box to a new position.
5. Click OK and save the form.

Quick fix

Wrong records in a text box You need to change the setting for the Enter Key Behavior property.

1. Open the form in Design view.
2. Right-click the text box in the form header, and then click Properties on the shortcut menu.
3. Click the Other tab. In the Enter Key Behavior property box, select Default.
4. Click the Save button.

Go to...

My subform doesn't show the data I expected, page 148.

Go to...

My form is blank where there should be data, page 146.

Are you having trouble typing data in a multiline text box?

yes

no

Go to...

I'm having trouble entering data in my combo box or list box, page 142.

Quick fix

Data entry in multiline text boxes You may be pressing Enter, which moves you to the next control instead of the next line.

1. For a temporary solution, press Ctrl+Enter. For a permanent solution, open the form in Design view.
2. Right-click the text box, and then click Properties.
3. Set the Enter Key Behavior property to New Line In Field.

If your solution isn't here, check these related chapters:

- Controls, placing and formatting, page 12
- Controls, viewing data, page 22
- Forms, designing, page 124

Or see the general troubleshooting tips on page xv.

I'm having trouble entering data in my combo box or list box

Source of the problem

Data entry forms are supposed to make life easier, not stubbornly decline to accept the data you try to enter. This is especially true for controls that are designed to speed things up, like combo boxes and list boxes. When you click in a combo box, a list of acceptable values is displayed and you can pick the one you want. List boxes display the values without you having to click the arrow. Sometimes you must choose from the list, but other times you can enter whatever you want.

If you're having trouble entering data in a list box or combo box control, you might have one of the following problems:

● With a combo box, you might have a bad setting in the Row Source, Control Source, or Bound Column property. The Row Source property tells Microsoft Access where to get the values to display in the list. The Control Source property tells Access the field in which to store the value you select from the list or type in the control. The Bound Column property indicates which column of data in the list should be stored in the Control Source field. If any of these properties are improperly set, you will see an error or an incorrect value will be entered.

● If you are trying to enter a value that's not listed in the combo box or list box, the Limit To List property might be set to Yes.

The following steps show you how to solve these problems.

How to fix it

1. In the database window, select the form with the combo box or list box and then click the Design button.

2. Right-click the combo box or list box control and then click Properties on the shortcut menu.

3. Click on the Data tab and in the Control Source property box, make sure that the field indicated is the one in which you want to store the value you select from the list. Make sure the name of the field is accurate and spelled correctly.

4. Review the information in the Row Source property box. It should be a structured query language (SQL) statement (as shown in the figure), the name of a lookup table, or an actual list of values. The Row Source Type property setting indicates where the values come from: Table/Query, Value List, or Field List. ▶

5. In the Bound Column property box, type the number for the column in the Row Source that contains the value you want stored.

Combo Box: CategoryID

CategoryID	▼

Format | **Data** | Event | Other | All

Control Source	CategoryID
Input Mask	
Row Source Type	Table/Query
Row Source	SELECT DISTINCT Categories.CategoryID, Categories.CategoryName FROM Categories ORDER BY Categories.C
Bound Column	1
Limit To List	Yes
Auto Expand	Yes
Default Value	
Validation Rule	

6. If you want to be able to enter a value that's not in the list, change the Limit To List property to No. Note that if the column displayed in the combo box is not the bound column, the Limit To List property is set to Yes. ▶

Combo Box: SupplierID

SupplierID	▼

Format | **Data** | Event | Other | All

Control Source	SupplierID
Input Mask	
Row Source Type	Table/Query
Row Source	SELECT DISTINCT Suppliers.SupplierID,
Bound Column	1
Limit To List	Yes
Auto Expand	Yes
Default Value	No
Validation Rule	

Tip

In the figure above, an SQL statement in the Row Source property box creates a query with two fields, both from the Categories table: CategoryID (column 1) and CategoryName (column 2). The category name is displayed in the list, but the value from CategoryID (column 1) is stored in the control.

My subform doesn't print the way I want

Source of the problem

You take it for granted that forms are more for online work than for printed documents, but sometimes you want to print a form and you want it to look right. Even when you've set all of the printer options and laid out the form the way it ought to look, things that could have gone wrong did. You might have encountered one of these problems:

● Your subform was definitely included in the form's design, but it didn't appear in Print Preview. The reason is probably that the subform doesn't include any records that are related to the current record in the main form. It is also possible that the Data Entry property for the subform is set to Yes, which would show an empty record in the subform.

● When you printed a form that includes a subform, not all the records in the subform that are related to the current record in the main form were printed. Or, when no records should have been displayed in the subform, and you want to save space, the subform printed anyway. These problems occur because the subform control is a fixed size.

The following solutions explain how to solve these problems.

How to fix it

If the subform appears empty in Form view or in Print Preview, and you know it should display related records, follow these steps:

1. In the database window, select the subform and then click the Design button.

2. On the toolbar, click the Properties button.

3. In the properties dialog box, click the Data tab and change the Data Entry property to No. ▶

4. Save the subform.

5. Look at the form in Form view or Print Preview and check the subform to be sure it is no longer empty.

If you want all the records in the subform to print with the record in the main form, follow these steps:

1. In the database window, select the main form and then click the Design button.

2. Click the border of the subform control.

3. On the toolbar, click the Properties button.

4. On the Format tab, set the Can Grow property to Yes. ▶

5. If you don't want to print the subform when it contains no related records, set the Can Shrink property to Yes.

6. Save the form.

More about problems with printer fonts

Another problem you might encounter when you print a form is that the printer you use prints the text in a crazy font—one you've never seen before, much less know the name of. Chances are the printer doesn't have the font you used when you designed the form and has substituted one similar to it. For example, if you format a form with Adobe PostScript fonts and send the document to a LaserJet printer, you may see unexpected results because some LaserJet printers don't use PostScript fonts. Try to use fonts such as TrueType fonts that are universally accepted and processed in the same way by all printers.

Also, try to print a form using the printer set up for your computer when you designed the form. When you select printer options and set up the page to fit the form when it prints, those settings are saved with the form. You don't have to worry about the settings unless you make changes to the form's layout or change printers.

My form is blank where there should be data

Source of the problem

It's bad enough when you see the wrong data or a weird error message instead of your familiar data. But when a form is blank, it's hard to know where to turn. Sometimes only one or two fields are blank; on other occasions, the whole form is blank. Here are some of the reasons for this apparent lack of cooperation:

- The form might not be bound to a table or query. Remember, a form has to get its data from somewhere. You can create an unbound form, of course, but you wouldn't expect to see data in it.

- The query the form is based on doesn't return any records. The query might include criteria that are so stringent that no records meet them. Or the query might have conflicting criteria, such as a combination of mutually exclusive conditions with the *And* operator.

- The form is in Data Entry mode. If the Data Entry property is set to Yes, a blank form appears rather than existing records when you open the form.

The following solutions show you how to get around these problems.

How to fix it

1. In the database window, select the form and then click the Design button.

2. Click the Properties button on the toolbar.

3. In the properties dialog box, click the Data tab and confirm that the Record Source property for the form is set to one of the tables or queries in the database. ▶

4. If it is, make sure the name of the table or query is spelled right.

Form	
Form	
Format	Data	Event	Other	All
Record Source	Quarterly Orders
Filter	
Order By	
Allow Filters	Yes
Allow Edits	No
Allow Deletions	No
Allow Additions	No
Data Entry	No
Recordset Type	Dynaset
Record Locks	No Locks

5. If it's not, click the arrow next to the Record Source property and select the table or query that contains the records you want to work with in this form. ▶

If the form is bound to a query but isn't displaying any data, check the criteria the query is using:

1. Close the form, select the query in the database window and then click the Design button.

2. In the query design grid, remove the first expression in the Criteria row. ▶

3. Click the View button to see whether the query now returns the records you want.

4. If the query still doesn't return the records you want, delete other criteria expressions one by one, switching to Datasheet view each time to check whether the correct records are displayed.

5. Once you get the right combination of criteria, save and close the query.

6. Open the form in Form view. The proper records should now appear.

If the form is completely blank, follow these steps:

1. Select the form in the database window and then click Design.

2. Click the Properties button on the toolbar and then click the Data tab.

3. Set the Data Entry property to No. ▶

My subform doesn't show the data I expected

Source of the problem

Subforms can be tricky. They present their own set of problems when you least expect them. The first thing to keep in mind when working with subforms is that the subform object is saved as a separate form in the database, while the subform control is part of the main form. The object and the control have different sets of properties.

Some of the problems with displaying data in a subform are as follows:

● When you open the form containing the subform in Form view, the subform displays all the records from the query or table it is based on instead of just the records related to the current record in the main form. If this is your problem, you may have used control names instead of field names to link the form and the subform.

● When the form starts to open, you see an unexpected parameter prompt. The problem here might be that the fields linking the main form and the subform aren't identified correctly.

● When you try to limit the Datasheet view of the subform to a single record, Access shows you as many records as will fit in the subform. This problem occurs because some of the subform's properties aren't set the way they should be.

The following steps show you how to solve these problems.

How to fix it

If you see all the records in the subform instead of the list of related records you expected, do the following:

1. In the database window, select the main form and click the Design button.

2. Right-click a border of the subform control and then click Properties on the shortcut menu.

3. In the Data tab, look at the names in the Link Child Fields and Link Master Fields property boxes. These properties should include the fields that link the record source for the subform (Child) to the record source for the main form (Master). ▶

Subform/Subreport: Customer Orders Subform1

Customer Orders Subform1

Format	Data	Event	Other	All

Source Object . . . . Customer Orders Subform1
Link Child Fields . . . . CustomerID
Link Master Fields . . . . CustomerID
Enabled . . . . Yes
Locked . . . . No

4. If the fields don't match, click the Build button to open the Subform Field Linker dialog box and choose different fields. Click OK. ▶

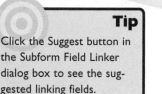

> **Tip**
>
> Click the Suggest button in the Subform Field Linker dialog box to see the suggested linking fields.

If you see an unexpected parameter prompt, Access may not recognize the name of one of the linking fields. Follow these steps to correct the problem: ▶

1. Click Cancel to close the prompt box, and then select the form in the database window and click the Design button.

2. Select the subform control and then click the Properties button on the toolbar.

3. Remove the table names from fields specified in the Link Child Fields and Link Master Fields property boxes. For example, if you see Products.Categories.CategoryID in the property box, delete the table name (in this example, Categories), including the period.

4. Save the subform.

To see a single record in the subform, do the following:

1. In the database window, select the subform and then click the Design button.

2. Click the Properties button on the toolbar.

3. On the Format tab, change the setting in the Default View property box to Single Form.

4. Set the Allow Form View property to Yes.

5. Set the Navigation Buttons property to Yes so that you can move through the records in the subform.

6. Set the Dividing Lines property to No to get rid of the line below the record data. ▶

7. Save the subform and open the main form in Form view.

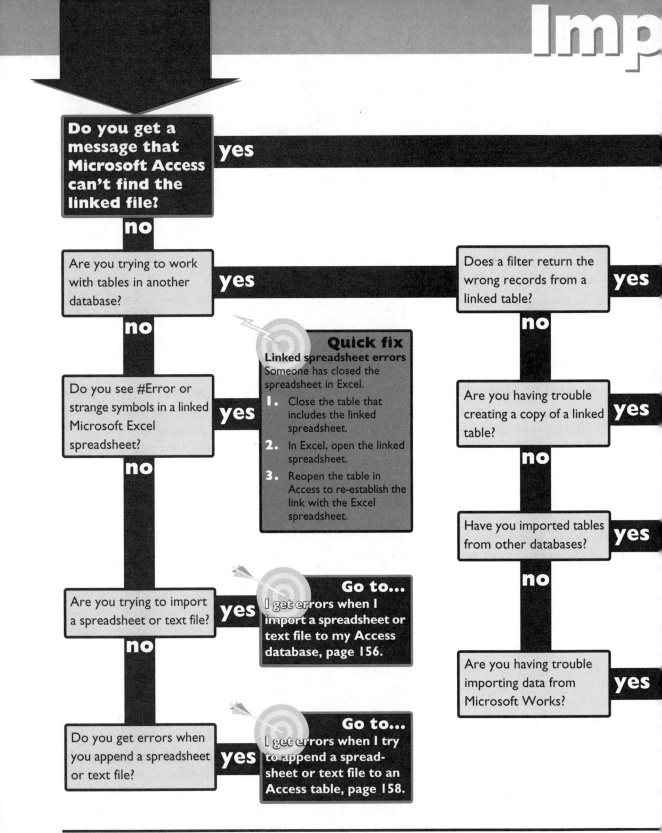

Do you get a message that Microsoft Access can't find the linked file?

yes

no

Are you trying to work with tables in another database?

yes

no

Does a filter return the wrong records from a linked table?

yes

no

Do you see #Error or strange symbols in a linked Microsoft Excel spreadsheet?

yes

no

Quick fix

Linked spreadsheet errors
Someone has closed the spreadsheet in Excel.

1. Close the table that includes the linked spreadsheet.
2. In Excel, open the linked spreadsheet.
3. Reopen the table in Access to re-establish the link with the Excel spreadsheet.

Are you having trouble creating a copy of a linked table?

yes

no

Have you imported tables from other databases?

yes

no

Are you trying to import a spreadsheet or text file?

yes

no

Go to...
I get errors when I import a spreadsheet or text file to my Access database, page 156.

Are you having trouble importing data from Microsoft Works?

yes

Do you get errors when you append a spreadsheet or text file?

yes

Go to...
I get errors when I try to append a spread-sheet or text file to an Access table, page 158.

Quick fix

Finding linked tables The file that contains the table might have been moved or renamed.

1. Open the database that contains links to tables.
2. On the Tools menu, point to Database Utilities and then click Linked Table Manager.
3. Click the check box for the tables whose links you want to refresh.
4. In the Select New Location dialog box, locate the database containing the tables you linked to, and then click Open.
5. Click OK.

Quick fix

Filtering linked records The values in the criteria are case-sensitive.

1. Open the table you're linked to.
2. Check for uppercase and lowercase field values.
3. Correct any mismatches.

Go to...

I copied a linked table, but it is still linked and doesn't show up in my database, page 152.

Go to...

I'm having trouble with an imported table, page 154.

Quick fix

Importing from Microsoft Works

1. Open the file in the host application.
2. Save the file in dBASE IV format.
3. Open Access, point to Get External Data on the File menu, and click Import.
4. Select the file and click Import.

If your solution isn't here, check this related chapter:

- Queries, action, page 192

Or see the general troubleshooting tips on page xv.

I copied a linked table, but it is still linked and doesn't show up in my database

Source of the problem

You've seen the advantages of linking to tables in another database for some time now. You've gotten access to the data in a useful table while someone else maintains that table in the source database. Nice going. But then you found that despite these advantages, having your own copy of the table in your database would be best. So, you created a copy of the table. When you peer at the database window, however, you can tell by the link icon (the arrow pointing to the right) that the table is still linked to its original source and is not a stand-alone copy. What went wrong? ▶

The problem is that with the Copy and Paste commands you are copying only the link, not the whole table. You need to use another method to actually construct a table based on the linked table.

The following solution shows you how to use the helpful Make-Table query to create the local table.

How to fix it

1. Open the database that contains the link to the outside table. In the database window, click Queries.

2. Click New. In the New Queries dialog box, click Design View and then click OK.

3. In the Show Table dialog box, select the linked table, click Add, and then click Close.

4. From the list of fields for the table, drag the asterisk to the first column in the query design grid. ▶

5. On the Query menu, click Make-Table query.

6. In the Make Table dialog box, type the name for the new table in the Table Name box. ▶

7. Click Current Database and then click OK.

8. On the Query menu, click Run.

9. Click Yes when asked to confirm that you want to create a new table and paste the records in it.

10. Close the query without saving it. You will not need to run it again.

11. Return to the database window and then click Tables in the list of objects. You'll see the new table listed. ▶

12. Select the linked table and delete it from the database.

Tip

Deleting a linked table object from the database window removes only the link to the table. The original source table is unaffected.

I'm having trouble with an imported table

Source of the problem

When you imported a table from another database program—instead of linking to it—you could treat the newcomer pretty much as one of your Microsoft Access tables. You might have run into problems, however, if the table you imported contained types of data that differ from the types Access recognizes.

When a table is imported, Access tries to convert the data types in that table to equivalent Access data types, but it isn't always successful. For example, the Paradox Graphic, Binary, and Formatted Memo data types have no equivalent in Access. If you want these types of data in an Access table, you need to enter the items in the appropriate format, such as the OLE Object field type, after importing the source table.

The Name AutoCorrect feature doesn't work automatically for imported tables. Access doesn't create a name map for imported tables as it does for tables you create in Access. If you rename an imported table and that name change doesn't carry through to places where you refer to the table in other database objects, you'll have problems. But even though Name AutoCorrect doesn't work automatically, you can apply it to an imported table.

The following steps describe how to resolve these problems.

How to fix it

If there are data types in a Paradox table that don't match Access field data types, do the following:

1. Open the table you're importing in Paradox and convert any Formatted Memo fields to Memo.

2. Save the Paradox table and then import the table again to Access.

3. In Access, select the table in the database window and then click Design.

4. If the Paradox table had a Paradox Graphic field (used to store image files), add an OLE Object field to the table design in Access. ▶

5. If the Paradox table included a Binary field (used to store other file types), add another OLE Object field to the table design in Access.

6. Click the View button to switch to Datasheet view.

7. Locate the files corresponding to the objects stored in the Paradox table and insert the data into the table in Access.

To turn on the Name AutoCorrect feature for imported tables, do the following:

1. With the database open, click Options on the Tools menu.

2. Click the General tab.

3. Select both the Track Name AutoCorrect Info and Perform Name AutoCorrect check boxes. Click OK. ▶

4. In the Access database window, select the imported table, click the Design button, and then click the Save button on the toolbar. Saving the table creates the name map Access will use.

Tip

The names of tables you have imported don't always give you a clue about what is stored in the table. Some applications limit field and table names to eight characters with no spaces. You can rename the tables in Access so that they have a more informative title. Renaming the imported table has no effect on the original table.

I get errors when I import a spreadsheet or text file to my Access database

Source of the problem

You're probably not surprised that importing files from different programs can cause problems. But what should surprise you is that so few big problems occur. And when they do, Access warns you that some of the information won't be imported. Access also keeps track of some common errors in a table named Import Errors so you can deal with them one at a time.

If, when importing a file, you told the Import Wizard that the first row in that file contained column headings that Access should use as field names, the column headings might not be valid as an Access field name. There could be a blank column heading, for example. In this case, Access displays a message and automatically assigns a valid field name such as Field1.

Access creates the table to receive an imported spreadsheet with enough fields to hold the first row of values from the spreadsheet. If later rows in the spreadsheet contain more fields than the first, Access adds a field name such as Field*nn*, representing the number of the last column. An extra field delimiter in a text file can also cause this error.

Sometimes data in a spreadsheet or text file can't be stored in a field in an Access table because of the data type that Access assigned to that field when it imported the information. Access assigns a data type to the field based on the data in the first row that's imported. You might have included a text value in a later row for a field where Access expects only numbers. Another cause for this type of error is a row in the text file or spreadsheet that contains summary data or extraneous characters that don't follow the type and size assigned to the field.

The following solutions show you how to address these problems.

How to fix it

If Access has created an Import Errors table, you will see the message shown in the figure. To correct the import errors, do the following:

Import Spreadsheet Wizard

ⓘ Finished importing file 'C:\My Documents\Products.xls' to table 'ProductsXLS'. Not all of your data was successfully imported. Error descriptions with associated row numbers of bad records can be found in the Microsoft Access table 'Products$_ImportErrors2'.

OK

1. In the database window, select the imported table and then click Open.

2. In the database window, select the Import Errors table and then click Open.

3. On the Window menu, click Tile Horizontally, so you can see both tables at once. ▶

4. Review the errors in the Import Errors table and then correct the data in the imported table.

5. After correcting the data, save the imported table and delete the Import Errors table.

If you see strange generic field names (such Field1 or Field13), do the following:

1. Select the imported table in the database window and then click Design.

2. If the fields contain valid data, rename the fields with useful names, replacing the generic names Access provided. ▶

3. Save the table.

4. If the generic fields are the result of having too many fields in a row in the spreadsheet or text file, open the file you're trying to import and delete the extra fields so that every row has the same number of columns.

5. Import the file into Access again and replace the original imported table.

If you think the field data type is correct but the data can't be stored in it, try this:

1. Open the text file or spreadsheet.

2. Edit the data to make it consistent. For example, remove text from a column that contains all numbers or delete extraneous characters.

3. Save the file.

4. Return to Access and import the file again.

I get errors when I try to append a spreadsheet or text file to an Access table

Source of the problem

You've found some really great information in a Microsoft Excel spreadsheet that needs to be added to a table in your Access database. You could spend all night typing in the data, of course, but you know there's a better way. Just tack the data in the spreadsheet onto the data that's already in the table. Sounds like a piece of cake, right? It should be, but sometimes things go wrong. It's possible that one or more rows in the spreadsheet you want to append contain more fields than your table does. See the section in this chapter called "I get errors when I import a spreadsheet or text file to my Access database" for solutions to this problem.

You might also have encountered other problems when you tried to append a spreadsheet or even a simple text file, such as the following:

● The field names in the spreadsheet or text file don't match those in the destination table. If you indicated that the first row contains the field names when you appended the data, the field names must match.

● The data you're appending might not be the right data type for the field you're adding it to. For example, the table field has a Number data type and the incoming data is text. Or, numeric data in the spreadsheet or text file might be too large for the field size specified for the destination field. If the Field Size property in the Access field is set to Byte, for example, the field can't hold a number greater than 255.

● The spreadsheet or text file might contain duplicate values in the field you designated as the primary key or a uniquely indexed field for the destination table.

The following solutions show you the steps to take to correct these problems.

How to fix it

If you see a message that the file was not imported, the field names probably don't match. ▶

> **Import Spreadsheet Wizard**
>
> ⓘ An error occurred trying to import file 'C:\My Documents\Employees2.xls'. The file was not imported.
>
> [OK]

1. Open the table you're appending records to in Design view.

2. Change the field names to match the headings in the spreadsheet or text file you are appending.

3. If any fields are missing, add them to the table design.

4. Save the table. Import the spreadsheet or text file again to append the records.

If you see a message indicating that Access couldn't append all the data, do the following:

1. Note in the message that Access displays how many records are missing data and how many records were lost. ▶

2. If only a few errors occurred and you'd like to deal with them manually, click Yes in the message box.

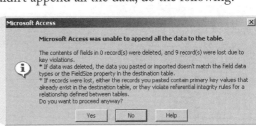

3. Open the table you appended the records to in Datasheet view and then click the column in which records weren't appended. This is the field that caused the data type or size mismatch problem.

4. Click Sort Ascending. Any blank fields will move to the top of the column.

5. Type the values from the spreadsheet or text file into the blank fields in the table. Repeat steps 3 through 5 for other fields that caused errors.

If too many errors occurred to correct manually, do the following:

1. Click No to clear the message.

2. Click Cancel to abandon the append operation.

3. Open the table you're appending records to in Design view.

> **Tip**
>
> You might have to return to the source spreadsheet or text file to find out what the value should be.

4. Select the primary key field and then click the Primary Key toolbar button to remove the primary key designation. ▶

5. Save and close the table and then append the spreadsheet or text file again.

6. Open the table you appended the records to in Datasheet view and edit the field you want as the primary key so that all records have unique values.

7. Return the table to Design view, set the primary key field again or add an AutoNumber field as the primary key field.

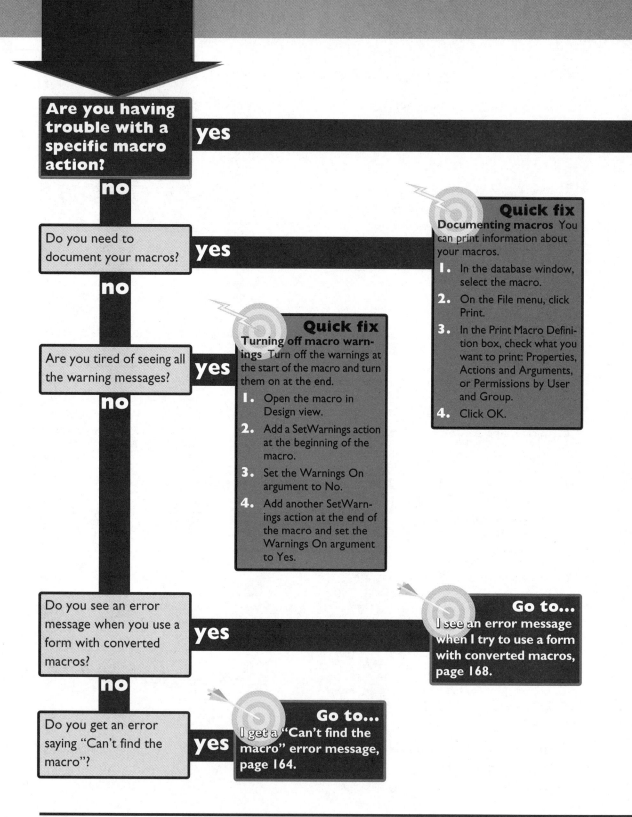

Are you having trouble with a specific macro action? → **yes**

no

Do you need to document your macros? → **yes**

no

Quick fix

Documenting macros You can print information about your macros.
1. In the database window, select the macro.
2. On the File menu, click Print.
3. In the Print Macro Definition box, check what you want to print: Properties, Actions and Arguments, or Permissions by User and Group.
4. Click OK.

Are you tired of seeing all the warning messages? → **yes**

no

Quick fix

Turning off macro warnings Turn off the warnings at the start of the macro and turn them on at the end.
1. Open the macro in Design view.
2. Add a SetWarnings action at the beginning of the macro.
3. Set the Warnings On argument to No.
4. Add another SetWarnings action at the end of the macro and set the Warnings On argument to Yes.

Do you see an error message when you use a form with converted macros? → **yes**

no

Go to...
I see an error message when I try to use a form with converted macros, page 168.

Do you get an error saying "Can't find the macro"? → **yes**

Go to...
I get a "Can't find the macro" error message, page 164.

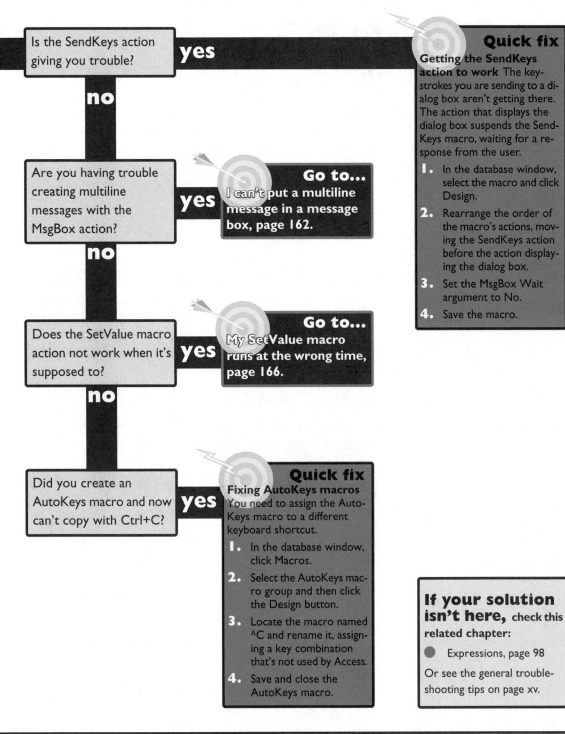

Is the SendKeys action giving you trouble?

yes

no

Are you having trouble creating multiline messages with the MsgBox action?

yes

no

Does the SetValue macro action not work when it's supposed to?

yes

no

Did you create an AutoKeys macro and now can't copy with Ctrl+C?

yes

Quick fix

Getting the SendKeys action to work The keystrokes you are sending to a dialog box aren't getting there. The action that displays the dialog box suspends the Send-Keys macro, waiting for a response from the user.

1. In the database window, select the macro and click Design.
2. Rearrange the order of the macro's actions, moving the SendKeys action before the action displaying the dialog box.
3. Set the MsgBox Wait argument to No.
4. Save the macro.

Go to...

I can't put a multiline message in a message box, page 162.

Go to...

My SetValue macro runs at the wrong time, page 166.

Quick fix

Fixing AutoKeys macros You need to assign the Auto-Keys macro to a different keyboard shortcut.

1. In the database window, click Macros.
2. Select the AutoKeys macro group and then click the Design button.
3. Locate the macro named ^C and rename it, assigning a key combination that's not used by Access.
4. Save and close the AutoKeys macro.

If your solution isn't here, check this related chapter:

● Expressions, page 98

Or see the general troubleshooting tips on page xv.

I can't put a multiline message in a message box

Source of the problem

Sometimes a short phrase such as "Needs a tune-up" doesn't quite convey enough information to get a message across. You need more information to help you or someone else make the right decision. Of course, the right decision can depend on whether you are repairing cars or selling them.

If you're having trouble creating a multiline message with the MsgBox macro action, you probably didn't type the text correctly. When you type a longish message, the text doesn't wrap, so the message box expands horizontally and could exceed the width of your screen. You need to use a special character (the @ sign) to break up the message into multiple lines.

The following solutions show you two ways to enter multiple-line messages in a message box. You'll also learn how to display the @ symbol in a message box for cases when you need to show it rather than use it as a special character.

How to fix it

If you are trying to display more than one line in a message box (similar to the built-in error messages that Microsoft Access displays), follow these steps:

1. In the database window, click Macros and then click New.

2. In the Action column, select MsgBox from the drop-down list.

3. In the Action Arguments section at the bottom of the window, click in the Message argument box and type the first line of the message you want to display. ▶

4. Type the @ character at the end of the first line and then type the second line.

5. Type another @ character and then type the third line of the message.

> **Tip**
>
> When you create a multiline message, the first line appears in bold at the top of the message box. The other lines appear in normal text below the first line. You can type up to 255 characters in the message box.

6. Click the Save button and then name the new macro.

7. Click the Run button on the toolbar. ▶

Another way to create a multiline message is to use an expression that includes the carriage return and line feed characters [indicated by the symbols Chr(13) and Chr(10)], which will move the text to the next line. Follow these steps:

1. Open the macro you're having trouble with in Design view.

2. In the Action column, select MsgBox from the drop-down list.

3. In the Message argument box, type an expression such as **="This is the first line" & Chr(13) & Chr(10) & "and this is the second" & Chr(13) & Chr(10) & "and this is the third line."**

4. Save the macro and then click the Run button.

If you want the @ character to appear in the message (very handy if you want to display an e-mail address), you need to type an expression such as the following, which uses the Chr function with the character code for @:

1. Open the macro in Design view.

2. Type an expression such as **="You can send me e-mail at vandersenz"& Chr(64) &"aol.com"**

3. Save the macro and click the Run button. ▶

> **Warning**
>
> If you don't precede the expression with an equal sign, you'll see the whole expression in the message box, including the quotation marks, the Chr functions, and the & symbols.

> **Tip**
>
> You can use Chr(64) to display the @ symbol only once in the expression. If you use it twice, the message is broken into three lines.

I get a "Can't find the macro" error message

Source of the problem

Access seems so helpless when it displays a message saying that it can't find a macro. You know that no macro was supposed to run when you opened a form or moved to a control. Why is Access looking for one, and why didn't Access tell you the name of the macro it was looking for? ▶

If no macro name appears in the message, someone (we won't name names or point fingers) might have inadvertently typed a space or two in one of the event property boxes for a form or a control. If the property box isn't totally blank, Access sniffs around for a macro to run.

If the message does show the name of the missing macro, the macro selected in the form might be misnamed or not spelled correctly.

The following solutions tell you how to cure these problems.

How to fix it

If the error message doesn't contain the name of a macro, follow these steps:

1. Open the form in Design view. Click the Properties button on the toolbar and then click the Event tab.

2. If the error message appeared when you opened the form, click in the On Load event property box.

3. If the property box is blank but the insertion point is not at the left end of the property box, press Backspace until the insertion point is at the far left, removing any spaces. ▶

4. Repeat steps 2 and 3 for the On Open and On Current event properties.

5. If the error message appeared when you tried to save the current record in the form, check the Before Update and After Update event properties and remove any spaces from the blank boxes.

6. If the message appeared when you moved to a control or changed the data in a control, click that control.

7. In the Properties dialog box for the control, click the Event tab and remove any spaces from the On Got Focus, Before Update, and After Update event properties.

8. Click the View button to switch to Form view.

9. If the message still appears, go through each event property box that is blank and press Backspace to clear any inadvertent spaces.

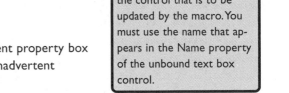

Tip

In the macro expression itself, make sure you have used the correct name for the control that is to be updated by the macro. You must use the name that appears in the Name property of the unbound text box control.

If the error message contains the name of the missing macro, that's some comfort, but you still have a problem. Try the following remedy:

> **Microsoft Access** ✕
>
> ⓘ Microsoft Access can't find the macro 'LoadMacro.'
>
> The macro (or its macro group) doesn't exist, or the macro is new but hasn't been saved.
> Note that when you enter the macrogroupname.macroname syntax in an argument, you must specify the name the macro's macro group was last saved under.
>
> [OK]

1. In the database window, select the macro associated with the form and click the Design button.

2. Compare the name of the macro with the name that was displayed in the error message.

3. If the names are different, click Save As on the File menu and save the macro with the name that appeared in the message.

4. If you want to keep the current macro name, open the form in Design view and click the Properties button on the toolbar.

5. Move to the property box for the event that caused the problem and select the name of the existing macro from the list. ▶

> **Form** ✕
>
> Form ▾
>
> | Format | Data | Event | Other | All |
>
> Before Del Confirm . . . .
> After Del Confirm . . . .
> On Open . . . .
> On Load . . . . LoadMacro
> On Resize . . . . [Event Procedure]
> On Unload . . . . AutoKeys
> On Close . . . . AutoKeys.^C
> On Activate . . . . Customer Labels Dialog
> On Deactivate . . . . Customer Labels Dialog.Cancel
> On Got Focus . . . . Customer Labels Dialog.Enable
> On Lost Focus . . . . Customer Labels Dialog.Preview
> On Click . . . . Customer Labels Dialog.Print

A word about grouped macros

Grouping macros is a good way to keep macros that apply to the same form or report together where you can find them. However, if an event is attached to one of the macros in a macro group and you have moved the macro to a different group or renamed the group without updating the name in the event property box, you will get the "Can't find the macro" error message. Remember, to refer to a macro in a macro group, use the identifying syntax MyNewMacroGroup.mymacro.

My SetValue macro runs at the wrong time

Source of the problem

In a database program like Access (which is often called an event-driven system), nothing happens until something else happens. If that doesn't make sense, think about not going to the refrigerator until a commercial comes on. Macros can automate some of your tedious tasks, but they have to be told when to perform; in other words, macros need to know the event that should make them run.

Sometimes macros don't go on when they're scheduled. For example, a SetValue macro you created is supposed to perform an act like adding 30 days to the date you enter in the Billing Date field and place the result in the Reminder Date field. When you enter the Billing Date, the Reminder Date is blank—it is not entered as planned. But the next time you open the form, the date is there. Clearly, the macro is doing its thing, but it's doing it at the wrong time. ▶

If you're having problems with the timing of a SetValue macro, you probably attached it to the wrong event. You might have attached the macro to a form event such as On Load or On Open, in which case the macro runs when you open the form in Form view, although your intent was to have the macro run when you entered or updated the information in a specific field.

The following solution shows you how to solve this problem.

How to fix it

1. Open the form containing the macro in Design view and then click the Properties button.

2. In the properties dialog box, click the Event tab.

3. Remove the name of the macro from the On Load or On Open property box.

4. On the form, click the control that you want to have run the macro.

5. On the Event tab, click the down arrow in the After Update event property, and select the macro you want to run from the list. ▶

6. Click View to return to Form view.

More about SetValue macros

You can use the SetValue macro action not only to set the value of a field or a control, you can also use it to set properties in a control, form, or report. The SetValue action is easy to use because it has only two arguments: the item that is the focus of the action and the expression that sets the value for the item.

But be warned! The expression you use with the SetValue action is a little different from one you would use in the Control Source property for a control in a form or report. When you use an expression in the Control Source property, you must precede it with an equal sign. But when you use an expression in the Expression argument of the SetValue action, you must not use an equal sign. If you do, you'll get unexpected results, such as a wrong date. ▶

I see an error message when I try to use a form with converted macros

Source of the problem

As part of entering the 21st century, you've upgraded to a new version of Access and are now converting the macros in your database to Microsoft Visual Basic procedures. That part isn't hard. You've simply used a command, and one that's clearly named—Convert Form's Macros to Visual Basic. And one would think that Access would know which Visual Basic methods to use in place of the old macro actions, but you're suddenly faced with an error message when you try to use a form. The message refers to the form's event property setting causing an ambiguous name. ▶

The source of this problem is that, at one time, your form had an event property set to a procedure, and then the property was changed to run a macro instead. The event procedure remained in the form's class module, so when you converted the macro to Visual Basic, Access created a duplicate procedure. You find this out when you try to use the form in Form view.

The following steps show you how to delete the duplicate macro.

How to fix it

1. In the database window, select the form and then click Design.

2. On the View menu, click Code to open the Visual Basic editor. ▶

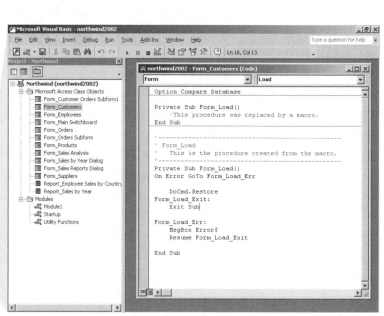

3. On the Debug menu, click Compile *<database name>*. ▶

4. The second copy of the procedure is highlighted, and a debug message is displayed. Click OK and locate the redundant copy of the event procedure. ▶

5. Select the entire procedure, including the Private Sub and End Sub statements and then press Delete.

6. On the View menu, click Microsoft Access.

7. Open the form in Form view, and you will see the error message no longer appears.

An ounce of prevention

To keep this problem from happening at all, go to the form's or report's class module and delete all the procedures that relate to the event properties you have set to macros. If you haven't mixed macros and code in the form or report design, you can get rid of all the Visual Basic procedures by setting the object's Has Module property to No. Then you can simply convert all the macros to Visual Basic.

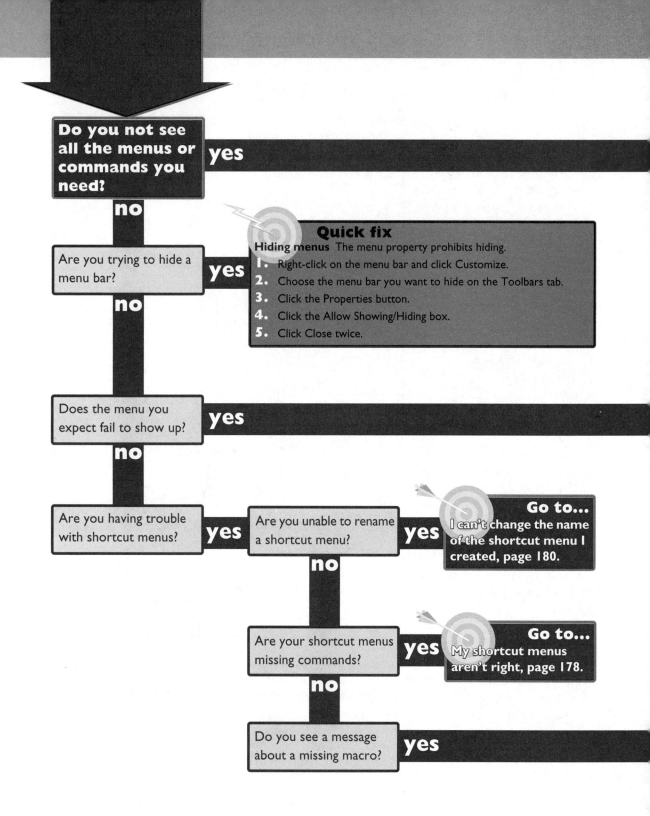

Do you not see all the menus or commands you need? — yes

no

Are you trying to hide a menu bar? — yes

Quick fix
Hiding menus The menu property prohibits hiding.
1. Right-click on the menu bar and click Customize.
2. Choose the menu bar you want to hide on the Toolbars tab.
3. Click the Properties button.
4. Click the Allow Showing/Hiding box.
5. Click Close twice.

no

Does the menu you expect fail to show up? — yes

no

Are you having trouble with shortcut menus? — yes

Are you unable to rename a shortcut menu? — yes

Go to...
I can't change the name of the shortcut menu I created, page 180.

no

Are your shortcut menus missing commands? — yes

Go to...
My shortcut menus aren't right, page 178.

no

Do you see a message about a missing macro? — yes

Menus

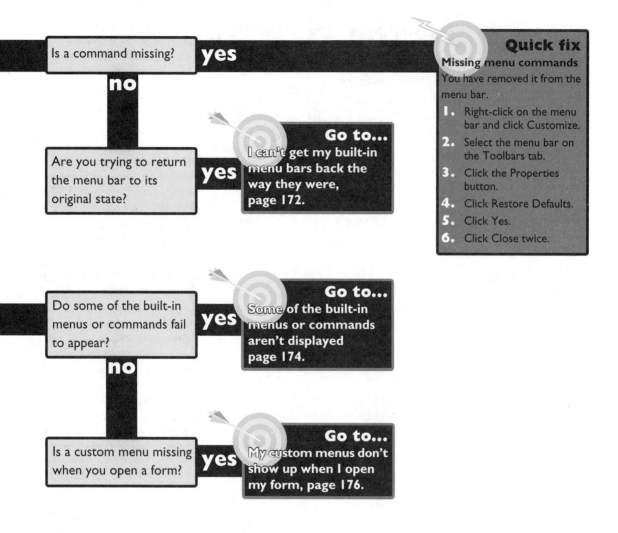

Is a command missing? **yes**

no

Are you trying to return the menu bar to its original state? **yes**

Go to...
I can't get my built-in menu bars back the way they were, page 172.

Quick fix
Missing menu commands
You have removed it from the menu bar.
1. Right-click on the menu bar and click Customize.
2. Select the menu bar on the Toolbars tab.
3. Click the Properties button.
4. Click Restore Defaults.
5. Click Yes.
6. Click Close twice.

Do some of the built-in menus or commands fail to appear? **yes**

no

Go to...
Some of the built-in menus or commands aren't displayed page 174.

Is a custom menu missing when you open a form? **yes**

Go to...
My custom menus don't show up when I open my form, page 176.

Quick fix
Missing macro messages If you see the message, "Microsoft Access can't find the macro '<name of the shortcut menu>' ", you probably have the wrong shortcut menu selected.
1. Open the form in Design view and then click the Properties button on the toolbar.
2. On the Other tab, click in the Shortcut Menu Bar property box and select the correct shortcut menu from the list.
3. Save the form design.

If your solution isn't here, check this related chapter:
- Toolbars, page 300
Or see the general trouble-shooting tips on page xv.

I can't get my built-in menu bars back the way they were

Source of the problem

When you made little changes to Microsoft Access menus and then made a few more, and then a few more, the menus wandered a long way from where they started. Someone might have had a hand in this migration, by modifying an entire menu bar by adding or deleting a whole group of commands or by changing the number, order, or function of commands in a single menu. You might not even recall what your menus used to look like, let alone what they could do for you.

And if the order or number of your menus isn't the problem, how a menu behaves might be. Default properties and other settings for a menu bar that were in effect when you first started Access—settings like allowing docking and moving, resizing, and showing and hiding menus—might have been changed so that the menu bar doesn't behave as you'd expect.

If you or someone else has changed a menu bar and you now want the menu bar back the way it was, you have a few remedies to consider. You can reset the entire menu bar or a single menu so that all the commands revert to their original appearance and arrangement. All the menus are in the same order on the menu bar, and all the commands do what they did before the changes. You can also restore the default properties and settings for a menu bar—its default screen location, size, and the options for how the menu behaves.

The following solutions show you how to restore your menu bar.

Tip

When we talk about a *menu bar*, we're referring to a group of menu titles that usually appears in a bar across the top of the screen. *Menu titles*, on the other hand, are the individual labels shown in the menu bar. *Menu commands* are the actions you select from after clicking a menu title to display the drop-down list of available actions. Most menu commands are also available on toolbars.

How to fix it

To reset a menu bar to its original structure, follow these steps:

1. On the View menu, point to Toolbars and then click Customize.

2. Click the Toolbars tab. In the Toolbars list, highlight the name of the menu bar you want to reset.

3. Click Reset and then click OK to confirm the change. ▶

4. Click Close in the Customize dialog box.

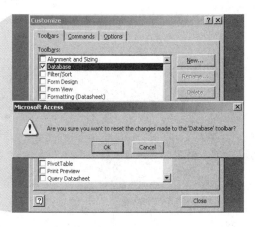

If you just want to reset a specific menu, do the following:

1. Right-click the menu bar and then choose Customize from the shortcut menu. The Customize dialog box will appear.

2. In the menu bar, right-click the menu you want to reset and then click Reset on the shortcut menu. ▶

3. Click Close in the Customize dialog box.

If you want to restore the default properties and settings for a menu bar, do the following:

1. On the View menu, point to Toolbars and then click Customize.

2. Click the Toolbars tab and then click the Properties button.

3. In the Selected Toolbar list, select the name of the menu bar you want to restore. ▶

4. Click Restore Defaults.

5. In the message box that appears, click Yes to confirm the action. ▶

6. When you're finished, click Close in the Toolbar Properties dialog box and then close the Customize dialog box.

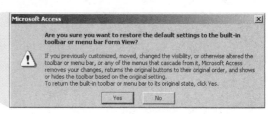

More about restoring and resetting menus

You might have noticed in the figure showing the Toolbar Properties dialog box that some of the properties are dimmed, which indicates that they are not available for changing. The Toolbar Name, Type, and Show On Toolbars Menu options can't be changed in a built-in menu.

In addition, the Restore Defaults button becomes available only after you have made a change to the original built-in menu. It is never available, however, for custom menu bars, and neither is the Reset button in the Customize dialog box. Makes sense, doesn't it?

Tip

After you open the Toolbar Properties dialog box, you can make changes to several menu bars without returning to the Customize dialog box to select the next one. Simply select the next victim from the Selected Toolbar list and make your changes.

Some of the built-in menus or commands aren't displayed

Source of the problem

It's confusing when you look at the menu bar you've been using for ages and sense something is missing. Maybe one of the menus is gone or one of the commands in a menu no longer appears when you click the menu.

Problems such as these arise for several reasons. You (or someone else) might have changed the startup settings to keep the menus or shortcut menus from appearing. You might have been viewing personalized menus. If that's the case, only the menu commands you use often or that Access expects you to use often are displayed in the menu bar. If you see a down arrow at the bottom of the menu, the command you're looking for might be in the expanded menu. If you don't want to expand the menu each time you use it, you can change the display option for menus so that menus appear every time in their full, expanded manner.

Another reason you don't see a menu is that it might have been moved to another menu bar. You can easily move it back or add another copy of the menu to the original menu bar.

The following solutions show how to deal with these problems.

How to fix it

To change the startup settings so that your full menus appear, follow these steps:

1. On the Tools menu, click Startup.

2. In the Startup dialog box, select the Allow Full Menus check box to restore a complete set of built-in menus. ▶

3. Select the Allow Default Shortcut Menus check box to restore the shortcut menus related to different views.

4. Click OK.

5. Close the database and then reopen it to activate the changes.

Startup dialog box

Application Title:

Application Icon:

☐ Use as Form and Report Icon

Menu Bar:
(default)

☑ Allow Full Menus
☑ Allow Default Shortcut Menus
☑ Use Access Special Keys

(Show Database Window, Show Immediate Window, Show VB Window, and Pause Execution)

Display Form/Page:
(none)

☑ Display Database Window
☑ Display Status Bar

Shortcut Menu Bar:
(default)

☑ Allow Built-in Toolbars
☑ Allow Toolbar/Menu Changes

OK   Cancel

Tip

If you're reluctant to change the startup options but still want to see all the built-in commands, hold down the Shift key when you open the database.

If you want to see all the commands in a menu without expanding the list, do the following:

1. On the View menu, point to Toolbars and then click Customize.

2. Click the Options tab.

3. Clear the Show Full Menus After A Short Delay check box.

4. Check the Always Show Full Menus option. ▶

5. Click Close in the Customize dialog box.

To add a missing menu to a built-in menu bar, follow these steps:

1. On the View menu, point to Toolbars and then click Customize.

2. Click the Toolbars tab and select the menu bar that is missing the menu.

3. Click the Commands tab and then click Built-in Menus in the Categories list.

4. Locate the missing menu name and drag it to the menu bar.

5. Drop the item when you see the dark I-beam. ▶

6. Click Close.

Tip

If you add a menu such as the Tools menu to a built-in menu bar that appears in more than one view, that menu will appear on the menu bar in all the views. Most of the commands in the added menu are carried over, depending on the context of the new menu bar.

My custom menus don't show up when I open my form

Source of the problem

You've created a neat data entry form with so many custom features that even your dog could enter data without a mistake. Well, maybe your cat. You built a custom menu bar with just the menus and commands that you need to use the form efficiently. You left out all the commands that could cause trouble, such as Design and Delete. You also created some quick shortcut menus to use with some of the controls in the form. The shortcut menus contain just the actions you need and nothing more—sorting and filtering records based on the data in a control, for example. Now, when you open the form to enter data, the same old vanilla menu bar shows up instead of your custom one, and when you right-click a control, no shortcut menu appears then either.

The most common source of these problems is that you have not told Access that the custom menu bar and the shortcut menus belong to the form and its controls. The menus are considered properties of the form and its controls, and you need to set these properties as you do others.

The following solution shows you how to resolve these problems.

How to fix it

If you have built a custom menu bar for a form, do the following:

1. Open the form in Design view.

2. Click the Properties button on the toolbar and then click the Other tab.

3. In the Menu Bar property box, click the down arrow and select the name of your custom menu bar from the list. ▶

4. Close the properties dialog box and then click the View button to switch to Form view to verify that the custom menu has replaced the standard menu bar.

If you don't see a shortcut menu that you created for one of the controls in a form, follow these steps:

1. Open the form in Design view and then click the control.

2. Click the Properties button on the toolbar and then click the Other tab.

3. In the Shortcut Menu Bar property, click the down arrow and select the menu name from the list. ▶

4. Switch to Form view and right-click the control you just added the shortcut menu to. ▶

5. If you still don't see the shortcut menu you designed, click the View button to return the form to Design view.

6. Double-click the form selector (the small gray square where the rulers meet in the upper left corner). The form's properties dialog box appears.

7. Click the Other tab and change the Shortcut Menu property to Yes. ▶

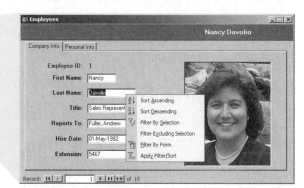

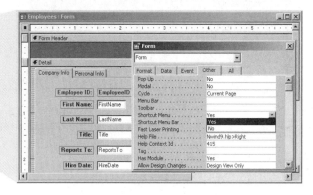

Tip

Don't select the name of the shortcut menu in the form's Shortcut Menu Bar property or it will appear when you right-click any-where in the form, not just in the control.

My shortcut menus aren't right

Source of the problem

The beauty of shortcut menus is that they're convenient and precise. When you need to do something now and you're where you need to do it, just right-click and the commands you need are there. But the shortcut menus that you see when you right-click in Access are not immune to modification. Commands might have been deleted or properties changed so that the shortcut menus aren't as useful as you want them to be.

That's the bad news. The good news is that Access provides an easy, pain-free way to restore and reset shortcut menus. In fact, you can restore the original structure and properties for all built-in shortcut menus all at once. You can even restore any changes you made to the shortcut menus. You can fix all the shortcut menus that appear in a single view with a single click.

How to fix it

To reset all the shortcut menus to their original structure, do the following:

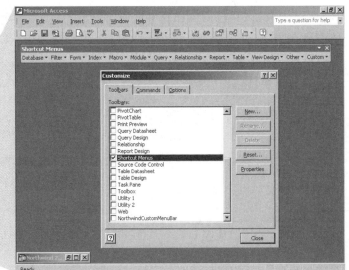

1. On the View menu, point to Toolbars and then click Customize.

2. In the Customize dialog box, click the Toolbars tab and then select Shortcut Menus from the Toolbars list. ▶

3. Click Reset.

4. Click OK to confirm the action.

5. Click Close in the Customize dialog box.

To reset specific shortcut menus, do the following:

1. On the View menu, point to Toolbars and then click Customize.

2. In the Customize dialog box, click the Toolbars tab and then select Shortcut Menus from the Toolbars list.

3. A menu bar showing the shortcut menus for different views will appear.

4. To reset the shortcut menus for a particular view, click the name of the view in the Shortcut Menus menu bar and then click the Reset button in the Customize dialog box. ▶

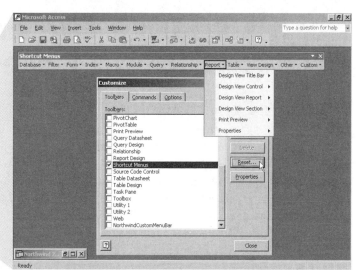

5. If you want to reset a specific shortcut menu in a view, click the down arrow next to the view name.

6. From the list that appears, select the shortcut menu you want to reset. The list of shortcut menus is organized by location and function. For example, to reset the shortcut menu that appears when you right-click in the query design grid, click Design View Grid to display the current menu commands. ▶

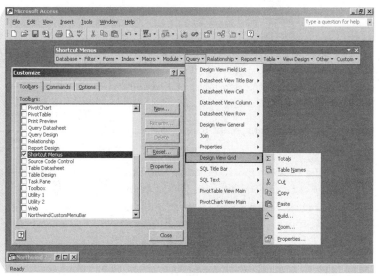

7. In the Customize dialog box, click the Reset button.

8. Click OK to confirm the change and then click Close in the Customize dialog box.

Tip

If you want to restore a single command on the shortcut menu, click the right arrow next to the shortcut menu name, select the command and then click the Reset button.

I can't change the name of the shortcut menu I created

Source of the problem

You've created a custom shortcut menu to use with a form you designed. The menu displays a list of actions you can take, such as filtering or sorting the records displayed in the form. Now you've added commands to the shortcut menu—say, ones for adding and deleting records—and you want to save the revised menu with a new name to reflect your additions. Good idea.

You open the Customize dialog box and select Shortcut Menus on the Toolbars tab to display the Shortcut Menus menu bar with your custom shortcut menu on it. Now you find that the Rename button is not available in the Customize dialog box. Bad luck.

The reason for your misfortune lies in the way Access stores shortcut menus in a single menu bar, not as separate items as it does with toolbars and custom menus. You need to (temporarily) turn the shortcut menu into a toolbar before you can change its name. After you've renamed it, you can return the shortcut menu to its natural state.

The following solution shows the steps to solve this problem.

How to fix it

1. Open the database in which you created the custom shortcut menu.

2. On the View menu, point to Toolbars and then click Customize.

3. On the Toolbars tab, scroll down the list of toolbars and select Shortcut Menus from the list. You can tell that you can't rename the shortcut menu because the Rename button in the Customize dialog box is dimmed. ▶

Tip
If you want to delete a specific shortcut menu, you need to change it to a Toolbar before you can delete it.

4. On the Shortcut Menus menu bar, click Custom to see the names of all the custom shortcut menus in the current database. ▶

5. In the Customize dialog box, click the Properties button.

6. In the Toolbar Properties dialog box, select the name of the shortcut menu you want to rename in the Selected Toolbar list.

7. In the Type list, select Toolbar. ▼

8. Click Close.

9. On the Toolbars tab, select the name of the converted shortcut menu and then click Rename.

10. Type the new name in the Rename Toolbar dialog box and click OK. ▶

To restore the shortcut menu to its original state, follow these steps:

1. On the Toolbars tab, click Properties.

2. In the Toolbars Properties dialog box, select the newly named toolbar from the Selected Toolbar list.

3. In the Type box, select Popup.

4. Access displays a message about changing the toolbar back to a shortcut menu. Click OK in the message box to complete the conversion. ▶

5. Click Close in the Properties dialog box and then click Close in the Customize dialog box.

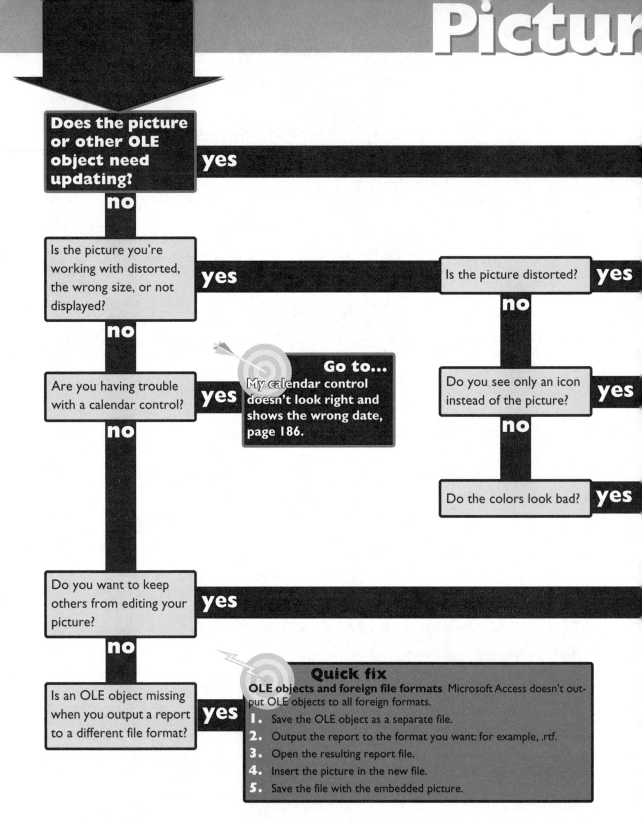

Does the picture or other OLE object need updating?

yes

no

Is the picture you're working with distorted, the wrong size, or not displayed?

yes

Is the picture distorted?

yes

no

Go to...
My calendar control doesn't look right and shows the wrong date, page 186.

Are you having trouble with a calendar control?

yes

no

Do you see only an icon instead of the picture?

yes

no

Do the colors look bad?

yes

Do you want to keep others from editing your picture?

yes

no

Is an OLE object missing when you output a report to a different file format?

yes

Quick fix

OLE objects and foreign file formats Microsoft Access doesn't output OLE objects to all foreign formats.

1. Save the OLE object as a separate file.
2. Output the report to the format you want: for example, .rtf.
3. Open the resulting report file.
4. Insert the picture in the new file.
5. Save the file with the embedded picture.

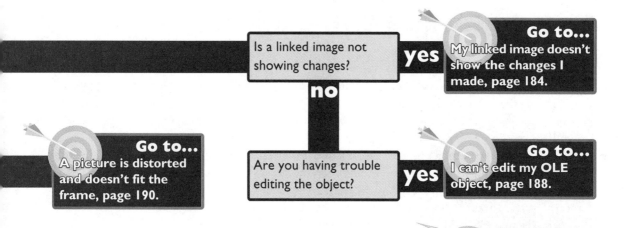

Is a linked image not showing changes?

yes → Go to... My linked image doesn't show the changes I made, page 184.

no

Go to... A picture is distorted and doesn't fit the frame, page 190.

Are you having trouble editing the object?

yes → Go to... I can't edit my OLE object, page 188.

Quick fix

Replacing an icon with an image You need to change a setting in Access to show the full image.

1. Open the form or report in Design view and then click the icon.
2. On the Edit menu, point to the Object command for the type of object you're working with and then click Convert.
3. Clear the Display As Icon check box.
4. Click OK and save the form.

Quick fix

Changing the color display The picture was probably created on a computer that supports more colors.

1. Open the form or report in Design view and click Properties.
2. Set the Palette Source property to the one used to create the picture, if it is available.

Quick fix

Keeping an image from being edited Others can edit the picture in an unbound object frame unless you change it to an image.

1. Open the form in Design view and select the picture.
2. On the Format menu, point to Change To and click Image.
3. Click OK to confirm the change.

If your solution isn't here, check these related chapters:

- Controls, viewing data, page 22
- Forms, designing, page 124

Or see the general troubleshooting tips on page xv.

My linked image doesn't show the changes I made

Source of the problem

You've spruced up your form with an image of your newly appointed company president—your cat—figuring that a little personal advertising never hurt. You made some changes to the image, perhaps adorning it with a playful mouse, but when you opened the form again, the image you so carefully linked doesn't show your changes.

The settings for several properties in Microsoft Access affect when and how a linked image is updated. One or more of these properties might be set incorrectly, and, if that's the case, the changes to your image won't be displayed. Changing the settings for these properties will set things right. If you don't want to go to that length, you can update the image manually.

The following solution shows you how to update your linked image.

How to fix it

To set the properties for the image so that changes are displayed automatically, do the following:

1. In the database window, select the form you're working with and then click Design. ▶

2. Right-click the linked object and then click Properties.

3. In the Properties dialog box, click the Data tab.

Tip

For more information about linking and embedding objects, see the sidebar "Is it bound or unbound? Linked or embedded?" on page 189.

4. In the Update Options property box, select Automatic. ▶

5. In the Enabled property box, select Yes.

6. In the Locked property box, select No.

7. Close the Properties dialog box and then save the form.

8. Switch to Form view. The image should be displayed with all the current changes. ▼

Unbound Object Frame: OLEUnbound0

OLEUnbound0

| Format | Data | Event | Other | All |

OLE Class . . . . Paint
Display Type . . . . Content
Update Options . . . . Manual
                Automatic
OLE Type . . . . Manual
OLE Type Allowed . . . .
Class . . . . Paint.Picture
Source Doc . . . . \\jpierce99\c$\PROJECTS\troub
Source Item . . . .
Enabled . . . . No
Locked . . . . Yes

Cat Products : Form

Cats, Cats, Cats

All you need for cats and more!

952 I Avenue
Seattle, WA 98117
1-800-555-1234

Our Company President, Sophie

Product Name: Chef Anton's Gumb

Category: Seafood

Supplier: Mayumi's

Record: 5 of 77

Tip

If you don't want to change the properties, you can update the image manually. Open the form in Design view, right-click on the linked image, click Linked Object in the shortcut menu, and then click Open. The object's native application opens, and you'll see the current version of the image or other object. Make any other changes you want and then close the application window. The image or other object will be updated in the Access form.

My calendar control doesn't look right and shows the wrong date

Source of the problem

You discovered the neat calendar control that you can use to dramatize a schedule of appointments. But much to your dismay, the calendar didn't match your way of scheduling meetings and other appointments, and what's worse, it displayed an incorrect date.

The problem with the calendar's schedule display has to do with how some of the calendar control's properties are set up. You might want to display a different day as the first day of the week, for example, or you might need to reduce the size of the labels. Changing the settings of the calendar's properties will correct these problems.

If your problem is an incorrect date, you probably set the calendar control's Control Source property to the wrong date field or didn't set it at all. If you don't set the Control Source property to a field, the calendar uses the current system date.

The following steps show you how to reset the calendar control.

How to fix it

To change the appearance of the calendar control, do the following:

1. Open the form in Design view and then click the calendar control. ▶

2. Click the Properties button on the toolbar and then click the Other tab.

3. Click in the Custom property box and then click the Build button (...).

4. In the Calendar Properties dialog box, make the changes you want. For example, choose Monday as the first day of the week or clear the Vertical Grid check box to remove the lines running between the days of the week. You can also clear the Month/Year Selectors check box to remove the drop-down lists from the calendar. ▶

5. Click Apply after each change to see its effect on the appearance of the calendar.

6. In the Calendar Properties box, click OK and then save the form.

To solve the problem of a wrong date showing in a calendar control, follow these steps:

1. Open the form in Design view and then click the calendar control.

2. Click the Properties button on the toolbar and then click the Data tab.

3. In the Control Source property box, select the date field you want the calendar to display. ▶

4. Save the form and then switch to Form view.

I can't edit my OLE object

Source of the problem

Since life isn't perfect, at some point you're going to want to make some changes to the image or other OLE object you placed in your handsome customized form. When you start to make the changes, you find that you can't edit the object in Form view, where you can actually see it as part of the form's full presentation. You double-click the object, and you see just the property sheet. The program you used to create the object doesn't open to help you edit the object in place.

Several possible reasons might explain why you can't change the object:

- The program the object was created in isn't installed on your computer. Without it, you're dead in the water.

- The object's properties are set to prevent editing in Form view even though you can edit the object in Design view.

- The OLE object was converted to a static image to save time when opening the form. Static images can't be edited in place, but you can resurrect the object from the original file.

The following solutions show you how to change the object properties to allow editing.

How to fix it

To set the object's properties to allow editing, do the following:

1. Open the form in Design view.

2. Select the object and then click the Properties button in the toolbar.

3. Click the Data tab and then set the Enabled property to Yes. ▶

4. Set the Locked property to No.

5. Save the form.

6. Switch to Form view and then double-click the object to open it in its native program.

7. Make the changes you want and then click outside the object in another part of the form.

8. Save the form.

Tip
You can tell whether you can edit the object in Form view by clicking on it. If you see small black handles inside the frame, the object can be edited in place.

Unbound Object Frame: OLEUnbound1

OLEUnbound1

Format | Data | Event | Other | All

OLE Class . . . . Package
Row Source Type . . . .
Row Source . . . .
Link Child Fields . . . .
Link Master Fields . . . .
Display Type . . . . Content
Update Options . . . . Automatic
OLE Type . . . . Embedded
OLE Type Allowed . . . . Either
Class . . . . Package
Source Doc . . . .
Source Item . . . .
Column Count 0
Enabled . . . . No
Locked . . . . Yes / No

If the object is a static image (and provided the original image file is on a computer you have access to), delete the image from the form and reinsert it by following these steps:

1. Open the form in Design view.

2. Click the image and then press Delete on your keyboard.

3. On the Insert menu, click Object.

4. Click the Create From File option, locate the object file you used before, and then click OK. ▶

5. Save the form.

> **Microsoft Access** ? X
>
> File: Microsoft Photo Editor 3.0 Photo
>
> ○ Create New   C:\My Documents\My Pictures\CompanyPresic
>
> ● Create from File   Browse... ☐ Link
>
> OK
>
> Cancel
>
> ☐ Display as Icon
>
> Result
>
> Inserts the contents of the file as an object into your document so that you may activate it using the application which created it.

Is it bound or unbound? Linked or embedded?

A few definitions may be in order at this point.

A *bound object* is stored directly in an Access table as part of the stored data. For example, an employee's picture is a bound object.

An *unbound object* is an element of a form or report design and has nothing to do directly with the table data.

When you *link* an object to an Access form or report, the original object remains in the source application. Access reaches it by means of a pointer to the location where the object is stored. Linking saves disk space and ensures that the latest version of the object is retrieved.

When you *embed* an object in an Access form or report, you are storing a static copy of it in the form or report. You can change the object in Access, but the original copy created in the source program does not reflect the changes.

A picture is distorted and doesn't fit the frame

Source of the problem

At the start of most videos you rent from your local shop, you often see a message stating that the film has been reformatted to fit your screen. Someone has kindly taken the time to make sure that the original film fits nicely on the TV screen. When you insert a picture in a form or report in Access, however, nobody sees to it that the picture looks right and fits the frame you drew. That's up to you.

An incorrect setting in the picture's Size Mode property can cause distortion. The default setting is Clip. With this setting, the picture stays at its original size, and, if it's bigger than the frame, only part of the picture shows. With the Stretch setting, however, Access resizes the picture to fit both the height and width of the frame. This setting can distort the picture if its original dimensions are much different from the frame you drew.

The Size Mode property not only leads to distortion, it also can be the reason a picture doesn't fit the frame. The picture may appear cropped, or too much white space might appear in the frame. This problem can be especially bothersome when you're storing pictures in a field and the pictures are not all the same size.

If the picture you're having trouble with is a background picture in a form, the form's Picture Size Mode property might be set incorrectly. The problem could also be that the picture's alignment is not set so that it will resize when you change the size of the form window.

The following steps show you how to resize images to fit properly in their frames.

How to fix it

To resize a distorted picture, do the following:

1. Open the form or report in Design view.

2. Click the picture and then click the Properties button on the toolbar.

3. In the properties dialog box, click the Format tab, and then change the Size Mode property to Zoom. ▶

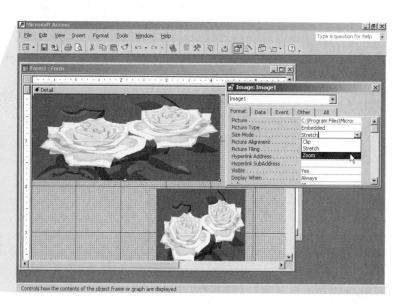

4. Drag the border of the picture frame to fit the picture.

5. Save the form or report.

If you are using a series of pictures that are bound to a field and the pictures are all the same size, use the previous steps to adjust the frame to fit the pictures. If the pictures are not the same size, do the following:

1. Open the form in Form view.

2. Click the picture and then click the Properties button on the toolbar.

3. Click the Format tab and then change the Border Style property to Transparent. ▶

4. Change the Back Color property so that it's the same color as the form's background.

5. Save the form.

If you're having trouble with a background picture in your form, try these steps:

1. Open the form in Design view and then click the Properties button on the toolbar.

2. In the properties dialog box, click the Format tab and set the Picture Size Mode property to Stretch.

3. If you want the picture to resize with the form window, set the Picture Alignment property to Center. If you don't want the picture to resize, set the Picture Alignment property to Form Center.

4. Switch to Form view and then save the form.

Tip

The Zoom setting is the best setting for pictures in the bitmap (.bmp) format because it preserves the picture's proportions. If you use the Stretch setting, the picture expands horizontally and vertically to fill the frame, which can cause distortion if the picture's proportions differ significantly from the proportions of the frame you drew.

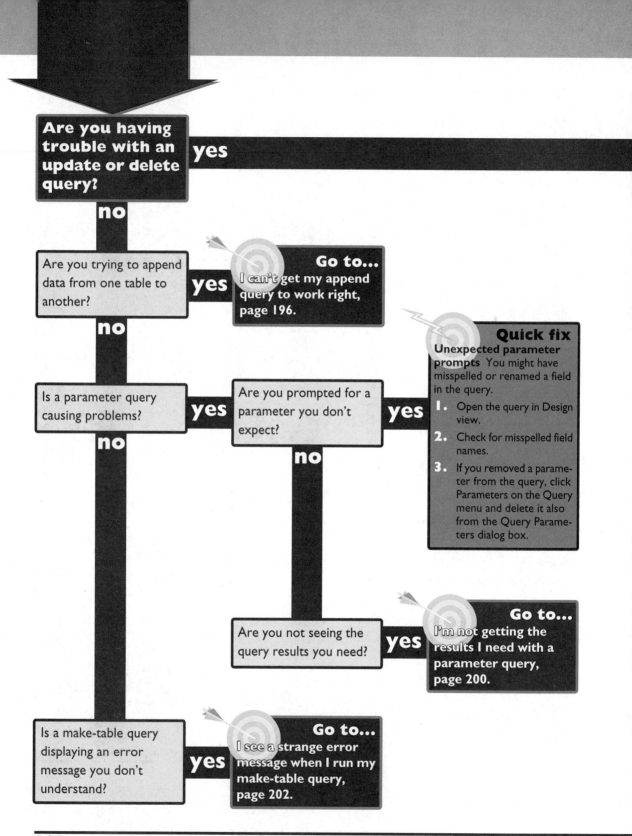

Are you having trouble with an update or delete query?

yes

no

Are you trying to append data from one table to another?

yes

Go to...
I can't get my append query to work right, page 196.

no

Quick fix

Unexpected parameter prompts You might have misspelled or renamed a field in the query.

1. Open the query in Design view.

2. Check for misspelled field names.

3. If you removed a parameter from the query, click Parameters on the Query menu and delete it also from the Query Parameters dialog box.

Is a parameter query causing problems?

yes

Are you prompted for a parameter you don't expect?

yes

no

no

Are you not seeing the query results you need?

yes

Go to...
I'm not getting the results I need with a parameter query, page 200.

Is a make-table query displaying an error message you don't understand?

yes

Go to...
I see a strange error message when I run my make-table query, page 202.

Queries, action

Do you see a type mismatch error message?

yes

no

Quick fix

Type mismatch messages You have an expression in the Update To cell that doesn't match the field data type.

1. Open the update query in Design view.
2. Click in the Update To cell of the field you need to change.
3. Put the correct expression for the new value in the Update To cell.
4. Save and run the query.

Are you updating a primary key field?

yes

Quick fix

Trouble updating primary key fields Referential integrity prevents changing the primary key value if there are child records.

1. Click the Relationships button on the toolbar.
2. In the Relationships window, right-click the line between the two tables and click Edit Relationships.
3. Select Cascade Update Related Records.
4. Click OK.
5. Run the update query again.

Are you getting a key violation or validation rule violation message?

yes

Go to...
My update query causes errors, page 194.

no

If your solution isn't here, check these related chapters:

- Queries, calculations, page 204
- Queries, selection criteria, page 224

Or see the general troubleshooting tips on page xv.

Are you trying to use a delete query to delete duplicate records?

yes

Go to...
Using a find duplicates query to delete duplicate records didn't work, page 198.

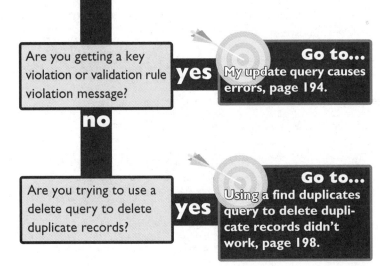

My update query causes errors

Source of the problem

Using an update query is a quick way to get work done, but it doesn't always work right. You can run into problems because Microsoft Access is very careful about what data you can add, delete, or update in a table. The following are common problems you can run into with update queries:

- You tried to update an AutoNumber field. This causes a not updateable error message.

- You tried to update records with primary key values that are already in the destination table. This causes a *key violation* error message.

- You tried to update records with field values that violate a validation rule set for the field, or you might have violated the record validation rule set for the table. Either of these actions causes a *validation rule violation* error message.

- You enforced referential integrity (which requires that every record on the "many" side of a relationship have only one matching record on the "one" side) and tried to update records that result in a violation of referential integrity rules for the related tables. This also causes a key violation error message.

The following steps show how to overcome these problems.

How to fix it

If you see the error message shown in the figure, you might have tried to change an AutoNumber field. Do the following: ▶

1. Click OK in the message box to return to the update query design.

2. Delete the value in the Update To cell in the column for the AutoNumber field.

3. Run the query and respond Yes to confirm the update action.

If the error message indicates that you have encountered key violation problems, do the following: ▶

1. Click No in the message box to abandon the update query.

---

2. Review the values entered in the Update To row for the fields in the query. You probably used a value in more than one record in a field that must be unique for each record—an ID field, for example.

3. Change the value in the Update To cell so each record still has a unique value in that field.

4. Run the query and then click Yes to confirm the update action.

If the error message includes a reference to one or more records violating validation rules, do the following: ▶

1. Click No in the error message to abandon the query for now.

2. Switch to the database window and then open the destination table in Design view.

3. Review each field in the table and look at its Validation Rule property in the Field Properties area of the window. Note any rules and the fields they apply to.

4. Click the Properties button on the toolbar and check the Validation Rule property box for a record validation rule for the table. Note any rule.

5. Return to the query design and edit the Update To cells as necessary to comply with the rules in the destination table.

6. Run the query again.

Tip

If you're planning to enforce the rules again after modifying the tables, be careful not to leave any field values that violate referential integrity.

If you see a message about violating referential integrity rules that are enforced between related tables, do the following:

1. On the Tools menu, click Relationships.

2. Right-click the relationship line between the source and destination tables being used in the query, and then click Edit Relationship on the shortcut menu.

3. Clear the Enforce Referential Integrity check box and click OK. ▶

4. Open the tables in Datasheet view, and modify the tables one at a time so all the child records you're adding have a matching record in the parent table. Also, make sure you're not deleting a record or changing the primary key value of a record in the parent table if that record has matching records in the child table.

I can't get my append query to work right

Source of the problem

Moving data from one table to another is only a little more complicated than dropping a bunch of folders in a file cabinet. All you need to do is tell Access what data you want to put in the table and in which fields you want the data to go. Sounds pretty simple, doesn't it? Then how come things go wrong and the data turns up in strange places or disappears altogether? You might have encountered one or more of several problems when creating and running an append query:

- When you created your append query, you placed the asterisk (*) from the source table's field list in the query grid's Field row to include all the fields from that table. Then you selected the asterisk for the destination table in the Append To cell as well. If one or more of the field names in the tables are not the same, you get an error message when you run the query because using the asterisk shortcut method requires that the field names in the source table and the destination table match. The error message tells you the name of the source field that has no match in the destination table.

- You have a source field and a destination field that are defined with incompatible data types. For example, trying to append text data to a hyperlink field can cause an error message whether you have used the asterisk shortcut or added the fields to the query grid manually.

- You selected the wrong field in the Append To row in the query grid, so the appended data ended up in the wrong field. If the field names match, Access fills in the Append To row but if they don't, you need to type the field names manually.

The following solutions show you how to overcome these problems.

How to fix it

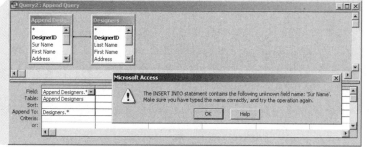

If you see an error message about an unknown field name and don't want to rename the table fields, do the following: ▶

1. Click OK to clear the message and then remove the asterisk column from the query grid.

2. From the list of fields for the source table, drag the first field to the query grid.

3. Click in the Append To row for that column and then select the corresponding field from the destination table.

---

4. Repeat steps 2 and 3 until all the fields are added to the query grid.

5. Save and run the query.

If you see a message about failing to convert data types, do the following: ▶

1. If you want to run the append query and accept blank values in the incompatible field, click Yes.

2. Open the source table in Datasheet view and fill in the missing values. You might also want to correct the mismatch in the types of data before trying to run the query again.

Tip

If you see error messages about key violations or validation rule violations, refer to the solution, "My update query causes errors," page 194.

3. If you want to correct the data type mismatch before appending the records, click No to abandon the append query.

4. Open either the source or destination table in table Design view and change the data type of the field to one that is compatible with the corresponding field in the other table.

5. Save the table and rerun the append query.

If the data turns up in the wrong fields after you run your append query, do the following:

1. Open the query in Design view.

2. Click the Show Table button and then select the destination table from the Show Table dialog box.

3. Click Add to add the table to the query and then click Close.

4. Compare the field names in the source table field list with those in the destination field list. (Be careful—the matching fields might not be in the same order.)

5. Change the field in the Append To cell for the fields that were misplaced.

6. Save the query and then run it again.

Tip

If the primary key field of the destination table is not an AutoNumber field, be sure to include the source field that corresponds to it in the append query.

Tip

If you're appending data to a table that's in another database, Access does not display a drop-down list of field names in the Append To row.

Using a find duplicates query to delete duplicate records didn't work

Source of the problem

After the tedious work of deleting duplicate records one at a time, you decide that turning the find duplicates query that the Query Wizard built for you into a delete query sounds like a good idea. You run the query, but all of a sudden the table has no records at all. Using the find duplicates query as a delete query can get you into trouble, as you can see.

A delete query deletes not only all the duplicate records, but also any record that had a duplicate, including the original record. The only records the delete query leaves in the table are those that had no duplicate values in the field in the first place.

The following solution provides a way to work around this problem, resulting in a table with only unique values in one or more fields.

How to fix it

Fixing this problem is a two-part process. First you create a new table. To do that, follow these steps:

1. In the database window, select the table with the duplicate values and then click the Copy button on the toolbar.

2. Click the Paste button on the toolbar.

3. In the Paste Table As dialog box, type a name for the copy of the table and select Structure Only in the Paste Options area. Click OK. ▶

4. Select the new table in the database window and then click the Design button. In Design view, select the field or fields in which you don't want duplicate values. Click the Primary Key button. Be sure you don't include any AutoNumber field that you used in the original table as the primary key. ▶

5. Save and close the table.

Queries, action

In the second phase of the process, append the records from the original table to the copy:

1. In the database window, click Queries and then click New.

2. Select Design View and then click OK.

3. In the Show Table dialog box, click the Table tab and select the original table.

4. Click Add and then click Close.

5. In the table field list, double-click the asterisk (*) to add all the fields to the query grid.

6. On the Query menu, click Append Query.

7. In the Append dialog box, select the table you created in the first phase of this solution and then click OK. ▶

8. Click the Run button on the toolbar and then click Yes. Notice that the message refers to all the records the original table contains.

9. Click Yes again in the message box about not being able to append all the records because of key violations. The records left out have duplicate values in the fields you chose as the primary key for the new table.

10. Open the new table and make sure there are no duplicates. Delete the original table and rename the copy.

> **Warning**
>
> Before running a delete or other action query, run it as a select query and look at the records that will be affected by the query. If the records are the right ones, return to query Design view and click Delete Query on the Query menu to change the type of query. Then, when you run the query, Access asks for confirmation that you want to delete all those records.

> **Warning**
>
> Always make a backup copy of a table you're using in an action query. Making a backup is especially important when working with delete queries because you can't undo the deletion. With a backup copy, you can restore any data you inadvertently deleted.

I'm not getting the results I need with a parameter query

Source of the problem

You create a parameter query to give yourself some flexibility in choosing the records you want to see from the underlying table. But like a lot of other conveniences, this flexibility comes with a risk. One of the problems you might encounter is seeing the cryptic error message "Can't bind name." What Access is trying to tell you is that you didn't do a good job indicating which parameters you needed. You need to explicitly indicate the data types if you're using the parameter for a chart or a crosstab query. You might also see this message if you used a Yes/No field as a parameter in the query, which is not permitted.

Using a lookup field in a parameter query can also produce unexpected results. You type a value you've been looking at in a table into the parameter prompt, but nothing shows up in the query results. As always, what you see in a lookup field is not the same as what is stored in the field. When you type a value that is not stored in the field, Access doesn't find any matches.

The following solutions provide remedies for these problems.

How to fix it

If you see the message "Can't bind name," do the following:

1. Open the query in Design view.

2. On the Query menu, click Parameters.

3. In the first Parameter row of the Query Parameters dialog box, type the first prompt you entered in the query design grid. Make sure you type it exactly as it appears in the design grid.

4. In the Data Type column to the right, select the data type that matches the field. ▶

5. Repeat steps 3 and 4 for each parameter whose data type you need to specify.

6. Click OK.

7. Save the query.

If the field you want to use as the parameter is a lookup field, do the following:

1. Open the query in Design view.

2. Click the Show Table button on the toolbar.

3. From the list of tables, select the table that contains the value you see in the lookup field. For example, if your query is based on a table that lists products and you want to enter the category of the product as a parameter, add the categories table to the query. After you make the selection, click Add and then click Close.

4. In the list of fields for the table with the lookup values, double-click the field that contains the displayed value to add it to the design grid.

5. In the Criteria row for that field, type a prompt. For example, type **[Enter Name]** in the Criteria row in the CategoryName column.

6. On the View menu, click Datasheet View to run the query.

7. In the parameter prompt, type the category name.

8. Save the query.

More parameter query tips

If you want to see all the records in the results of a parameter query, you can add criteria to the parameter field column to allow that option instead of creating a separate query without the parameter prompt. After typing the prompt in the Criteria row, move down to the Or row and type the same prompt followed by **Is Null**. When you click OK without typing a value in the parameter prompt, all the records are displayed because the parameter you don't enter is a null value, one of the acceptable criteria.

After you save the query, Access converts the Or criterion to an expression in its separate column in the query grid.

I see a strange error message when I run my make-table query

Source of the problem

Anyone who has worked with such a comprehensive and flexible database management system as Access has undoubtedly experienced the gentle slap on the wrist of an error message from time to time. Most of the messages give you a clear idea of why you goofed up, but once in a while they just don't seem to make sense.

Running a make-table query to create a new table from the information in other tables can be just such a case. If you are trying to use data from two related tables to populate a new table and you see a cryptic message about Variant data types and null values, you know the frustration. This is not what you were trying to do. ▶

What's happening is that one of the fields you're working with is an AutoNumber field, and the make-table query is trying to place a null value in it, which is not allowed. The culprit here is the type of join used for the relationship in the query design. You specified an outer join, in which all records from one table are included in the query results even though no matching record exists in the other table. The "other" table is the one with the AutoNumber field, and this wholesale retrieval results in a null value being left in the AutoNumber field.

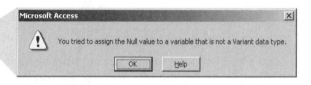

The simplest solution is to delete the AutoNumber field from the query and make the new table without it. But you might need that field in the table you're creating, so you have to find another way around this problem. The following solution shows how to solve the problem.

How to fix it

The first step is to modify the make-table query to use an inner join to relate the tables, so only those records that have matches in both tables are included.

1. Open the make-table query in Design view. The arrow at one end of the join line indicates that the existing join is an outer join. ▶

2. Double-click the join line. In the Join Properties dialog box, select the first option in the list to create an inner join between the tables and then click OK. ▶

3. Save the query with a new name, for example, FixIt.

4. On the Query menu, click Run. In the Paste confirmation dialog box, click Yes to complete the new table.

5. In the database window, select the new table. On the Edit menu, click Copy. On the Edit menu, click Paste.

6. In the Paste Table As dialog box, type a name for the copy of the table (for example, **FixedTable**), click Structure Only, and then click OK. ▶

7. Select the FixedTable table in the database window and then click Design.

8. Select the AutoNumber field and then choose Number from the Data Type drop-down list. ▶

9. Save and close the table.

Now you're free to populate the new FixedTable with the data from the original tables without causing the error message. Here's how:

1. Open the FixIt query in Design view.

2. Double-click the join line. In the Join Properties dialog box, select the second option to create an outer join and then click OK.

3. On the Query menu, click Append Query to change the make-table query to an append query. ▶

4. In the Append dialog box, choose FixedTable in the Table Name box and then click OK. ▶

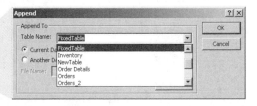

5. On the Query menu, click Run. Click Yes when asked once again to confirm the paste operation.

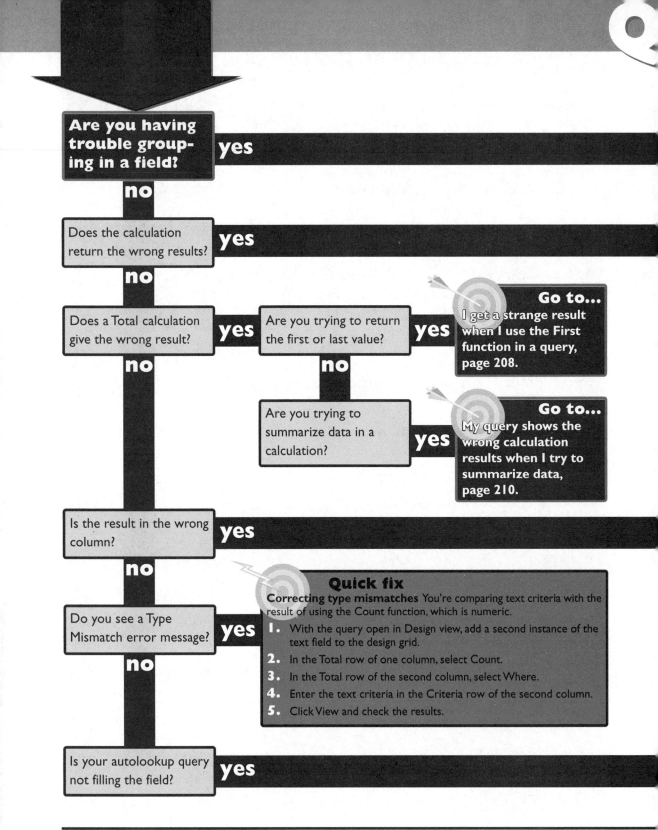

Are you having trouble grouping in a field? **yes**

no

Does the calculation return the wrong results? **yes**

no

Does a Total calculation give the wrong result? **yes**

Are you trying to return the first or last value? **yes**

no

Go to...
I get a strange result when I use the First function in a query, page 208.

Are you trying to summarize data in a calculation? **yes**

Go to...
My query shows the wrong calculation results when I try to summarize data, page 210.

Is the result in the wrong column? **yes**

no

> ### Quick fix
> **Correcting type mismatches** You're comparing text criteria with the result of using the Count function, which is numeric.
>
> 1. With the query open in Design view, add a second instance of the text field to the design grid.
> 2. In the Total row of one column, select Count.
> 3. In the Total row of the second column, select Where.
> 4. Enter the text criteria in the Criteria row of the second column.
> 5. Click View and check the results.

Do you see a Type Mismatch error message? **yes**

no

Is your autolookup query not filling the field? **yes**

Quick fix

Grouping records in a field
You used the asterisk (*) to add fields to the query grid.

1. Remove the asterisk from the query grid.
2. Add the field you want to group by to the query grid.
3. Add the field you want to calculate with to the query grid.
4. In the Total row for the field you want to group by, select the function you need.
5. Click the View button to check the results.

Does the calculation fail to return any value?

yes

Go to...

I keep getting blanks instead of real values, page 206.

no

Is the currency symbol missing from your calculation?

yes

Quick fix

Retaining currency formatting You need to apply the currency formatting in the query itself.

1. Open the query you are working with in Design view.
2. Right-click in the column that contains the currency calculation and then click Properties on the short-cut menu.
3. Click the General tab.
4. In the Format property box, select Currency.
5. Save the query and then run it again to see the results.

Quick fix

Misplaced functions You placed the function in the wrong column.

1. Open the query in Design view.
2. Replace the function in the Total cell with Group By.
3. Select the function in the Total cell of a different column.
4. Click View to check the results.

Go to...

My autolookup query isn't working, page 212.

If your solution isn't here, check these related chapters:

- Queries, calculations, page 204
- Queries, selection criteria, page 224

Or see the general trouble-shooting tips on page xv.

I keep getting blanks instead of real values

Source of the problem

You've seen the response a 12-year-old gives when he doesn't know the answer to your question. He just shrugs his shoulders in the universal gesture for "I don't know." That's sort of what Microsoft Access does when you ask it to calculate a value in a query and it doesn't have the answer. In Access, the shrug is called null. Access believes it's better to leave the result blank than to guess at the answer.

The reason Access comes up blank in a query is that one of the fields you used in the expression for the calculated field includes blank records. In an arithmetic expression, if any of the values used in the expression are blank (null), the entire expression is evaluated as null and Access shows blank values, as shown in the figure. ▶

Another cause of a blank result in a query is that you're combining text values in an expression by using the *Plus* (+) operator instead of the concatenation symbol, the ampersand (&). The *Plus* operator usually works, but if one of the text values is blank, the entire expression is null. ▶

The following steps show how you can solve problems with blank records.

How to fix it

To fix the calculation problem resulting from blank records, use the Nz function to convert null values to zero.

1. Open the query you're working with in Design view.

2. In the Field row for the field that includes blank records (Current Level in the figure), type an expression such as **Nz([InStock],0)+ Nz([OnOrder],0)- Nz([BackOrder],0)**. (For InStock, OnOrder, and BackOrder, you should substitute the field names from your own database.)

3. Save and run the query.

Current Stock Level : Select Query

Stock Levels
QuantityPerU
UnitPrice
InStock
OnOrder
BackOrder

Field:	ProductName	UnitPrice	Current Level: Nz([InStock],0)+Nz([OnOrder],0)-Nz([BackOrder],0)
Table:	Stock Levels	Stock Levels	
Sort:			
Show:	☑	☑	☑
Criteria:			
or:			

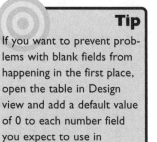

Tip

If you want to prevent problems with blank fields from happening in the first place, open the table in Design view and add a default value of 0 to each number field you expect to use in calculations.

Current Stock Level : Select Query

Product Name	Unit Price	Current Level
▶ Chai	$18.00	16
Chang	$19.00	37
Aniseed Syrup	$10.00	68
Chef Anton's Cajun Seasoning	$22.00	53
Chef Anton's Gumbo Mix	$21.35	0
Grandma's Boysenberry Spread	$25.00	77
Uncle Bob's Organic Dried Pears	$30.00	15
Northwoods Cranberry Sauce	$40.00	-4
Mishi Kobe Niku	$97.00	29
Ikura	$31.00	6
Queso Cabrales	$21.00	52
Queso Manchego La Pastora	$38.00	86
Konbu	$6.00	24
Tofu	$23.25	25
Genen Shouyu	$15.50	29
Pavlova	$17.45	29
Alice Mutton	$39.00	0
Carnarvon Tigers	$62.50	42

Record: ◀◀ ◀ 1 ▶ ▶◀ ▶* of 77

If you see blank records instead of the text values you tried to combine with the plus sign (+), do the following:

1. Open the query in Design view.

2. In the Field row for the field causing the problem, replace each plus sign (+) with an ampersand (&) and then save the query.

3. Run the query.

Full Name : Select Query

Employees2
*
EmployeeID
LastName
MI
FirstName

Field:	FirstName	MI	LastName	Full Name: [FirstName] &" "&[MI] &" "&[LastName]	
Table:	Employees2	Employees2	Employees2		
Sort:					
Show:	☑	☑	☑	☑	☐
Criteria:					
or:					

Tip

To place spaces between the text values, include a space between the field names enclosed in quotation marks.

I get a strange result when I use the First function in a query

Source of the problem

You tally up your recent rush of orders from all your faithful customers and want to look at the range of your success. So you create a query and figure you'll just sort the orders in descending order of total dollar amount. If you pick the first record in the query result (you used the First function in your query after all), you'll see the order with the highest total amount, right?

Wrong! The First function (like the Last function) ignores the sort order you set for a query. These functions also ignore indexes and primary keys. What they do is return the first or last record on the basis of record number—the order in which the records were entered in a table—not by the first or last record in the current sort order. ▶

The following solutions describe how to solve this problem.

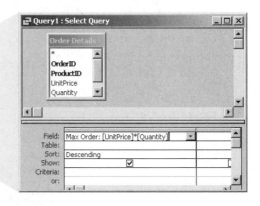

How to fix it

To correct the problem, do the following:

1. Create a new query, making sure you include the table with the values you want to sort.

2. In the Field row in the first column, type an expression such as **Max Order: [UnitPrice]*[Quantity]**. Use the fields that calculate the values you want to sort. ▶

3. Click the Totals button on the toolbar.

4. In the Total row, choose Max from the drop-down list.

5. To see the smallest value among the records, copy the expression you used in step 2 to the Field row in the second column in the query grid and change the name in the expression to Min Order.

6. From the drop-down list in the Total row, click Min.

7. Save and run the query. ▶

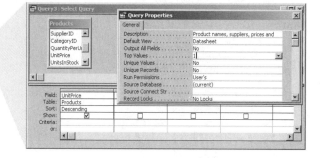

If you're looking for the highest or lowest value in a single field, you can use the Top Values property by following these steps:

1. Start a new query based on the table that contains the values you're interested in.

2. Drag the field name that contains those values to the first column in the design grid.

3. Choose Ascending in the Sort row if you want to see the lowest value in the field at the start of the query results, or choose Descending to see the highest value.

4. Right-click in the background of the upper pane of the query window and then click Properties.

5. In the Top Values property, type 1. ▶

6. Run the query.

> **Tip**
>
> When you close and reopen a query that uses one of the summarizing functions with an expression, you see that the function has been added to the expression in the Field row and the Total cell is changed from the function to Expression.

> **Tip**
>
> You can also simply type 1 in the Top Values box on the Query Design toolbar. The number you type there is copied to the Top Values property in the query property sheet.

My query shows the wrong calculation results when I try to summarize data

Source of the problem

The whole point of grouping records in a query is to come up with summary information such as average time on a job or total orders by month. Access tries to make such summaries so easy that you can do them blindfolded. If, when you run your query, you find that you worked an average of 36 hours per day or that your orders totaled $1,599,900,108 in March—it was a busy month— something has gone wrong somewhere. One of the following actions probably caused your problem:

- You grouped records on the wrong field.

- You placed the function you're using to summarize the data in the wrong column, or you chose the wrong function from the list.

- You're counting records with blanks in certain fields. If you're trying to count all the records, including the ones with blanks, you need to create a calculated field based on a special function.

The following solutions describe ways to solve these problems with summarized data.

How to fix it

To correct a problem caused by grouping records on the wrong field, follow these steps:

> **Tip**
>
> All the functions used to summarize data can be used with Number, Date/Time, Currency, and AutoNumber fields. Only the Min, Max, and Count functions can be used with Text fields. The only function you can use with Yes/No and OLE Object fields is Count.

1. Open the query in Design view.

2. If the Total row isn't showing in the query grid, click the Totals button on the toolbar.

3. Verify that you have included the field you want to group by in the query grid.

4. In the Total row for that field, select Group By. ▶

5. Move to the Total row for the field whose values you want to summarize and select the function you need from the drop-down list. The list on the next page will help you figure out which function to choose.

If you want to include blank values when counting the number of records, do the following:

1. Create a new query, basing it on the table with the records you want to count, but don't add any fields to the grid.

2. Click the Totals button on the toolbar.

3. In the first Field row, type an expression such as **TotalCities: Count(*)**.

4. In the Total row, choose Expression from the drop-down list. ▶

Tip

To see how results differ between this method and counting field values that might include blanks, drag the City field name to the grid and choose Count in the Total cell.

5. Run the query. ▶

If you want to	Choose
Add all the values in the field	Sum
Find the average of the field values	Avg
Show the lowest value in the field	Min
Show the highest value in the field	Max
Count the number of non-null field values	Count
Compute the standard deviation of the values	StDev
Compute the variance of the values	Var

My autolookup query isn't working

Source of the problem

Just when you think you made data entry easier with autolookup, nothing happens. The insertion point just sits there blinking at you. Let's say you're entering new orders from your customers, and after you type the customer's name you want the autolookup query to fill in the customer's address, phone number, and other boring information for you. If Access doesn't automatically fill in the data, you could have one of several problems:

- The fields in the query might not be from one or more tables that are part of a one-to-many relationship.

- The linking field you used in the query design might be wrong. The linking field must be the field from the table on the "many" side. For example, when you are working with orders and customers, the customer table is on the "one" side (the parent table) and the orders table is on the "many" side (the child table). One customer can place many orders, but an order is sent to a single customer.

- AutoLookup also does not work if the field joining the tables from the "one" side includes duplicate values. All the records in this field must be unique. The trouble is that a field like a customer name can't be the primary key or a unique index in an orders table (the "many" side of the relationship).

- The record you want to look up might not exist in the table on the "one" side. If Access is going to look up information in a table that it will use to fill in fields in another form, that information had better exist.

> **Tip**
>
> A *one-to-many relationship*, the most common type, relates a single record in one table to any number of records in another table. A *one-to-one relationship* is used mainly as a lookup tool that relates a single record in one table to a single record in another table, possibly containing augmenting but seldom-used data. A *many-to-many* relationship exists in theory, but in Access it's implemented as two one-to-many relationships with a table in between. The "junction" table contains only those fields needed to link the two original tables with a one-to-many relationship.

How to fix it

The first thing to do is check the relationship between the tables and fields that are in the query design grid:

1. With your database open, click the Relationships button on the toolbar.

2. Right-click the relationship line linking the tables you're working with (Orders and Customers in this example) and then click Edit Relationship on the shortcut menu.

3. Check the related fields and make sure the relationship type is One-To-Many. ▶

4. Click OK, close the Relationships window, and then open the query in Design view.

5. If the linking field in the query grid is from the table on the "one" side, delete the column containing the field from the query grid.

6. Drag the linking field from the table on the "many" side to the query design grid.

7. Save and run the query.

If the field you're using in your AutoLookup query includes duplicate values, try the following:

1. Open the table on the "one" side in Design view and then click the field that links this table with the table on the "many" side.

2. In the Field Properties area, change the field's Indexed property to Yes (No Duplicates).

3. Save the table.

4. Open the table on the "many" side in Design view.

5. Click the field that links this table with the table on the "one" side.

6. Change the Indexed property to No. ▶

7. Save the changes.

8. Run your query again.

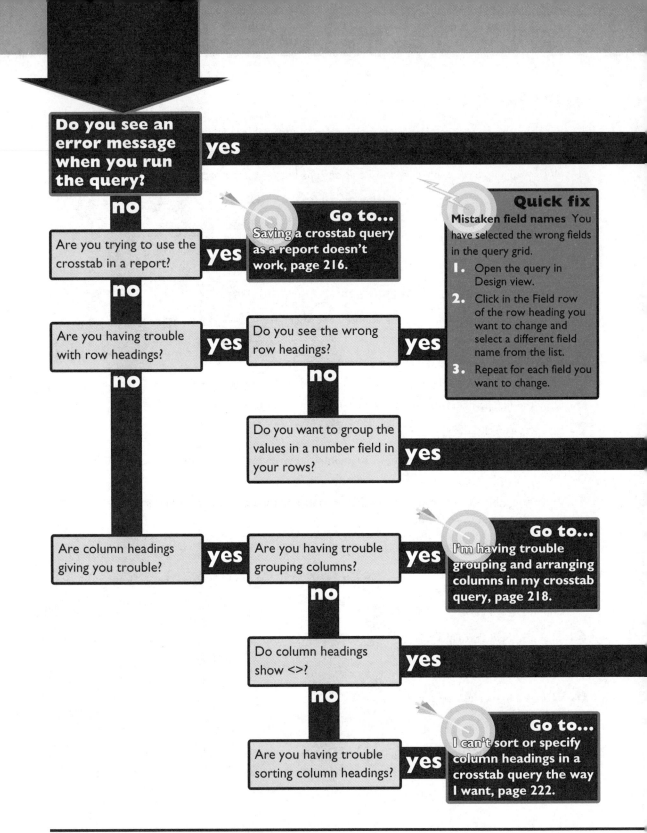

Do you see an error message when you run the query? **yes**

no

Are you trying to use the crosstab in a report? **yes**

Go to... Saving a crosstab query as a report doesn't work, page 216.

no

Are you having trouble with row headings? **yes** Do you see the wrong row headings? **yes**

Quick fix

Mistaken field names You have selected the wrong fields in the query grid.

1. Open the query in Design view.
2. Click in the Field row of the row heading you want to change and select a different field name from the list.
3. Repeat for each field you want to change.

no

no

Do you want to group the values in a number field in your rows? **yes**

Are column headings giving you trouble? **yes** Are you having trouble grouping columns? **yes**

Go to... I'm having trouble grouping and arranging columns in my crosstab query, page 218.

no

Do column headings show <>? **yes**

no

Are you having trouble sorting column headings? **yes**

Go to... I can't sort or specify column headings in a crosstab query the way I want, page 222.

Queries, crosstab

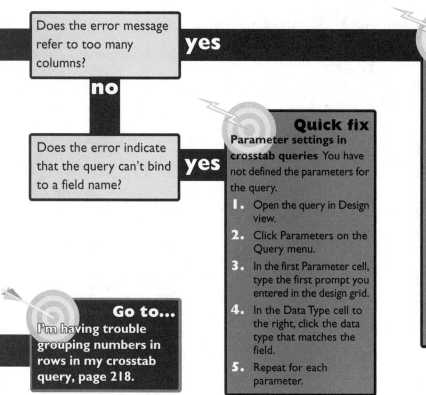

Does the error message refer to too many columns?

yes →

Quick fix

Too many columns You have too many distinct values in the field you designated as the column heading.

1. Click OK to clear the message.
2. In the Field row for the field that's resulting in too many column headings, add an expression that groups the values in the field. You could group date values by quarter by entering an expression such as **Expr1:Format ([DateField],"q")**, which extracts the numeric value of the quarter in which the date falls.

no ↓

Does the error indicate that the query can't bind to a field name?

yes →

Quick fix

Parameter settings in crosstab queries You have not defined the parameters for the query.

1. Open the query in Design view.
2. Click Parameters on the Query menu.
3. In the first Parameter cell, type the first prompt you entered in the design grid.
4. In the Data Type cell to the right, click the data type that matches the field.
5. Repeat for each parameter.

Go to...

I'm having trouble grouping numbers in rows in my crosstab query, page 218.

Quick fix

Empty columns A column heading field contains a null value.

1. Return to the query Design view and enter **Is Not Null** in the Criteria row of the field.
2. Run the query again.

If your solution isn't here, check these related chapters:

- Queries, selection criteria, page 224
- Queries, simple select, page 236
- Reports, creating, page 258

Or see the general troubleshooting tips on page xv.

Saving a crosstab query as a report doesn't work

Source of the problem

The Crosstab Query Wizard did just what you ordered it to and produced a very useful summary of your company's performance. Now all you need to do is put that info in a report and distribute it to all your admiring stockholders.

Unfortunately, the tools you think will do the job backfire. Using a make-table query to create a table you can use as the basis for the report undoes all the summarization that the crosstab query so carefully calculated. Instead, the report expands to include the detailed records in a plain vanilla format. (If you were summarizing orders by customer and quarter, the table would show a record for each customer and each quarter in which an order was placed. Each customer would have up to four records, one for each quarter.)

The clever Save As command provides nothing more than a default tabular report, which has all the data but not in the form of a crosstab—it doesn't show the columns, values, and rows with the summarized and coordinated values you want. Using the AutoReport tool results in the same flat report.

To get the results you need, you have to group the records within the report. The following solution shows how to correct the problem and create a report from a crosstab query.

How to fix it

1. In the database window, click Reports and then click New.

2. In the New Report dialog box, select the crosstab query you want to save as a report and then click OK.

3. On the View menu, click Sorting And Grouping.

4. In the Field/Expression column, select the field you want to use to group records so you can summarize associated data. This should be one of the fields you used as a row heading in the crosstab query. ▶

5. In the Group Properties area of the Sorting And Grouping dialog box, select Yes in the Group Header box and then close the Sorting And Grouping dialog box.

6. Click the Field List button on the toolbar if the field list is not already showing.

7. From the field list, drag the fields you used as the query's row headings to the grouped field's header section in the report design window. ▶

8. Drag the column heading fields to the Detail section of the report design window.

9. In the Detail section, remove the attached labels from the column heading fields.

10. In the toolbox, click the Label icon and add labels for the column headings to the group header section. (If the toolbox isn't displayed, first click the Toolbox button on the toolbar.)

11. Click the Label icon again and then add a title for the report in the Page Header section. ▶

12. Preview the report. ▶

Tip

You can save space in your report by placing the column heading labels in the Page Header section. Then the labels are not repeated in each group.

Tip

You can't update data in a crosstab query. The crosstab query creates a static snapshot. To update the data in the crosstab with the latest table data, close and reopen the crosstab query.

I'm having trouble grouping numbers in rows in my crosstab query

Source of the problem

Creating summaries of your sales activities doesn't help much if what you end up with is a table with a record for each individual order and a column for each employee who made the sale. That information won't fit on a slide or in a report. There must be a way to group some of these numbers to get a better overall picture of your data.

Unfortunately, the Crosstab Query Wizard can work on only one table or query at a time, but in a relational database the data you need to summarize is likely to be contained in related tables. Another problem with the Crosstab Query Wizard is that you can't always group values into rows the way you need them. The wizard can group records only with specific data types, such as dates. It can't, for example, group numbers such as sales totals by numeric ranges.

The following solution shows how to solve this problem using a helpful function named Partition. This is a two-phase solution that uses a select query as the basis for the crosstab query.

How to fix it

First create a select query that summarizes the numeric values you want to group in the crosstab query:

1. In the database window, click Queries and then click New. In the New Query dialog box, click Design view and then click OK.

2. In the Show Table dialog box, click the Both tab. Select the tables or queries that contain the data you want in the crosstab query, click the Add button, and then click Close.

3. In the query window, make sure the tables or queries are linked by a matching field. If they are not, select a matching field in one table or query and drag it to the matching field in the other.

4. From the field list for the parent table, drag the field whose values will appear in the body of the crosstab query to the query grid.

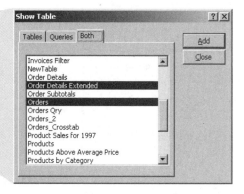

5. Drag the field containing the values you want to group and summarize in the crosstab rows to the query grid.

6. In the Field row for the summary field you just added, type a heading such as **Amount:** in front of the field name to create an expression.

7. In the next empty column, type an expression such as **Year: Year([*DateField*])** to use as the crosstab column heading. (The Year function extracts the year value from the date field.)

8. Click Totals on the View menu. In the Total cell for the Amount column, select Sum. ▶

9. Save and name the query and then run the query.

Now create the crosstab query based on this select query:

1. Start a new query as you did in the preceding steps 1–3, basing it on the query you just created.

2. On the Query menu, click Crosstab Query.

3. In the first column of the design grid, type an expression such as **SalesRange: Partition([Amount],0,100000,10000)**. This expression uses the Partition function to group the values in the Amount field beginning with 0 and ending with 100,000, in intervals of 10,000.

4. In the Crosstab row for this column, select Row Heading and then select Ascending in the Sort row.

5. Drag the field you want to use as column headings to the query grid. In the Crosstab row, select Column Heading.

6. Drag the field you want to use as a value to the query grid. In the Crosstab row for this column, select Value. In the Total row, select Count.

7. Save and run the query. ▶

I'm having trouble grouping and arranging the columns in my crosstab query

Source of the problem

It's easy to group column headings in a crosstab query by year or quarter in a date field, but it's not so easy to group by other data types. For example, in a crosstab query that links customers with the amount of each order they placed, you get thousands of columns—and an error message, by the way. To solve this problem, you need to find a different way to group values in the column heading field.

You can do this with the Switch function, which looks at a list of expressions you enter and returns a value related to the first expression that turns out to be true. You can use this handy function in a crosstab query to group columns by numeric ranges. When you see the results, however, the columns aren't likely to be in the right order. They're arranged alphabetically instead of in numeric order.

The following solutions show you how to fix your column groups with the Switch function.

Tip

You can also add a final expression to the Switch function that will take care of any values that don't fit the others. For example, add **True, "Others"** to the end of your Switch function expression. The values that don't meet the criteria in the numeric ranges you define will appear in a column of their own labeled Others.

How to fix it

1. In the database window, click Queries and then click New.

2. In the New Query dialog box, click Design view and then click OK.

3. In the Show Table dialog box, click the Both tab and then double-click the tables or queries that contain the records you want in the crosstab query. Click Close.

4. On the Query menu, click Crosstab Query.

5. Drag the field you want to use as the crosstab row heading to the design grid.

6. In the Crosstab row, select Row Heading and then select Ascending in the Sort row. ▶

7. Drag the field whose values you want to show in the body of the crosstab to the design grid.

8. In the Total row for that field, select Count. In the Crosstab row, select Value.

9. In the Field row in the next column, type an expression such as **Expr1: Switch([ExtendedPrice]<250, "<$250",[ExtendedPrice] Between 250 And 1000, "$250-$1,000", [ExtendedPrice]>1000, ">$1,000")**. This expression uses the Switch func-

tion to compare the values in a number field (ExtendedPrice) with numeric ranges. If the first comparison is true, the column heading is set to the value enclosed in the next set of quotation marks. For example, if a record's value in ExtendedPrice is less than 250, the column heading is set to <$250 and the record is included in the count value for that column. ▶

10. In the Crosstab row for that column, select Column Heading.

11. Run the query.

Warning

Be sure to identify the ranges of values to include all possible values. If the value in a record doesn't fit in any of the ranges, the crosstab will show a column with <> in the column heading.

If your column headings are numeric values, the columns might not appear in the right order. To fix this problem, do the following: ▶

1. Return to the query design.

2. Right-click in the background of the upper pane, away from any of the field lists, and click Properties on the shortcut menu.

3. In the Column Headings property box, type the column headings in the order in which you want them to appear in the query results. Separate the column headings with commas and enclose the headings in quotation marks. ▶

I can't sort or specify column headings in a crosstab query the way that I want

Source of the problem

Limiting the row heading fields in a crosstab query isn't that difficult. You just add criteria to the row heading fields in the query design grid. Working with column headings creates more problems, however.

You can add criteria to the column heading field in the query design grid, but you can't set the order of the columns there. If you're having trouble with the order of the columns, there's probably a conflict between criteria you used and the query's property settings. The selection and arrangement of column headings in a crosstab query is actually a property of the query rather than part of the query design structure. If you enter criteria in the query design grid to limit the values to use as column headings and then specify the order of the columns in the Column Headings query property, you'll likely see some conflict between the field values, and one or more of the columns might be blank.

The following solution shows how to solve problems with column headings in a crosstab query.

How to fix it

1. In the database window, click Queries and then click New.

2. In the New Query dialog box, select Design view and then click OK.

3. In the Show Tables dialog box, click the Both tab and then select the tables or queries you want to include in the crosstab query. Click Add and then click Close.

4. On the Query menu, click Crosstab Query.

5. From the field lists, drag the fields you want to use as the column heading, row headings, and values to the query design grid and then select the corresponding setting in the Crosstab row. In this example, ShipCountry provides the row headings, CategoryName is used as the column heading field, and ExtendedPrice provides the values for the crosstab. ▶

6. In the Row Heading field, select Ascending in the Sort cell.

7. In the Total cell of the Value field, select Sum (or another aggregate function).

8. Run the query.

To limit and arrange the columns the way you want, do the following:

1. Click the View button on the toolbar to return the query to Design view.

2. Right-click in an empty area of the upper pane of the query design window and then click Properties on the shortcut menu.

3. In the Column Headings property box, type the values you want to appear in the crosstab columns in the order you want them to appear. Enclose each value in quotation marks and separate them with commas. ▶

Query Properties	
General	
Description	
Default View	Datasheet
Column Headings	"Condiments","Beverages","Proeduce"
Run Permissions	User's
Source Database	(current)
Source Connect Str	
Record Locks	No Locks
Recordset Type	Dynaset
ODBC Timeout	60

4. If, when you run the query, one of the columns is blank, check the spelling in the Column Headings property box. Each value you type there must match the value in the field that is used as the column heading. To fix any misspellings, return to the Query Design view and correct the entry in the Column Headings property box.

5. Run the query again.

Crosstab Queries 101

Crosstab queries are useful tools for illustrating trends over time and relative proportions of totals. You can think of them as spreadsheet-like versions of charts or graphs. A crosstab query summarizes the data you use, rather than showing each and every record. The data is correlated with two types of information. In the example in this solution, orders are counted and grouped both by customer and by the quarter in which the order was placed.

Fields in your database are used as the three building blocks in a crosstab query: a row heading, a column heading, and a value. The values for the row heading field appear in a column at the left side of the crosstab, and the values for the column heading field are displayed (surprise!) at the top of each column. The field you select as the value is summarized as the number of records, the total of the values, or the average of the values. These values are displayed in the body of the crosstab.

Whether you use a field as a row or column depends on what you want to emphasize. You can easily switch back and forth to get the result you want. But if you want to use subgroupings of one of the fields (individual cities within each state, for example), you must specify that field as a row heading. You can use only one field as the column heading.

You can select up to three fields as row headings that act as subgroupings for the data values. Each additional row heading multiplies the number of records in the query result. Two row headings doubles the number and three row headings triples it. If you use more than one row heading, be sure to arrange your row headings in the query grid in the order you want the results grouped.

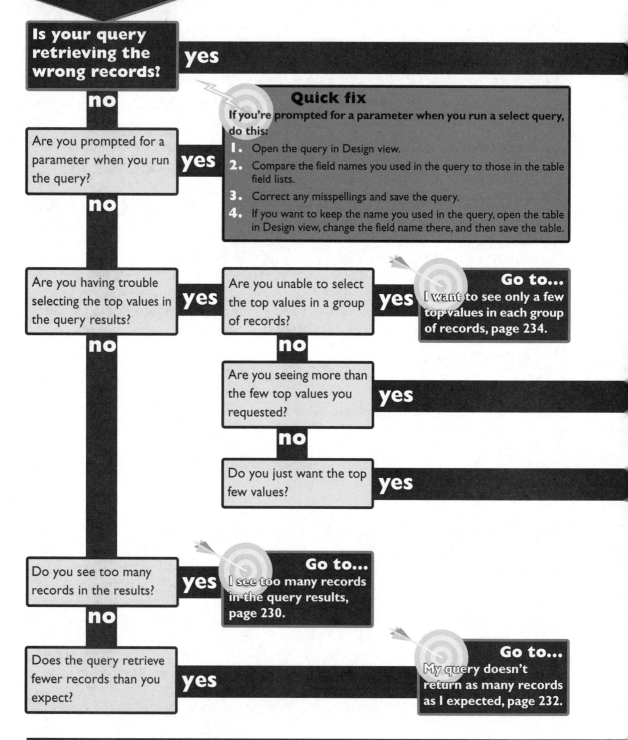

Is your query retrieving the wrong records?

yes

no

Are you prompted for a parameter when you run the query?

yes

no

Quick fix

If you're prompted for a parameter when you run a select query, do this:

1. Open the query in Design view.
2. Compare the field names you used in the query to those in the table field lists.
3. Correct any misspellings and save the query.
4. If you want to keep the name you used in the query, open the table in Design view, change the field name there, and then save the table.

Are you having trouble selecting the top values in the query results?

yes

no

Are you unable to select the top values in a group of records?

yes

no

Go to...
I want to see only a few top values in each group of records, page 234.

Are you seeing more than the few top values you requested?

yes

no

Do you just want the top few values?

yes

Do you see too many records in the results?

yes

Go to...
I see too many records in the query results, page 230.

no

Does the query retrieve fewer records than you expect?

yes

Go to...
My query doesn't return as many records as I expected, page 232.

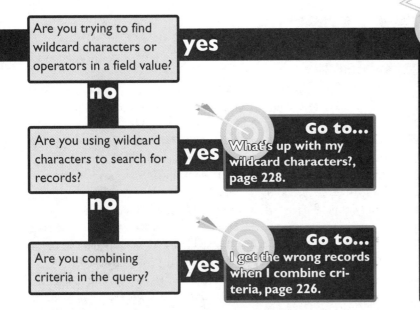

Are you trying to find wildcard characters or operators in a field value?

yes

no

Are you using wildcard characters to search for records?

yes

no

Are you combining criteria in the query?

yes

Go to...
What's up with my wildcard characters?, page 228.

Go to...
I get the wrong records when I combine criteria, page 226.

Quick fix
You need to treat wildcards and operators differently in a criterion.

1. If you're looking for one of the wildcard characters or an operator in a field by itself, use the = operator instead of Like. Access adds quotation marks around the character.

2. If you're looking for a wildcard character or operator that's part of a string, enclose the wildcard or operator in brackets: Like "[*]" returns all values that begin with an asterisk.

Quick fix
You need to set the Unique Records property of the query to Yes.

1. Open the query in Design view.

2. In the Top Values box on the toolbar, select the number of values you want to see. (If the number you want is not in the list, you can enter the number of values you want in the Top Values box.)

3. On the View menu, click Properties.

4. Set the query's Unique Records property to Yes.

Quick fix
You need to select which records you want to see:

1. If you want the highest values, click Descending in the Sort row of the field you're using as the criterion.

2. If you want the lowest values, click Ascending in the Sort row.

3. On the Query toolbar, click the Top Values list and select the number or percentage of records you want to see.

If your solution isn't here, check these related chapters:

- Filtering, page 110
- Queries, calculations, page 204
- Queries, simple select, page 236

Or see the general troubleshooting tips on page xv.

I get the wrong records when I combine criteria

Source of the problem

You want to see a list of all books about dogs and cats, except for any books about the moot subject of training cats. Everyone knows those books would just be empty covers. To find exactly the combination of information you want to see, you need to combine search criteria. The query design grid provides the Criteria and the Or rows where you place criteria in various arrangements.

If you're getting the wrong results with your query, you might have entered the correct criteria but in the wrong place. You might, for example, have tried to combine two values with the *And* operator in the Criteria row for a single field. Doing this rarely works for text fields because one field can't have two values at the same time. The only reason you combine criteria in this way is to find a memo field with both text values somewhere in the field. What you might have wanted to see are records with either of the two values in a text field. In this case, you need to use the *Or* operator in the Criteria row to combine the two values or simply place the second value in the Or row by itself.

Another problem you might have stems from combining criteria in two rows and two columns. If you place criterion A in the Criteria row and criterion B in the Or row of one column and then enter criterion C in the Criteria row of another column (without any criteria in the Or row), you see records that meet criteria A and C, plus all the records that meet only criterion B.

The following steps show how to solve these problems.

How to fix it

If you want to find records with two values in a memo field, do the following:

1. In the database window, select the query and then click the Design button.

2. In the query grid, click in the Criteria row for the memo field and type an expression such as **"*dog*" And "*cat*"**. When you move to another cell, Microsoft Access adds the *Like* operator to both values. ▶

3. Run the query. You see all records that have the words *dog* and *cat* in the same memo field.

> **Tip**
>
> The asterisk wildcard character represents any number of characters. The words *dog* and *cat* can be embedded anywhere in the memo text, and the expression will locate them even if they are part of another word, such as *catatonic* or *dogmatism*. The *Like* operator is case-insensitive.

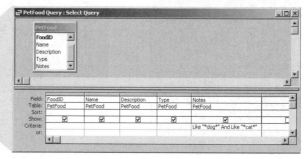

If you're trying to find records with either of two values in a single field, do the following:

1. Open the query in Design view.

2. In the Criteria row of the field you're searching, type the first criterion—for example, **"*cat*"**. Again, Access adds the *Like* operator.

3. Click in the Or row of the same column and then type the second value you want—for example, **"*dog*"**. ▶

4. Click the Run button to display the results of the query.

If you're combining criteria in more than one column, you might not have arranged the criteria correctly. Try the following:

1. Type a statement in the Criteria row of the first column and in the Or row of the same column.

2. Add a statement in the Criteria row in another column. This statement is combined with the statement you typed in the Criteria row of the first column with the *And* operator.

3. To apply the criterion in the Criteria row of the second column to both groups of records from the first column, copy that statement to the Or row of the second column. ▶

4. Run the query, and you will see records that meet both pairs of criteria.

The logic might not seem so logical

Combining selection criteria with And and Or can get rather confusing. Whether the record is included in the query results depends on the outcome of the full expression. And the outcome of the expression depends on the outcome of each of its components and on how they're combined. An expression using an *And* combination is true only when both criteria are true. If only one of them is true, the whole expression is false and the record is not selected. On the other hand, when criteria are combined with the *Or* operator, if either of the criteria is true, the whole expression is true and the record is selected.

Tip

You can use the Cut, Copy, and Paste commands to move or copy criteria from one cell to another.

What's up with my wildcard characters?

Source of the problem

When you send out invitations to your gala open house, you better get all the details right or the wrong guests will show up on the wrong day wearing the wrong outfits. The last thing you want is to have your boss show up at midnight in her bathing suit for a slide show of your latest ski trip! If you leave any gaps in the information and expect Access to come up with the right answers, you better give it a clue about what fits in the gaps. Wildcards can do just that if you choose them wisely.

Query criteria are requests for certain records to show up in certain circumstances when you run the query. If you see the wrong records or the wrong values in the query results, the criteria in the request might be goofed up. One of the following is probably your problem:

- You used the wrong operator with a wildcard character. For example, using the equal sign (=) with a wildcard character causes Access to look for the wildcard character itself rather than use it to represent other characters. ▶

- You used a wildcard in a field other than a text data type field, which resulted in an error message. For example, typing the question mark (?) wildcard to replace a number in a date field causes an error. The question mark wildcard character is intended to replace any single character in a text field.

The following steps show you ways to cure these problems.

How to fix it

If you're having trouble using a wildcard character to search for records, follow these steps:

1. In the database window, select the query and then click the Design button.

> **Tip**
>
> To find dates before a certain date, use the < operator combined with the actual date. To find a date in a specific month and year, use the * wildcard in place of the day value. Similarly, you can use the * wildcard in place of the month or year as well.

---

2. Click in the Criteria row for the fields where you typed wildcard characters.

3. Replace the equal sign (=) with Like or the not equal to sign (<>) with Not Like. ▶

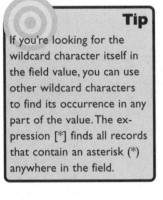

If you see a message about an invalid value, do the following: ▶

1. Click OK to close the error message.

2. In the Criteria row for the field where you used a wildcard, replace the wildcard character (in this case the ?) with a date value such as 01.

3. Run the query again.

Wildcards aren't so wild after all

Wildcard	Purpose
*	Used as the first or last character in the criteria. The * matches any number of characters in the field value. For example, "c*" finds any word that begins with the letter c.
?	Matches any single alphabetic character in a text field. For example, "c??e" finds care, cave, core, and so on.
#	Matches any single numeric character. For example, 25# finds 251, 252, 253, and so on.
[ ]	Used to enclose specific characters and matches any one of them. For example, "c[aou]ll" finds call, coll, and cull but not cell or cill.
!	Used within the square brackets. The exclamation point matches any character not in the brackets. For example, "c[!ao]ll" finds cell and cull but not call or coll.
-	Used within the square brackets. The hyphen defines an ascending or descending range of characters to match. For example, "c[a-d]d" finds cad, cbd, ccd, and cdd.

I see too many records in the query results

Source of the problem

You open the door just a crack, and half the world shows up. Too many records crash the party when you tried to invite just a few selected ones. That's what criteria are for in a query; they're like a formal invitation to a party. So why do you see so many unwanted guests in your query results?

One reason you can be flooded with records is that the query you're running is based on more than one table, but the tables aren't related in the query's design. In this case, you're swamped with what mathematicians call a *Cartesian product*—for each record in one table you get the whole set of records from the other table, not just a matching record. In other words, if one table has 100 records and the other has 250, the result will show 25,000 records.

Other causes of seeing too many records aren't so dramatic:

● The tables are not joined in the right way.

● Criteria in the query are not selective enough to narrow down the result. The criteria might be combined with the *Or* operator, which increases the number of records that meet the criteria.

The following steps give you some pointers on how to solve these problems.

How to fix it

If the tables you included in the query aren't related at all, do the following:

1. In the database window, select the query and then click the Design button.

2. In the query window, select a field in one table that matches a field in another and drag it to the matching field in the other table. ▶

3. Save and run the query.

To change the way two tables are joined, follow these steps:

1. In the database window, select the query and then click the Design button.

2. In the query window, right-click the relationship line between the two tables and then click Join Properties on the shortcut menu.

3. In the lower section of the Join Properties dialog box, select the first option (labeled with the number 1) to create what Access calls an inner join. ▶

4. Click OK and then repeat for other relationships between tables in the query.

5. When finished creating relationships, save the query.

Join Properties `? ×`

Left Table Name	Right Table Name
Products	Suppliers

Left Column Name	Right Column Name
SupplierID	SupplierID

- ● 1: Only include rows where the joined fields from both tables are equal.
- ○ 2: Include ALL records from 'Products' and only those records from 'Suppliers' where the joined fields are equal.
- ○ 3: Include ALL records from 'Suppliers' and only those records from 'Products' where the joined fields are equal.

OK   Cancel   New

Tip

The type of join determines which records are returned by the query. It has nothing to do with the type of relationship. An *inner join* returns only records that have matches in both tables. *Outer joins* return all the records from one of the tables and only the matching records from the other table.

If you want to enter criteria that will limit the records further, try one or more of the following steps:

1. In the database window, select the query and then click the Design button.

2. In the query grid, click in the Criteria row for a field without selection criteria and add criteria. This criteria will be combined with criteria entered for other fields to reduce the number of records.

3. Move criteria for a field from the Or row to the Criteria row. This further restricts the number of records that appear in the query results.

4. Add selection criteria to existing criteria using the *And* operator.

5. When you have the results you want, save the query.

Tip

Be careful not to specify mutually exclusive conditions when using the *And* operator—for example, **Animal is Dog AND Animal is Cat**. No record can meet both of these criteria.

My query doesn't return as many records as I expected

Source of the problem

It's hard to know which is worse—having the whole town crash your party or having no one show up at all. You keep wondering what you might have said that keeps everyone away. If your query displays very few or no records at all, it might indeed be something you said. In the form of the selection criterion, that is.

If you see fewer records than you expected, one of these situations is probably the source of your problem:

- You accidentally entered criteria that no record could meet. For example, you might have combined two values with an *And* operator in a text field. The field can't have two values in the same record, so no records will meet these criteria.

- You placed criteria in the Criteria row of too many columns. Access interprets this combination of criteria using an implied *And* operator. That means few records will meet all the criteria.

- The criteria values you used are too limiting. Using wildcard characters can add some leeway.

- You want to include records that have no value in the field you're setting criteria for, but you didn't enter criteria that will select blank records.

The following steps give you some ways to correct these problems.

How to fix it

First select the query in the database window and click the Design button. Then do the following:

1. In the query design grid, check criteria you typed for misspellings, spaces in the wrong place (for example, in field names not enclosed in brackets in an expression), and extra characters that might be in the way.

2. Remove any mutually exclusive values from criteria combined with the *And* operator or change the *And* operator to an *Or* operator to allow both values. For example, change the criteria "cat" And "dog" to "cat" Or "dog".

3. If criteria are entered for more than one field, remove criteria from the Criteria row for one or more fields or move those criteria to the Or row for that column.

To make the criteria more flexible (which should result in the display of more records), use wildcard characters as follows:

1. Replace one or more characters with a wildcard character. The question mark (?) can be used to represent a single character; the asterisk (*) represents any number of characters.

2. If you're already using wildcards, check to make sure you're using the right wildcard for that data type. (See the table in the solution "What's up with my wildcard characters?" on page 229 for examples of other wildcard characters you can use in selection criteria.) ▶

3. Switch to Datasheet view to see the results. ▼

Tip

If you use = or <> with wildcards, Access looks for the wildcard character itself, not what it represents.

To include records with blank (or null) values in a field, do the following:

1. Open the query in Design view.

2. In the Or row for a field that already contains criteria in the Criteria row, type **Is Null**. ▶

3. Save and run the query.

I want to see only a few top values in each group of records

Source of the problem

The fiscal quarter is coming to a close, and now it's time to figure out which salespeople in each region have been the most successful. Or maybe you need to determine how best to spend your marketing budget and want to know the three most expensive products in each category. Those products deserve more sales promotion if the return is high.

Creating a query that displays the records with the top few values from an entire table is pretty simple. You use the Top Values box on the Query Design toolbar to choose the number or percentage of values you want to see. But you can't use the Top Values box if you have arranged the records by the values in a particular field, such as product categories. The following solution describes how to find the top values among records you have already sorted.

How to fix it

The first step in fixing this problem is to create a query that sorts the records into the groups you want to look at—for example, by product category or sales region. Then you use an expression to sort and limit the number of records within the groups to show the top values.

1. In the database window, click Queries and then click New.

2. In the New Queries dialog box, click Design view and then click OK.

3. In the Show Table dialog box, select the table with the field you want to sort records by and the table that contains the field whose top values you want to see. Click Add.

4. Repeat step 3 to add any other tables you need in the query and then click Close in the Show Table dialog box.

5. Drag the fields you want in the query result to the grid, including the one you want to sort records by first and the field you want to select the top values from.

6. In the Sort row for the field you want to sort records by first, select Ascending as the sort order.

7. On the View menu, click Datasheet view to see the results returned by the query. In this example, the records are sorted by Category Name. ▶

8. On the View menu, click Design view.

9. In the Sort row for the field whose top values you want to see, choose Descending as the sort order. (If you want to see the lowest values, you set the sort order to Ascending.)

Category Name	Product Name	Unit Price
Beverages	Ipoh Coffee	$46.00
Beverages	Chai	$18.00
Beverages	Lakkalikööri	$18.00
Beverages	Rhönbräu Klosterbier	$7.75
Beverages	Laughing Lumberjack Lager	$14.00
Beverages	Chartreuse verte	$18.00
Beverages	Côte de Blaye	$263.50
Beverages	Steeleye Stout	$18.00
Beverages	Sasquatch Ale	$14.00
Beverages	Guaraná Fantástica	$4.50
Beverages	Chang	$19.00
Beverages	Outback Lager	$15.00
Condiments	Sirop d'érable	$28.50
Condiments	Gula Malacca	$19.45
Condiments	Original Frankfurter grüne Soße	$13.00
Condiments	Louisiana Hot Spiced Okra	$17.00
Condiments	Vegie-spread	$43.90
Condiments	Northwoods Cranberry Sauce	$40.00
Condiments	Grandma's Boysenberry Spread	$25.00
Condiments	Chef Anton's Cajun Seasoning	$22.00
Condiments	Aniseed Syrup	$10.00

Record: 1 of 77

10. In the Criteria row for that field, type an expression such as **In (SELECT Top 3 [UnitPrice] FROM Products WHERE [CategoryID]=[Categories].[CategoryID] ORDER BY [UnitPrice] DESC).** ▼

Field:	ProductName	UnitPrice
Table:	Products	Products
Sort:		Descending
Show:	✓	✓
Criteria:		In (SELECT Top 3 [UnitPrice] FROM Products WHERE [CategoryID]=[Categories].[CategoryID] ORDER BY [UnitPrice] DESC)
or:		

11. Save and name the query and then run the query to see the results. ▶

Tip

The *In* operator uses the SQL SELECT statement in this example to generate a list of the top three items from the Products table within each category group. The WHERE clause specifies the match between the CategoryID fields in the Products and Categories tables. The ORDER BY clause with the DESC argument specifies a descending sort order within the list.

Category Name	Product Name	Unit Price
Beverages	Côte de Blaye	$263.50
Beverages	Ipoh Coffee	$46.00
Beverages	Chang	$19.00
Condiments	Vegie-spread	$43.90
Condiments	Northwoods Cranberry Sauce	$40.00
Condiments	Sirop d'érable	$28.50
Confections	Sir Rodney's Marmalade	$81.00
Confections	Tarte au sucre	$49.30
Confections	Schoggi Schokolade	$43.90
Dairy Products	Raclette Courdavault	$55.00
Dairy Products	Queso Manchego La Pastora	$38.00
Dairy Products	Gudbrandsdalsost	$36.00
Grains/Cereals	Gnocchi di nonna Alice	$38.00
Grains/Cereals	Wimmers gute Semmelknödel	$33.25
Grains/Cereals	Gustaf's Knäckebröd	$21.00
Meat/Poultry	Thüringer Rostbratwurst	$123.79
Meat/Poultry	Mishi Kobe Niku	$97.00
Meat/Poultry	Alice Mutton	$39.00
Produce	Manjimup Dried Apples	$53.00
Produce	Rössle Sauerkraut	$45.60
Produce	Uncle Bob's Organic Dried Pears	$30.00
Seafood	Carnarvon Tigers	$62.50
Seafood	Ikura	$31.00
Seafood	Gravad lax	$26.00

Record: 1 of 24

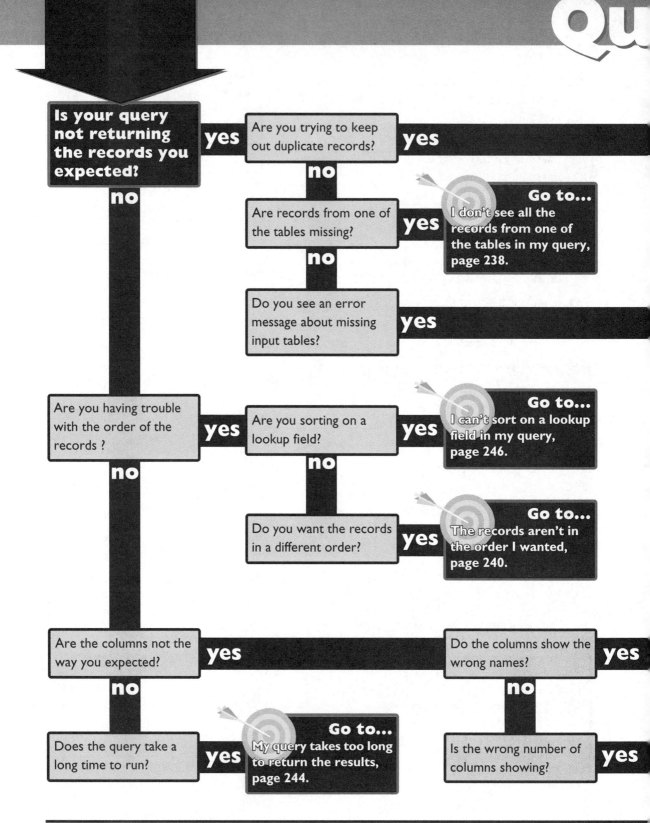

Is your query not returning the records you expected?

yes → Are you trying to keep out duplicate records? **yes** →

no

Are records from one of the tables missing? **yes** →

Go to...
I don't see all the records from one of the tables in my query, page 238.

no

Do you see an error message about missing input tables? **yes** →

no

Are you having trouble with the order of the records? **yes** → Are you sorting on a lookup field? **yes** →

Go to...
I can't sort on a lookup field in my query, page 246.

no

Do you want the records in a different order? **yes** →

Go to...
The records aren't in the order I wanted, page 240.

no

Are the columns not the way you expected? **yes** → Do the columns show the wrong names? **yes** →

no

Does the query take a long time to run? **yes** →

Go to...
My query takes too long to return the results, page 244.

Is the wrong number of columns showing? **yes** →

Quick fix

Keeping duplicate values at bay You need to change the query properties.

1. In Query Design view, click the Properties button on the toolbar.

2. If the query includes only one field, change the Unique Values property to Yes.

3. If you want unique records based on all the fields in the data source (whether they are in the query or not), change the Unique Records property to Yes.

Quick fix

Missing input tables A table that the query refers to has probably been deleted.

1. Open the query in Design view and then click Show Table on the View menu.

2. Right-click the field list for the table that was deleted and then click Remove Table. In the query grid, delete the fields from the table that was deleted.

3. Select the table you want to use in the query, click Add, and then click Close. Drag the fields from the new table to the query grid.

4. Save and run the query.

Quick fix

Correcting column names The query usually shows the field names from the underlying table.

1. To change the name in the query result, select the column in the design grid.

2. Click Properties.

3. Change the field's Caption property to the name you want to use.

If your solution isn't here, check these related chapters:

- Queries, calculations, page 204
- Queries, selection criteria, page 224
- Relationships, page 248
- Sorting, page 280

Or see the general troubleshooting tips on page xv.

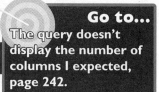

Go to...
The query doesn't display the number of columns I expected, page 242.

I don't see all the records from one of the tables in my query

Source of the problem

You know that your favorite customer, Paris Specialties, is in your database but when you run your query, you don't see their name. Did they forget to pay their last bill or what? You open the Customers table and, sure enough, their record is still there. That's a relief, but why didn't they show up in the query?

When you don't see a record you expect to see in a query, it's probably because of the type of join that's used in the query to relate the tables the query is based on. If the tables have a one-to-many relationship and are using the most common type of join—the inner join—the query displays only those records where the fields joining the tables have a match. In a query that matches customers with orders, if a customer doesn't have a matching order, the customer isn't included in the query results. Likewise, if an order isn't related to a customer, the order record isn't included.

By changing the type of join, you can return records without a match in the related table. The following solution shows you how you can create a query to show all the records on the "one" side of a table relationship (all the customers, in this example) even if there are no related records on the "many" side (the orders).

How to fix it

To change the type of join used in the query, do the following:

1. In the database window, select the query and click the Design button.

2. Right-click the relationship line between the two tables you're concerned with and then click Join Properties on the shortcut menu.

3. In the Join Properties dialog box, select option 2, which returns all the records from the table on the "one" side of the relationship (Customers, in this example). ▶

4. Click OK.

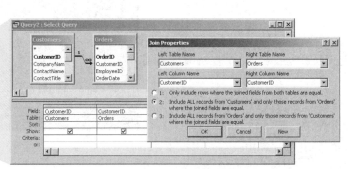

5. You can repeat these steps to change the type of join for other relationships in the query.

6. Click the View button on the toolbar to show the results of the query in Datasheet view.

Joining a table to itself can be useful

Suppose your table includes a field that refers to another field in the table. How are you going to retrieve the value from another record in the same table? Searching out each one by yourself might work, but a better idea is to use a self-join.

A great example of a self-join is a query that returns employees' names and the names of their managers, who are also employees and have records in the same table. You can see this example using the Employees table in the Northwind sample database that comes with Microsoft Access. The Employees table includes data about all the employees, including the managers, but the Reports To field contains the employee ID value, not the name of the manager. To see the manager's name in a query result instead of the employee ID, you need to put two copies of the same table in the query design. Then draw a relationship between the tables to link the fields in a self-join.

To avoid having two column headings that are the same in the query result, right-click in the column with the self-joined field and then click Properties. In the Field Properties dialog box, click the General tab and type a name, such as **Reports To**, in the field's Caption property. When you run the query, you see records only for those employees who have a value in the EmployeeID field. The employee ID value in the query result is replaced by the last name of that employee because of the self-join.

> **Tip**
>
> If you change the type of join in the relationships window, all instances of the related tables are affected. Changing the type of join in the query design window affects the relationship only for that query.

> **Tip**
>
> If you have enforced referential integrity, you won't see any order records without matching customers in the database when you run your query. The 1 at one end of the relationship line in the query design window and the ∞ symbol at the other end indicate that you have enforced referential integrity. If you haven't, no symbols appear.

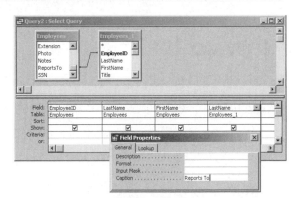

The records aren't in the order I wanted

Source of the problem

Ducks are often easier to line up than the results of an Access query, in spite of all the help you can get with the query design. In the tables, the records are orderly but when you combine them in a query, the order of things seems to get turned around. You might have selected the wrong sort order, or set it for the wrong field in the query design grid. If you're sorting on more than one field, you might not have arranged the fields in the right order in the query.

Here are a couple more reasons the records might not be in the order you want:

- You hid the field you're sorting on in the query results.
- You're trying to sort on a field added to the query by dragging the all-fields asterisk (*) to the query grid.

The following steps show ways to overcome these difficulties.

How to fix it

To select the field to sort on and set up the sort order, do the following:

1. In the database window, select the query and then click Design.

2. In the query design grid, examine the sort order selected in the Sort row of the fields.

3. For any field you don't want to sort by, remove the sort settings by choosing Not Sorted from the Sort row's drop-down list.

4. In the Sort row for the field you do want to sort by, select the sort setting you want.

5. If you selected a setting in the Sort row for more than one field, make sure the field you want to sort by first is at the left, with the other sorting fields arranged in sort precedence from left to right.

6. If the sorted field doesn't appear in the query result, make sure the Show box is selected for that field.

If you added all the fields to the grid by dragging the asterisk from the field list and want to sort by one of the fields, do the following:

1. Open the query in Design view.

2. From the list of fields, drag the field you want to sort by to the query design grid.

3. In the Sort row, set the sort order for the field.

4. Clear the Show box to keep from displaying two copies of the field and then run the query. ▶

5. Repeat these steps with other fields if you want to sort on more than one field. Be sure to arrange them from left to right in the order you want the sort carried out.

Seeing is believing

You might want to see the fields in the result of a query in an order that's different from the one in which they're set up in the query design grid. If you sorted on multiple fields in the design grid, you can add a copy of the field you want in a different position to the query grid, placing it as it should appear in the query result. (In the figure, you see that a copy of the City field has been added.) Clear the Show box in the columns used for multiple-field sorting so that you won't see two copies of the field values in the query results. ▶

The query doesn't display the number of columns I expected

Source of the problem

What you expect and what you get can be very different, whether you're opening a gift or dropping a quarter in a slot machine in Las Vegas. Sometimes you expect a lot more than you see, and sometimes you expect a lot less. Access queries can surprise you just as much.

If you see too many columns in the query result, you might have included more fields than you need in the query design. You might have used the asterisk (*) shortcut to place all the fields from a table in the design grid. You might also have set one of the default options that includes all the fields from the tables and queries underlying a query, whether or not you add them to the query design grid.

If your query shows too few columns, you might not have included the fields or tables you need. Another cause of this problem could be that you hid the fields by clearing the Show box in the design grid. If you do this, the columns don't show up in the results. Hidden columns can further complicate things because they don't always stay where you left them in the design grid. When you save and close a query, Access, in a frenzy of removing clutter, moves hidden columns to which you added selection criteria or sort settings to the far right of the design grid, possibly off the screen and out of view. If a field has no criteria or sort settings, it's removed altogether from the design grid, and when you reopen the query in Design view, the field is no longer there.

The following steps show you how to address these problems.

How to fix it

If you see too many columns, try this:

1. Open the query in Design view.

2. If you added the fields to the query design grid using the asterisk shortcut, delete the column with the asterisk from the design grid and add the fields you need in the query, one at a time, by dragging the field name from the field list to the query grid.

3. If you need some of the fields for selection criteria, sorting, or calculations but don't want to see these fields in the query results, hide them by clearing the Show box for those fields.

4. If you still see all the fields from the underlying tables even though they're not included in the design grid, click Options on the Tools menu.

5. Click the Tables/Queries tab and then clear the Output All Fields check box. ▶

6. Click OK.

Tip

Changing the Output All Fields setting affects all new queries, not existing ones. So if you're starting a new query and you change this option afterward, delete the query and start over so the change will take effect.

[Options dialog box showing the Tables/Queries tab with Table design settings: Default field sizes (Text: 50, Number: Long Integer), Default field type: Text, AutoIndex on Import/Create: ID;key;code;num. Query design section with Show table names checked, Output all fields unchecked, Enable AutoJoin checked. Run permissions with User's selected. SQL Server Compatible Syntax (ANSI 92) options.]

If you see too few columns in your query, do the following:

1. In the database window, select the query and then click the Design button.

2. In the list of fields for the table, double-click the name of the field you want to add to the query. If you want a field in a specific place in the query design grid rather than in the first empty column, click the field name in the list of fields and drag it to that position in the grid.

3. To add another table or query to the query you're working with so you have access to those fields as well, click the Show Table button on the toolbar.

4. In the Show Table dialog box, click the Both tab and select the table or query you want to add. Then click Add.

5. Click Close in the Show Table dialog box and then add the fields you want to the query, following the process described in step 2.

6. To restore any fields that Access doesn't display in the query result, scroll right in the grid and select the Show box. ▶

[Query2: Select Query window showing three tables: Products, Order Details, and Suppliers, with the query design grid below.]

Field:	ProductID	ProductID	CategoryID	ProductName	SupplierID	CompanyName	ContactName
Table:	Products	Order Details Exten	Products	Order Details Exl	Products	Suppliers	Suppliers
Sort:			Ascending			Descending	
Show:	☑	☐	☐	☑	☐	☐	☐
Criteria:							
or:							

My query takes too long to return the results

Source of the problem

If you have time to refill your coffee cup while your query is running, the query is too slow. If the coffee cools off before the results of the query appear, it's *really* too slow. A lot of factors can affect a query's performance. You can correct or at least minimize many of these. The following list includes the most common causes of poor query performance:

● A field linking the tables isn't indexed, or fields used for sorting or selection criteria in the query aren't indexed.

● Some of the fields in the query are defined with an unnecessarily large data size. This wastes disk space and slows the query.

● You included more fields than you need in the query. Queries with lots of fields take more time to display their results.

The following solutions describe how to correct or avoid these problems.

How to fix it

To create indexes for the fields in the tables the query is based on, do the following:

1. In the database window, select a table included in the query and then click Design.

2. In the Field Name column, select the field that is used to link the tables in the query.

3. In the Field Properties area, click the General tab, click in the Indexed property box, and select Yes (Duplicates OK). ▶

4. Repeat step 3 for each field you plan to sort on or set criteria for in the query.

5. Look at the fields with Text as their data type and reduce the Field Size property to the smallest size that will hold your data. The default field size for a text field is 50 characters, but your field might require fewer.

6. Look at the fields with Number as their data type, and reduce their field size if possible. The Field Size property setting determines the amount of disk space used by the number field. For example, the Byte field size setting can be used to store positive integers from 1 through 255 and uses only 1 byte of disk space. An Integer field size setting can be used to store larger positive or negative integers and uses only 2 bytes. ▶

7. Save and close the table.

To reduce the number of fields in a query, do the following:

1. Open the query in Design view.

2. In the query design grid, remove any fields you don't need in the query results.

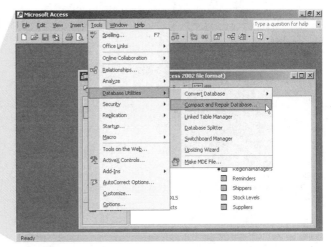

3. If you need a field for sorting or for criteria but don't need to see the field in the query result, clear the Show box for that field.

More help speeding up queries

Access has a couple of other tools you can use to help speed up your queries. The Performance Analyzer looks at your query design and comes up with suggestions, recommendations, and ideas that might help the query's performance. To run the Performance Analyzer, point to Analyze on the Tools menu and click Performance. Click the Queries tab and select all the queries you want to examine, or click Select All to give them all the once-over. Click OK. After a few moments, the Analyzer displays its advice. You can review and accept the recommendations individually or all at once.

As you work with your database, it becomes scattered around on the disk. Queries take longer to find records for display or update. Access provides a tool you can use to consolidate your database for easier data retrieval. Point to Database Utilities on the Tools menu and then click Compact And Repair Database. ▶

I can't sort on a lookup field in my query

Source of the problem

Lookup fields were invented to make entering data faster and more accurate. All you need to do is select a value from the list, and you're home free. Unfortunately, that's not quite true—in spite of the old saying "What you see is what you get." What you see in a lookup field is a far cry from what Access stores in the record. And when you try to sort on a lookup field in a query, you're sorting on the stored value not the value you're looking at. If your query results aren't in the order you expected, you might be sorting on a lookup field.

It's easy to find and fix the problem, as the following solution demonstrates.

How to fix it

If you think the field you're trying to sort on is a lookup field, do the following:

1. Open the table the query is based on in Design view.

2. Select the field you're trying to sort on and then click the Lookup tab in the Field Properties area. If you see a SELECT statement in the Row Source property, the field is getting its value from another table or query. ▶

Tip
You might encounter a similar problem if you try to filter records in your query based on the value in a lookup field. When you filter on a lookup field, you must type the stored value in the Criteria row in the query grid. Unlike the sort order, a filter is not saved with the query design.

3. Close the table design window and open the query in Design view.

4. Run the query. You see that the records are not sorted correctly (by Supplier name in this example). ▶

5. Click in the column that contains the lookup field and then click Sort Ascending or Sort Descending on the toolbar. ▶

6. Click the View button to return to the query design and then click Save.

7. Click the View button again, and you see that the records are now sorted in the correct order because the sort order you set in the Datasheet view is saved with the query. ▶

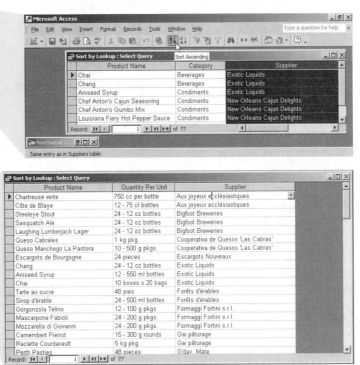

Where do lookup fields look?

The most popular sort of lookup field gets its values from another table or query. This is called a "lookup list." The biggest advantage of this type of lookup field is that the tables with the lookup field and the table with the values are related. When the values in the list change, the list is still available to the lookup field.

Another type of lookup field gets values from a list called a "value list." These values are entered in the Row Source property of the lookup field itself. This property is found on the Lookup tab in the Field Properties area of the table design window. Other properties of a lookup field determine which value is bound to the field and which is displayed on the screen.

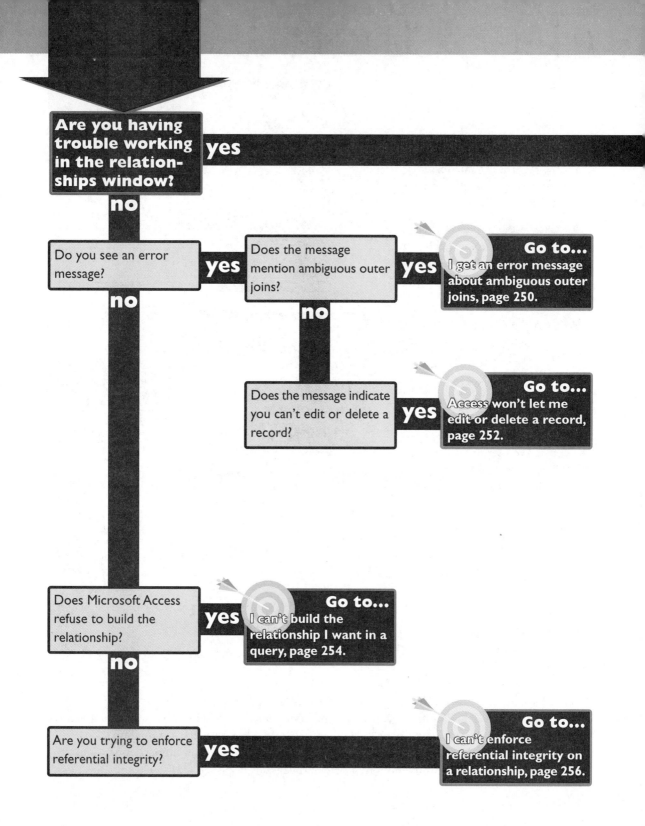

Are you having trouble working in the relationships window?

yes

no

Do you see an error message?

yes → Does the message mention ambiguous outer joins?

yes → **Go to...**
I get an error message about ambiguous outer joins, page 250.

no

Does the message indicate you can't edit or delete a record?

yes → **Go to...**
Access won't let me edit or delete a record, page 252.

no

Does Microsoft Access refuse to build the relationship?

yes → **Go to...**
I can't build the relationship I want in a query, page 254.

no

Are you trying to enforce referential integrity?

yes → **Go to...**
I can't enforce referential integrity on a relationship, page 256.

Relationships

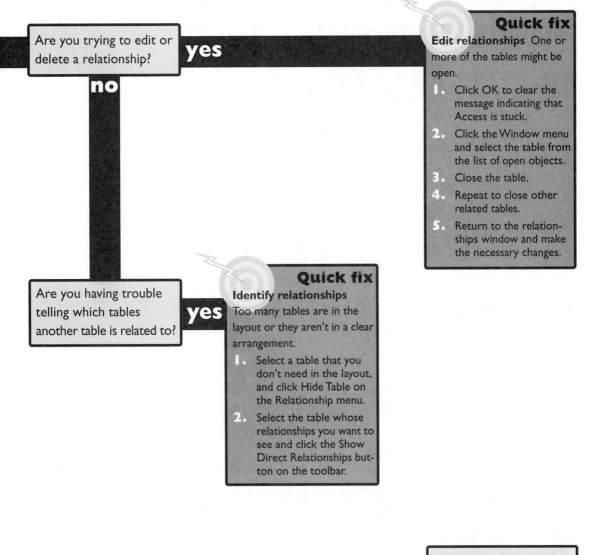

Are you trying to edit or delete a relationship?

yes

no

Are you having trouble telling which tables another table is related to?

yes

Quick fix

Edit relationships One or more of the tables might be open.

1. Click OK to clear the message indicating that Access is stuck.
2. Click the Window menu and select the table from the list of open objects.
3. Close the table.
4. Repeat to close other related tables.
5. Return to the relationships window and make the necessary changes.

Quick fix

Identify relationships Too many tables are in the layout or they aren't in a clear arrangement.

1. Select a table that you don't need in the layout, and click Hide Table on the Relationship menu.
2. Select the table whose relationships you want to see and click the Show Direct Relationships button on the toolbar.

If your solution isn't here, check these related chapters:

- Queries, simple select, page 236
- Table design, page 290

Or see the general troubleshooting tips on page xv.

I get an error message about ambiguous outer joins

Source of the problem

Microsoft Access is usually pretty good about understanding what you want it to do. But even Access becomes confused once in a while, especially when your instructions can be interpreted in a couple of ways. That's sometimes the case when you create a query with several tables and at least one of the joins is an outer join. An outer join selects all the records in one table but only those records from the related table that have matching values in the field joining the tables. Access informs you of its confusion by showing an error message complaining of "ambiguous outer joins." This means you related the tables in such a way that you get different results depending on the sequence in which you applied the table relationships.

The best way to fix this problem is to create two queries—the first to process one of the joins between two tables and the second to use the results of the first query with the third table. Here are the steps to follow.

How to fix it

1. Click OK to clear the error message and then close the query design window. You don't need to save changes to the ambiguous query. ▶

   > **Microsoft Access**
   >
   > The SQL statement could not be executed because it contains ambiguous outer joins. To force one of the joins to be performed first, create a separate query that performs the first join and then include that query in your SQL statement.
   >
   > OK   Help

2. In the database window, click Queries and then click New. In the New Query dialog box, click Design view and then click OK.

3. On the Tables tab in the Show Table dialog box, select the tables you want to join with an outer join, click Add to place them in the query, and then click Close.

4. In the field list, select the primary key field from one table and drag it to the matching field in the other table.

5. Right-click the relationship line between the tables and then click Join Properties on the shortcut menu.

6. In the Join Properties dialog box, select the outer join (option 2 or 3) that results in the records you want and click OK. ▶

   > **Join Properties**
   >
   > Left Table Name: Supervisor
   > Right Table Name: Jobs
   > Left Column Name: SuperID
   > Right Column Name: SuperID
   >
   > ○ 1: Only include rows where the joined fields from both tables are equal.
   > ○ 2: Include ALL records from 'Supervisor' and only those records from 'Jobs' where the joined fields are equal.
   > ● 3: Include ALL records from 'Jobs' and only those records from 'Supervisor' where the joined fields are equal.
   >
   > OK   Cancel   New

Relationships

7. From the field lists, drag the fields you want to display in the query results to the design grid.

8. Save and name the query.

9. Start a new query as you did in steps 1 and 2. In the Show Table dialog box, click the Queries tab, select the query you just created, and then click Add. Then, click the Tables tab and add the third table you want to use in your query. Click Close.

10. Drag the linking field from the query to the table. Access creates an inner join by default.

11. From the field lists, drag the fields you want to display in the query to the design grid.

12. Save and name the query.

13. Click the Run button. You see only the records with matching values in both linking fields. ▶

More about joins

Time out here for a few definitions to be sure we're on the same page. The type of join you specify tells Access to include specific records from specific tables in the query results. The most common type of join, the *inner join*, retrieves only those records with matching values in the fields linking the tables. An *outer join*, on the other hand, is one in which all records from one table are included, but only matching records from the other table are included. An outer join can be either left or right. A *left outer join* includes all the records from the parent table (the table on the "one" side of a one-to-many relationship) but only the matching records from the child table. A *right outer join* includes all the records from the child table and only the matching records from the parent table.

Access won't let me edit or delete a record

Source of the problem

All you're trying to do is clean up some of the tables in your database. Sounds simple enough—just change some field values and delete records you don't need anymore. But Access has a different slant on the edits and deletions you want to make and shows you a message that says, "The record cannot be deleted or changed because table '*tablename*' includes related records." The message shows the name of a table that's related to the one you're working with—a table that would be left with loose ends if your changes were carried out. This message appears because the tables are bound by *referential integrity*. Referential integrity helps preserve the relationships between the data in your database, but it also can cause error messages. For example, when you try to change the value of the primary key field in a record in the parent table that has one or more related records in the child table. You will also see a message when you try to delete a record from the parent table that still has related records in the child table.

Access realizes that keeping your data up-to-date and free of errors can be a time-consuming problem, so it provides two options for you to use when referential integrity is in force.

Here are the steps for how to implement these options.

How to fix it

To fix the problem with editing a table's primary key field, do the following:

1. With your database open, click Relationships on the Tools menu.

2. Right-click in the middle of the relationship line that links the two tables you want to work with, and then click Edit Relationship on the shortcut menu.

3. In the Edit Relationship dialog box, select the Cascade Update Related Fields check box.

4. Click OK.

5. Repeat steps 2 through 4 to add the Cascade Update Related Fields option to any other relationships involving the table you want to edit.

6. Close the relationships window.

7. In the database window, select the parent table and click Open. Make the necessary changes in the primary key values. Access doesn't prompt for confirmation for the updates.

Relationships

If you're trying to delete a record from the parent table and you are sure you want to delete related records from the child table, do the following:

1. Open the Edit Relationship dialog box, following steps 1 and 2 in the previous solution.

2. Select the Cascade Delete Related Records check box.

3. Click OK.

4. Follow steps 1, 2, and 3 to edit each relationship line that involves the table you want to delete records from.

5. Close the relationships window.

6. In the database window, select the parent table and click Open. Delete records as necessary.

7. Click Yes to confirm the deletion of all the related records in the child table as well as the parent record. ▶

> **Tip**
>
> You can set one cascade option or the other—you don't need to set them both.

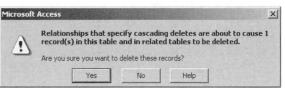

What exactly is referential integrity?

Referential integrity is a set of rules that tries to keep a database intact and free of loose ends. In a one-to-many table relationship, referential integrity ensures that no related records on the "many" side exist without a matching parent record on the "one" side. This means you can't accidentally delete a parent record that still has child records, and you can't change the primary key field in a record in the parent table if that record still has related records in the child table. The rules also apply to tables in a one-to-one relationship.

For you to set referential integrity, the matching field from the parent table must be a primary key or have a unique index. Both tables in the relationship must be in the same database, and the related fields must have the same data type, with this exception: an AutoNumber field can be related to a Number field with a field size set to Long Integer.

You can tell whether referential integrity has been enforced on a relationship by looking at the symbols that appear at the ends of the relationship line in the relationships window. In a one-to-many relationship, the line will show a 1 at the "one" end and an infinity sign (∞) at the "many" end. A one-to-one relationship shows a 1 at both ends of the line.

I can't build the relationship I want in a query

Source of the problem

When you first recognized the magic of relational databases, the sky was the limit. At last you had a tool to help you store all the data you needed and turn it into worthwhile information with the click of a button. You could relate tables just the way you wanted to and draw out all the information you needed. But now, when you try to get the most from your Access database, there seems to be relationship rules that tie your hands. The source of your problem might be your choice of where to create these relationships. You can create some relationships in the relationships window that you can't create when building a query. Here are a couple of problems you might run into when trying to relate two tables in a query design:

- You're trying to relate the tables using fields with different data types. For example, you're trying to relate an AutoNumber field to a text field. If you're doing this, you'll likely see an error message about a type mismatch.

- You're trying to use a memo, OLE Object, or hyperlink field in the relationship, which is not permitted.

  The following solutions describe ways to correct these problems.

How to fix it

If you see an error message in the Query Design view about a type mismatch, do the following:

1. Click OK to clear the message.

2. Right-click the relationship line between the tables and click Delete on the shortcut menu.

3. If the primary key field in the parent table is an AutoNumber field, select that field and drag it to the matching Number field in the child table. This creates the relationship line between the tables.

4. If the child table has no matching field with the Number data type, close the query design window. Then, in the database window, select the child table and click Design.

5. Add a field to the table, selecting Number from the Data Type list. On the General tab in the Field Properties area, set the Field Size property to Long Integer.

6. Save the table design.

7. If no data has been entered in either table in the query or if data has been entered only in the parent table, return to the query design and set the relationship between the AutoNumber field in the parent table and the new Number field in the child table. If you have already entered data in the child table, open that table in Datasheet view and edit the records to include values in the new number field to match values in the AutoNumber field of the parent table. Then return to the query design.

If you have tried to relate the tables with a memo field and you get an error message, try the following:

1. Click OK to clear the message and then close the query design. ▶

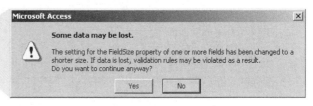

2. In the database window, select the table with the memo field and then click Design.

3. If the memo field doesn't contain more than 255 characters in any record and you know you won't ever need more than that, simply change the field data type by selecting the memo field and choosing Text from the Data Type list. Click the Save button on the toolbar.

4. If you get an error message because a record contains too many characters, switch to Datasheet view and edit the memo field data to fewer than 256 characters or click Yes to truncate the excessive text if you know you don't need it. ▶

5. Save the table and return to the query design.

6. Draw the relationship line between the tables and continue with the query design.

I can't enforce referential integrity on a relationship

Source of the problem

Creating happily related tables is one thing, but it's another to insist that they all toe the line and obey the house rules. When you first build relationships between your tables in the relationships window, you're the one responsible for making sure the fields creating the relationships have the same data type and content. After all, if one field contains dates and the other contains text, no values are going to match.

To help you crack the whip and get your tables to play by the rules, Access provides a tool. This tool could have been named something simpler than "referential integrity," but that's what we've got. Referential integrity keeps records in a database tightly integrated. Choosing to enforce referential integrity is easiest before you enter any data in the tables, but you can try to do it later. If you tried to apply referential integrity to a table relationship in the relationships window and encountered a problem, the existing data in the tables already violates referential integrity. A record in the child table might have no matching record in the parent table. The field in the parent table you are using to form the relationship might also not be a primary key.

The following steps show how to correct these problems.

How to fix it

If you see a message that existing data violates referential integrity, follow these steps:

1. Click OK to clear the message.

2. Clear the Enforce Referential Integrity option and then click Create to go ahead with the relationship.

If the matching field in the child table is a primary key field, you must follow these steps to remove the designation and change it to an indexed field that allows duplicates first:

1. Open the table in Design view and select the primary key field.

2. Click the Primary Key toolbar button.

3. Change the Indexed property in the Field Properties area to Yes (Duplicates OK). If you have created a one-to-one relationship, you can set the Indexed property to Yes (No Duplicates).

4. Save and close the table.

Next, create a query that compares matching fields in the parent and child tables as follows:

1. Switch to the database window, click Queries, and then click New. In the New Query dialog box, select Design view and then click OK. On the Tables tab in the Show Tables dialog box, select the two tables and click Add to place them in the query. Click Close.

2. Drag the primary key field in one table to the matching field in the other table to create the relationship line.

3. From the field lists, drag the matching fields from both tables to the design grid.

4. Right-click the join line and then click Join Properties on the shortcut menu.

5. In the Join Properties dialog box, select the join type that includes all the records on the many (child) side and only those on the one (parent) side that match. This way you can see which child records have no parent.

6. Click OK, and then click the Run button.

7. In the query datasheet, edit the records so that each field in the child table matches one in the parent table and then close the datasheet.

8. On the Tools menu, click Relationships. In the relationships window, right-click the relationship line between the tables and choose Edit Relationship. In the Edit Relationship dialog box, select Enforce Referential Integrity.

If you see a message about the parent table not having a unique index, try these steps: ▶

1. Click OK to clear the message.

2. Right-click in the parent table title bar and click Table Design on the shortcut menu.

3. Select the field you want to use in the relationship and set the Indexed property to Yes (No Duplicates). ▶

4. Save and close the table design window.

5. In the Edit Relationships dialog box, select the Enforce Referential Integrity check box and then click OK.

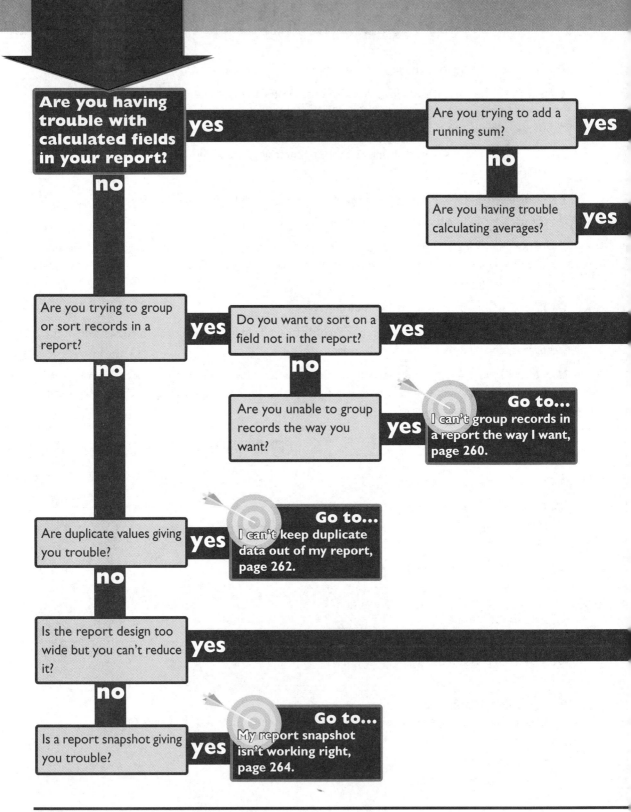

Are you having trouble with calculated fields in your report? — **yes**

Are you trying to add a running sum? — **yes**

no

Are you having trouble calculating averages? — **yes**

no

Are you trying to group or sort records in a report? — **yes**

Do you want to sort on a field not in the report? — **yes**

no

Are you unable to group records the way you want? — **yes**

Go to...
I can't group records in a report the way I want, page 260.

no

Are duplicate values giving you trouble? — **yes**

Go to...
I can't keep duplicate data out of my report, page 262.

no

Is the report design too wide but you can't reduce it? — **yes**

no

Is a report snapshot giving you trouble? — **yes**

Go to...
My report snapshot isn't working right, page 264.

Reports, creating

Go to...

I can't calculate averages without including the zero values, page 266.

Quick fix

Calculating running sums You need to place the control for the running sum in the detail section of the report, not the group footer section.

1. Add a text box control to the detail section of your report.
2. Right-click the control, and then click Properties.
3. On the Data tab, enter the name of the field you want to tally in the Control Source property box.
4. In the Running Sum property, select Over All to keep the sum going through the report or Over Group to reset the sum to zero at each new group.

Quick fix

Sorting on absent fields You don't have to show the field in the report to sort records on it.

1. Make sure the field you want to sort on is in the table or query used by the report.
2. Click Sorting And Grouping on the View menu.
3. Enter the field name in the Field/Expression box and choose the Sort Order.

Quick fix

My report is too wide A line is probably drawn across the report design.

1. Drag the report section boundaries down one at a time to locate lines drawn to the right margin.
2. Resize the lines to fit the width you want.
3. Restore the section heights to their original settings.

If your solution isn't here, check these related chapters:

- Controls, viewing data, page 22
- Controls, placing and formatting, page 12
- Reports, previewing and printing, page 268

Or see the general troubleshooting tips on page xv.

I can't group records in a report the way I want

Source of the problem

They say there's safety in numbers. If that old adage is true, a report that groups a bunch of records to come up with conclusions can be a big help at the next corporate get-together. Microsoft Access makes it so easy to group records to display summaries of your data that it's hard to imagine anything going wrong. But Murphy is alive and well—even in Access.

Some of the problems you might have faced include the following:

● Your records aren't really grouped. You might have failed to include a group header or footer in the report design. You must set one of these properties to Yes in the Sorting And Grouping dialog box, or the records will be just sorted and not grouped.

● You're grouping by two different fields, and you grouped the fields in the wrong sequence. For example, if you're trying to group by category and then by country, you might have set the country group above the category group in the Sorting And Grouping dialog box. This would group by country first and then by category sold to each country. ▶

The following solutions provide ways to overcome these problems.

How to fix it

To make sure your records are grouped, follow these steps:

1. In the database window, select the report and then click Design.

2. On the View menu, click Sorting And Grouping.

3. In the Field/Expression column, click in the row for the field you entered earlier for grouping the records.

Tip

If you don't want to show any information in the Group Header or Group Footer section, you can reduce its height to nothing.

4. In the Group Properties pane, set either the Group Header or Group Footer property to Yes. You can set both to Yes, if you like. ▶

5. Close the Sorting And Grouping dialog box, click the Save button, and then preview the report.

To change the order of record grouping in the report, do the following:

1. Open the report in Design view and then click Sorting And Grouping on the View menu.

2. In the Sorting And Grouping dialog box, click the row selector (the small gray box at the left end of the row) for the field you want to move. ▶

3. Drag the row selector up or down to position the field where you want it.

4. Close the Sorting And Grouping dialog box and then click the Preview button to view the report.

Heads up on headers

When you have large groups of records that span more than one page in your report, it's handy to have the group header information printed on the spillover pages. By doing this, you can keep track of the column headings and other information without having to look back at the page that contains the group header. To do this, click the section boundary for the Group Header section and then click the Properties button on the toolbar. Set the Repeat Section property to Yes. Unfortunately, if a new group happens to start at the top of a page, you might see two lines of the group header information.

Tip

If you change the Group Header or Group Footer property to No, you delete any controls you placed in those sections of the report.

I can't keep duplicate data out of my report

Source of the problem

Long lists of duplicate values not only clutter up a report, they can also cause someone studying your report (like your boss) to doze off as her eye follows the tedious repetition. A report is cleaner and more effective if you remove duplicate data and print the value only once. But the other values in the records are important too, so you can't simply leave the records out. You might have had trouble in a couple of situations:

- You created a report with records that are sorted on one or more fields and have found many records with the same values in those fields clustered together. Although all the information is important, you still don't need the repetition. ▶

- You grouped the records by one or more fields, and the duplicate values all appear in the Detail section because they occur in each record.

The following solutions describe ways to solve problems with duplicate data in reports.

How to fix it

If your report is based on sorted records, follow these steps:

1. In the database window, select the report and then click Design.

2. Click the control for the field in which duplicate values are showing and then click the Properties button on the toolbar.

3. In the property dialog box, set the control's Hide Duplicates property to Yes. ▶

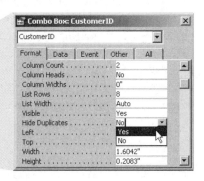

4. Repeat steps 2 and 3 for controls for other fields you sorted on that found duplicate values.

5. Click the Save button and then preview the report. ▶

If you grouped records in the report and don't want to see the duplicates in the detail section, you can use one of the two following ways to solve the problem, depending on whether you want the detail value printed on the same line or in the group header. If you want to print the duplicate value on the same line as the first record in the detail section, leave the field in the detail section of the report and then follow steps 2 and 3 in the previous solution for each control that contains duplicate values. If you don't need the duplicate value printed on the same line as the first detail record, follow these steps:

1. Open the report in Design view.

2. Drag the Detail section border down to make room in the Page Header section.

3. Click the field in the Detail section and drag it to the Page Header section. ▶

4. Click the Preview button to view the report.

My report snapshot isn't working right

Source of the problem

Whoever invented the report snapshot is a genius and an honest supporter of preserving our forests. Report snapshots, which were introduced in Microsoft Access 2000, provide a way to distribute a high-fidelity version of a report, preserving the layout, graphics, and other embedded objects without printing a gazillion copies on paper. A snapshot is a separate file that can be e-mailed to anybody. Then they can print as much of the report as they need to read.

But just because the report snapshot is a great invention doesn't mean it can't cause trouble. For example, you might have had a problem creating or opening a snapshot. If you have permission to open the file and it is in fact a snapshot file (with an .snp file extension), it might be too big for the disk space available on your computer. Or you might not have the Snapshot Viewer program installed. Access usually installs the viewer when you create a report snapshot, but you might not have created and saved one yet.

Another problem you might have encountered is that you created and saved the report snapshot, and now you can't find it. The snapshot is saved as a separate file outside the Access database. You decide where to store the file when you export the report as a snapshot.

The following solutions describe how to address these problems.

How to fix it

If you see a message that the snapshot file is too big for remaining disk space, do the following:

1. On the Windows desktop, click the Start button and point to Programs.

2. Click Windows Explorer. (Depending on your version of Windows, you might need to point to Accessories first.)

3. Select a folder that you use often, such as My Documents, and on the View menu, click Details.

4. On the View menu, point to Arrange Icons and click By Size.

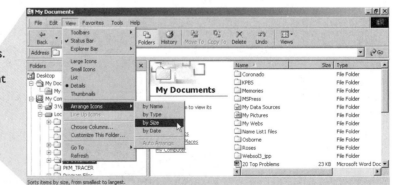

5. Scroll down to the bottom of the list, select large files that you no longer need, and then click Delete on the File menu.

6. Continue deleting files until you have enough disk space to save the report snapshot.

If the Snapshot Viewer isn't installed, you have not created any report snapshots yet. Run the Microsoft Office Setup program again to add it.

1. To start the setup, click Start on the Windows taskbar, point to Settings, and then click Control Panel.

2. Double-click Add/Remove Programs and then select Microsoft Office XP.

3. Depending on your version of Windows, click Add/Remove or Change. Follow the instructions in the series of dialog boxes to install the Snapshot Viewer, which is found in the Microsoft Access for Windows expanded list of features.

If you exported a report to a report snapshot and can't find the snapshot, the first place to look is where the file would be stored by default:

1. In the database window, select a report.

2. On the File menu, click Export.

3. In the Export Report dialog box, select Snapshot Format in the Save As Type box. ▶

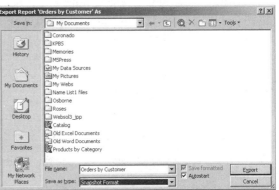

4. If you see the file you want, note the folder that's open, click Cancel, and return to the database window.

5. On the Windows desktop, click Start, point to Programs, and then click Windows Explorer. (Depending on your version of Windows, you might need to point to Accessories first.)

6. In the Folders pane, open the folder you viewed in step 4. ▶

7. In the right pane, double-click the snapshot file you want to view. The Snapshot Viewer starts automatically.

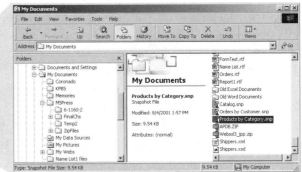

I can't calculate averages without including the zero values

Source of the problem

It's time to work on income projections for the next few quarters, and you need to figure out how the discounts you gave your best customers worked out. In a report to your manager, you want to include the average discount that was awarded on each product.

You've handled null values in your number and currency fields by setting the default value of the fields to 0. But now those zeros are coming back to bite you when you want to find the average of the values in that field. The null-turned-zero values are giving you the wrong results. What you need to see in the report is the average of all the non-zero values.

To do this, you need to count the non-zero values and use that number when you compute the average. The following steps show you how.

How to fix it

1. Open the report you're working with in Design view.

2. If the toolbox is not displayed, click the Toolbox button on the toolbar.

3. In the toolbox, click the Text Box icon and then click in the report's Detail section to add an unbound text box.

4. Click the Properties button on the toolbar.

5. Click the Data tab. In the Control Source property box, type an expression that counts the records with values in them, excluding records with zero values. For example, type an expression such as **=IIf([Discount]=0 Or [Discount] Is Null,0,1).** The IIf function adds 1 to the number of records counted only when the value in the field in which you are calculating the average (in this example, Discount) is not 0 or null.

Text Box: Text10	✕
Text10	▼

Format | Data | Event | Other | All

Control Source	=IIf([Discount]=0 Or [Discount] Is Null,0,1)
Input Mask	
Running Sum	No

6. Click in the Running Sum property box and select Over Group to restart counting with each new group.

7. Click the Other tab. In the Name property box, type a name for the control, such as **CountDisc**. Close the Properties dialog box. ▶

```
Text Box: Text10                                    ×
Text10                                  ▼
Format | Data | Event | Other | All
Name . . . . . . . . . . . . . . . CountDisc
Vertical . . . . . . . . . . . . . No
Tag . . . . . . . . . . . . . .
```

8. On the View menu, click Sorting And Grouping. Set the Group Footer property to Yes and then close the Sorting And Grouping dialog box. ▶

```
Sorting and Grouping                                ×
      Field/Expression              Sort Order
ProductID                      Ascending

                     Group Properties
Group Header      Yes
Group Footer      Yes
Group On          Yes        Display a footer for this group?
Group Interval    No
Keep Together     No
```

9. In the toolbox, click the Text Box icon and add a text box control to the report's Group Footer section. Click the Properties button on the toolbar.

10. Click the Data tab. In the Control Source property box, type an expression that computes the average for the records; for example, **=Sum([Discount])/[CountDisc].** The Sum function totals the values in the Discount field, including the records containing 0. That total is then divided by the number of non-zero and non-null values, which is calculated by the expression you typed in the control named CountDisc. ▶

```
Text Box: Text19                                    ×
Text19                                  ▼
Format | Data | Event | Other | All
Control Source . . . . . . . . . =Sum([Discount])/[CountDisc]  ▼ ...
Input Mask . . . . . . . . . . .
Running Sum . . . . . . . . . . No
```

11. Edit the label for the text box you added to the Group Footer section so it reflects the value you are calculating.

12. Right-click the section label for the report's Detail section and then click Properties.

13. On the Format tab, set the Visible property to No. ▶

```
Report1 : Report                                    _□×
  . . . 1 . . . 2 . . . 3 . . . 4 . . . 5 . . . 6
Report Header
Order Details          Section: Detail               ×
Page Header       Detail                        ▼
  Product ID      Format | Data | Event | Other | All
ProductID Header  Force New Page . . . . . . . None
                  New Row Or Col . . . . . . . None
  ProductID       Keep Together . . . . . . . Yes
Detail            Visible . . . . . . . . . . No
                  Can Grow . . . . . . . . .  Yes
           Discount         No          =IIf([Discount]=0 Or [Discount]
ProductID Footer
  Average Discount            =Sum([Discount])/[CountDisc]
Page Footer
=Now()                            ="Page " & [Page] & " of " & [Pages]
Report Footer
```

Reports, previ

Are you trying to preview a report? — **yes** → **Is data missing from the report preview?** — **yes**

no ↓   **no** ↓

Do you see blank pages? — **yes** →

Go to...
When I print my report, every other page is blank, page 270.

Are you prompted for a report title you don't expect? — **yes**

no ↓

Are your grouped records split over pages? — **yes** →

Quick fix

The Keep Together properties are not set correctly.

1. Open the report in Design view and then click Sorting And Grouping on the View menu.
2. Set the Keep Together group property to With First Detail.
3. Close the Sorting And Grouping dialog box.
4. Right-click the group section bar and then click Properties.
5. Set the Keep Together property to Yes.

no ↓

Are you printing a mailing label report? — **yes**

no ↓

Are you having trouble with a multiple-column report? — **yes** →

Go to...
My multiple-column report isn't printing right, page 274.

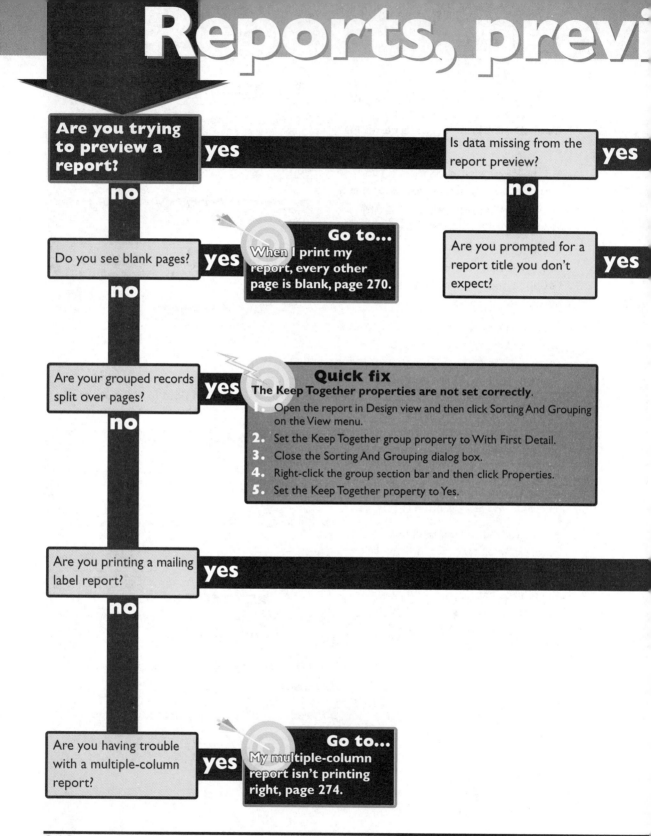

Quick fix

A report with missing data
You might be looking at the report in Layout preview, which shows just enough data for you to see how each section will look.

1. To preview the full report, close Layout preview by clicking Design View on the View menu.

2. On the View menu, click Print Preview.

Quick fix

The report's title control has been set up so that you can print the report with a different title each time.

1. Open the report in Design view.

2. Look for a text control in the report or page header containing a prompt expression —for example, =[Enter report title].

3. Delete the control.

4. Add a label to the report and add a fixed title.

5. Save the report design.

Are some of the mailing labels blank?

yes

Go to...
Some of my mailing labels are blank, page 272.

no

Do you want to print only specific labels?

yes

Go to...
I'm trying to print only selected labels, but Microsoft Access won't let me, page 276.

If your solution isn't here, check this related chapter:

- Reports, creating, page 258

Or see the general troubleshooting tips on page xv.

When I print my report, every other page is blank

Source of the problem

That you have to print on only one side of the page is bad enough, but to find that your report printed on only every other page is really too much. A quick look at the pages with words and numbers on them convinces you that you aren't missing any data from your report. Was your printer just taking a quick breath after pumping out each page?

Probably not. The real reason this problem occurs—and it occurs often—is very simple. Something in the design of your report is at odds with the page you're trying to print on. For example:

- The total width of the report plus the right and left margins exceeds the specified page width.

- Some controls have been placed outside the page dimensions, so some of the data appears on a spillover page or the page might be blank. This could occur if you used the Report Wizard.

- The settings in the Page Setup dialog box are overriding the settings in the report itself.

Here are the steps you need to take to solve these printing problems.

How to fix it

If every other page is printed blank, follow these steps:

1. In the database window, select the report and then click Design.

2. Look at the controls near the right edge of the report. Move or resize these controls so they're not as close to the edge.

3. Click the right edge of the report page (not the report design window) and drag it to the left to reduce the report width.

4. Click the Print Preview button and look at several pages.

5. If these steps didn't work, close the print preview window, click Page Setup on the File menu, and then click the Margins tab. ▶

6. Reduce the width of the right or left margin, or both, and then click OK.

7. Click the Print Preview button to view the report.

> **Tip**
>
> If you're previewing a report after making some design changes and you click Print Preview on the File menu, you will switch to Design view. This command is like a toggle—click once to turn it on and click again to turn it off.

Page Setup dialog box:

Margins	Page	Columns

Margins (inches)

Top: 1
Bottom: 1
Left: 1
Right: 1

Sample

☐ Print Data Only

OK   Cancel

If you used the Report Wizard to create the report, you probably didn't select the check box for the option named Adjust The Field Width So All Fields Fit On A Page. Because you can't go back and change settings in the Report Wizard, you have to correct this setting by hand.

1. With the report open in Design view, move the controls in all the sections to fit within the page width you need. For example, if you're printing on standard 8.5-by-11-inch paper, narrow the report design to 6.5 inches. Custom size paper might require a narrower printing width.

2. Click the right border of the report page and drag it to the width you want.

3. Click the Print Preview button to see whether you still have empty pages. If you do, return to Design view.

4. On the File menu, click Page Setup and then click the Columns tab.

5. In the Column Size area, select the Same As Detail check box. ▶

6. Click OK and then click the Print Preview button to view the report.

Page Setup

Margins	Page	Columns

Grid Settings
Number of Columns: 1
Row Spacing: 0"
Column Spacing: 0.25"

Column Size
Width: 5.5" Height: 1.375"
☑ Same as Detail

Column Layout
◉ Down, then Across
○ Across, then Down

OK   Cancel

Tip

Whenever you can, practice good report management. To avoid problems such as the ones mentioned in this solution, it's always a good idea to preview several pages of a report before printing it. It's even more important to catch errors before they show up in print if you're printing on expensive paper stock or mailing labels.

Tip

Even if most of the pages in your report contain text, your report could end up with a blank last page, which indicates that the report footer section is too large. To fix this, open the report in Design view, select the Report Footer section, and click the Properties button on the toolbar. Set the Height property to 0. Preview the report to see the results. You can also simply drag the lower boundary of the report footer up to reduce the height to 0.

Some of my mailing labels are blank

Source of the problem

One of the prized talents of Microsoft Access is its ability to take a table full of names and addresses and turn it into pages of printed mailing labels. Access can do this with the help of the Mail Merge feature in Microsoft Word or all on its own. Mailing label stock is expensive, and when you see a page of printed labels missing a few addresses, it's not a trivial problem. You can't really put the page back through the printer to fill up the blanks. Here are two reasons you might encounter blank mailing labels:

- If the blanks occur in groups, the underlying table might have no values in the fields you're sorting the records on. (This can also be true if the blank labels are scattered, but the problem isn't as obvious that way.)

- If you see a blank row at the bottom of the label page, you might be using a printer that skips the last row. Some printers set a large top margin by default, which causes the last row of labels to be printed on the next page. You don't lose any of the data, but the last row of labels on the sheet is wasted.

The following steps show how to solve these problems.

How to fix it

If you see groups of blank labels, do the following:

1. In the database window, click Queries and then click New.

2. In the New Query dialog box, select Design View and then click OK.

3. In the Show Table dialog box, click the Table tab, select the table that contains the names and addresses for the labels you're printing, click Add, and then click Close.

4. From the field list, drag the fields you want to use in the labels to the query grid.

5. In the Criteria row of each field, type **Is Not Null**. ▶

6. Click the Run button on the toolbar.

7. If you're happy with the results, save the query. If you're not, return to the Query Design view and make more changes to the selection criteria.

8. When you're satisfied with the query results, re-create the mailing labels based on the new query instead of the original table.

> **Tip**
>
> If you don't specify a sort order when you create labels with the Label Wizard, the labels are arranged in ascending order based on the first field in the table. If you base the labels on a query, they're sorted by the values in the column that is farthest to the left in the query grid.

If the last row of your labels is blank, try the following to fix the problem:

1. With your label report open in either Design view or Print preview, click Page Setup on the File menu.

2. Click the Margins tab and change the Top setting in the Margins section to 0.25. ▶

3. Click OK.

You don't have to depend on the Label Wizard

You can always create your own label design by starting a new multiple-column report with only a Detail section. After you set up the report, you can use several neat tools to create just the right disk label or personalized bookplates for the books in your library. The three functions that eliminate spaces when you put variable-length text values together are very useful for creating labels. The RTrim function removes spaces after the last character of text, while LTrim removes the spaces before the first character. Plain old Trim removes both the leading and trailing spaces. When you use these functions, be sure to add a space between the text controls or they will run together. For example, the expression **=Trim([FirstName]&" "&[LastName])** displays the first and last names separated by a space but without any leading or trailing spaces.

The Can Shrink and Can Grow field properties are also very useful. Setting Can Shrink to Yes prevents blank lines in mailing labels. Setting Can Grow to Yes adjusts the field vertically to accommodate extra lines in the printed label.

My multiple-column report isn't printing right

Source of the problem

You have a long list of items to print in a report, and you figured it can save space if you build the report to show the data in multiple columns. The Access Report Wizard is no help in this project, so you're on your own.

Multiple-column reports can present some unique problems that you don't have to worry about when designing regular reports. They require special consideration when it comes to arranging the data on the page and making sure that the report is readable—that the header information actually points to the corresponding data, for example. You might have encountered one of the following problems while building a multiple-column report:

● You told Access you wanted to see the data arranged in three columns in the report, but when you preview the report you see only one.

● You decided to add another column to the report, but Access warns you that there isn't enough room for the new column. In another case, the additional column is printed on the next page instead of with the other columns the way you wanted.

Here are the steps to take to combat these and other problems with multiple-column reports.

How to fix it

If you see only one column instead of the number you specified in the Page Setup dialog box, do the following:

1. In the database window, select the report and then click Design.

2. On the File menu, click Page Setup.

3. On the Columns tab, in the Column Size section, clear the Same As Detail check box.

4. In the Width box, type a smaller number. For example, if you're building a three-column report, type **2"** as the column width. Click OK.

5. In the report design window, right-click the group header bar and then click Properties on the shortcut menu.

6. On the Format tab, set the New Row Or Col property to Before Section. Set the Keep Together and Repeat Section properties both to Yes. ▶

7. Click the Print Preview button to view the report.

If you chose to arrange the columns across and then down in the Page Setup dialog box, you might see the warning message shown in the figure. ▶

Section: GroupHeader0

GroupHeader0

Format	Data	Event	Other	All

Force New Page . . . . None
New Row Or Col . . . . Before Section
Keep Together . . . . Yes
Visible . . . . Yes
Can Grow . . . . No
Can Shrink . . . . No
Repeat Section . . . . Yes
Height . . . . 0.25"
Back Color 16777215
Special Effect . . . . Flat

Tip

You won't see this warning message if you have the columns arranged down and then across. The column that doesn't fit on the page just moves to the next page in the report.

Microsoft Access

Some data may not be displayed.

There is not enough horizontal space on the page for the number of columns and column spacing you specified.

Click Page Setup on the File menu, click the Columns tab, and then reduce the number of columns or the size of the columns.

[OK]   [Cancel]

1. Click Cancel in the message box to return to the Report Design view.

2. On the File menu, click Page Setup.

3. On the Columns tab, reduce the number of columns and reduce the column width. Click the Margins tab, and reduce the width of the left and right margins. Click OK.

4. In the report design window, move or rearrange the controls in the report design to fit in the narrower column width.

Tip

The formula for calculating the maximum width of your multiple-column report is *Column width*Number of columns + Column spacing*(Number of columns − 1) + right margin + left margin*, which must add up to less than or equal to the page width.

5. Click the Print Preview button to view the report.

Designer tips for multiple-column reports

In a multiple-column report, the record data can all run together and be very confusing if you don't add a few cosmetic touches. If you arranged the columns so that the data reads down and then across the page ("snaking columns"), put a dividing line in the Group Footer section and set the Group Header section's New Row Or Col property to Before Section.

If you arranged the columns across and then down, put a dividing line in the Detail section beneath the detail controls and set the Group Header section's New Row Or Col property to Before & After.

I'm trying to print only selected labels, but Access won't let me

Source of the problem

You're trying to send a mailing to a sampling of your customers, but this group doesn't have anything in common that you can filter or sort on. For example, you can sort records to see everyone in a certain zip code or to see customers who are interested in cats. But you don't have a way to pick a few customers at random to send a letter to, asking what you're doing right and wrong.

Creating a filter or a query to select the records that you want to print a mailing label for is one thing, but selecting records at random is another. Not only do you want the records to be random this time, but you also want your choice to be different each time you round up a group of customers to send something to. The problem lies in the lack of a field you can use to select the records. If you had such a field, you could use it to line up records for printing. You could then clear the field after printing the selection so the slate is clean the next time around.

The following steps show you how to solve this problem.

How to fix it

Start by adding a field to the table that stores information about your customers.

1. Open your customer's table in Design view.

2. Add a field to the table's design and name it something like PrintYesNo.

3. From the Data Type drop-down list, select Yes/No.

4. On the General tab in the Field Properties area, be sure the Required property and the Indexed property are set to No. ▶

5. Save and close the table.

> **Tip**
>
> It is always a good idea to work with copies of any tables, forms, or reports that are operational in your application. When the new designs prove to be all right, you can rename them to replace the original objects.

Now add the new Yes/No field to a form in which you view customer information.

1. Open the customer's form in Design view.

2. On the View menu, click Properties.

3. In the Properties dialog box, change the Record Source property to the name of the table with the new Yes/No field. Keep the Properties dialog box open.

4. Open the toolbox and add a check box control to the form.

5. Click the Data tab in the Properties dialog box, click in the Control Source property, and select the name of the Yes/No field (PrintYesNo in this example).

6. Click the All tab and then type a name such as **YesPrint** in the Name property of the check box control. ▶

7. Change the label for the check box to read something like "Print this record."

8. Save and close the form.

Check Box: YesPrint	
YesPrint	

Format	Data	Event	Other	All

Name	YesPrint
Control Source	PrintYesNo
Default Value	
Validation Rule	
Validation Text	
Status Bar Text	
Visible	Yes
Display When	Always
Enabled	Yes
Locked	No
Triple State	No

In the next steps, create a query that selects the records with Yes in the PrintYesNo field.

1. On the Queries tab, click New, click Design View, and then click OK.

2. In the Show Table dialog box, select your updated customer's table, click Add, and then click Close.

3. Double-click the asterisk (*) in the customer's table field list.

4. Drag the PrintYesNo field to the first empty column in the query grid.

5. Clear the Show check box for the PrintYesNo field and type **Yes** in the Criteria row for this field. ▶

6. Save the query and name it something like SelectPrint.

7. Close the query design.

8. Open the report you use to print mailing labels in Design view and then click Properties on the View menu.

SelectPrint : Select Query	

CopyofCustomers	
PostalCode	
Country	
Phone	
Fax	
PrintYesNo	

Field:	CopyofCustomers.*	PrintYesNo				
Table:	CopyofCustomers	CopyofCustomers				
Sort:						
Show:	☑	☐	☐	☐	☐	
Criteria:		Yes				
or:						

I'm trying to print only selected labels, but Access won't let me

(continued from page 277)

9. In the Properties dialog box, click the Data tab and change the Record Source property to the name of the new query (SelectPrint in this example). ▶

10. Save and close the report.

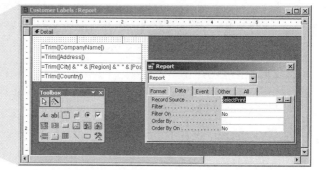

The last step in this process is to create a query that resets the Yes/No field to No.

1. In the database window, click Queries and then click New. Click Design View and then click OK.

2. In the Show Table dialog box, select the customer's table, click Add, and then click Close.

3. On the Query menu, click Update Query.

4. Drag the PrintYesNo field to the query design grid.

5. In the Update To row for the PrintYesNo field, type **No**.

6. In the Criteria row for the field, type **Yes**.

7. Save the query and give it a name like ClearYesNo. ▶

8. Close the query.

Now try out the selection process.

1. Open the customer's form in Form view.

2. Click the Print Record check box in a few records. Jot down the record number or customer name.

3. Close the form.

4. Open the label report in Print preview. You should see the labels only for those records you checked. ▶

5. Close the report.

6. In the database window, click Query and select the ClearYesNo update query.

7. Click Open.

8. Respond Yes twice to confirm that you want the records updated.

9. Open the customer form again to verify that all the records now have the PrintYesNo field cleared.

```
Customer Labels                                    _ □ ×

   Bon app'                 Blondel père et fils      Alfreds Futterkiste
   12, rue des Bouchers     24, place Kléber          Obere Str. 57
   Marseille  13008         Strasbourg  67000         Berlin  12209
   France                   France                    Germany

   Antonio Moreno Taquería  Berglunds snabbköp
   Mataderos 2312           Berguvsvägen 8
   México D.F.  05023       Luleå  S-958 22
   Mexico                   Sweden

Page: |◀ ◀        1    ▶ ▶| ◀
```

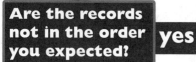

Are the records not in the order you expected? **yes**

no

Did you use the asterisk (*) to build the query and can't sort on one of the fields? **yes**

no

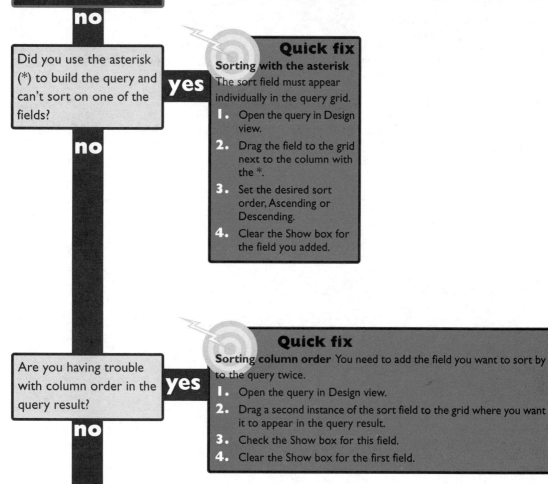

Quick fix

Sorting with the asterisk The sort field must appear individually in the query grid.

1. Open the query in Design view.
2. Drag the field to the grid next to the column with the *.
3. Set the desired sort order, Ascending or Descending.
4. Clear the Show box for the field you added.

Are you having trouble with column order in the query result? **yes**

no

Quick fix

Sorting column order You need to add the field you want to sort by to the query twice.

1. Open the query in Design view.
2. Drag a second instance of the sort field to the grid where you want it to appear in the query result.
3. Check the Show box for this field.
4. Clear the Show box for the first field.

Are you trying to sort a text field in numeric order? **yes**

Go to...

I can't sort a text field in numeric order, page 286.

Sorting

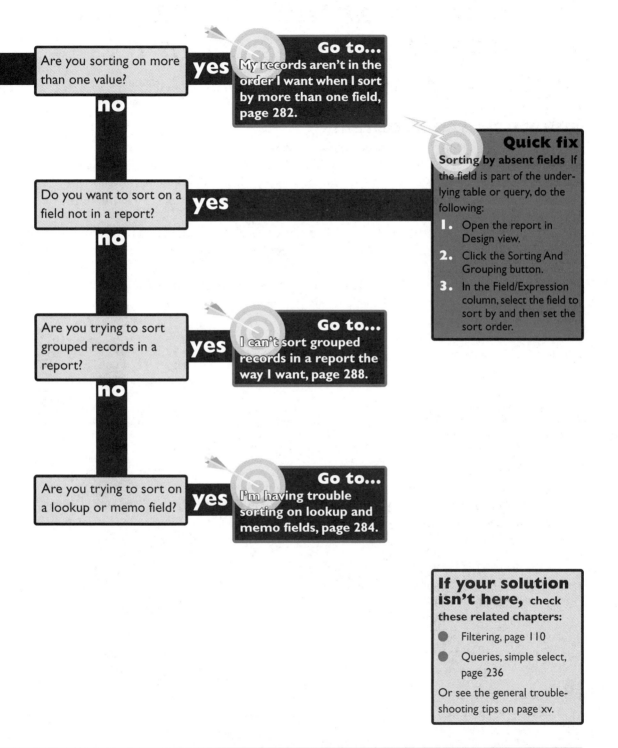

Are you sorting on more than one value?

yes → **Go to...** My records aren't in the order I want when I sort by more than one field, page 282.

no

Do you want to sort on a field not in a report?

yes → **Quick fix**

Sorting by absent fields If the field is part of the underlying table or query, do the following:

1. Open the report in Design view.
2. Click the Sorting And Grouping button.
3. In the Field/Expression column, select the field to sort by and then set the sort order.

no

Are you trying to sort grouped records in a report?

yes → **Go to...** I can't sort grouped records in a report the way I want, page 288.

no

Are you trying to sort on a lookup or memo field?

yes → **Go to...** I'm having trouble sorting on lookup and memo fields, page 284.

If your solution isn't here, check these related chapters:

● Filtering, page 110

● Queries, simple select, page 236

Or see the general troubleshooting tips on page xv.

My records aren't in the order I want when I sort by more than one field

Source of the problem

Sorting records in Microsoft Access can be easier than sorting your laundry on wash day. It's a very mechanical process that you shouldn't have to think about too much. But to make it simple and achieve the correct results, you have to get all the pieces together in the right places at the start. Access, like all computer programs, does only what you tell it to do, not what you wish or hope for. If you sort on the wrong field or in the wrong order, you'll get the wrong results.

When you're sorting on more than one field and you get the wrong results, the problem is usually that you sorted your data in the wrong sequence. Access first sorts by one field and then, within each group of equal values in that field, sorts by the next field, and so on. You tell Access which field to start with by where you place fields in a datasheet or the query grid. Access sorts in order of precedence, from left to right. In a report, you can sort on more than one field by using the Sorting And Grouping feature.

The following steps show you how to sort records by more than one field in a datasheet, query, and report.

> **Tip**
>
> If you're going to use a sort order often, save it with the table by clicking Yes when asked whether you want to save changes.

How to fix it

If you're sorting records by more than one field in a datasheet, follow these steps:

1. In the datasheet, drag the column containing the field you want to sort by first to the left of any other columns you want to sort by. This column doesn't need to be at the far left of the datasheet. ▶

2. Drag the other columns you want to sort by into position to the right of and adjacent to the first column. Each column will have precedence in sorting order over the column to its right.

3. Select the columns for the fields you want to sort by.

4. On the toolbar, click the Sort Ascending or Sort Descending button. The records will be sorted following the order in which you arranged the fields. ▶

If you need to sort by more than one field in a query, follow these steps:

1. In the database window, select the query and then click Design.

2. In the query grid, position the fields from left to right according to the sort order. The fields don't need to be in contiguous columns.

3. In the Sort row, set the sort order for each field. ▶

To sort records in a report by more than one field, do the following:

1. In the database window, select the report and then click Design.

2. On the View menu, click Sorting And Grouping.

3. In the Field/Expression list, select the name of the field by which you want to sort first.

4. In the Sort Order column, select the sort order you want.

5. Select the second field you want to sort by and then set the sort order for that field. ▶

6. Click the Preview button on the toolbar to see the results of the sort process.

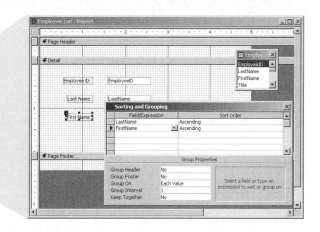

Tip

If you're sorting records in a form, you can sort on only one field so you have to use other methods to fine-tune the sort order. If you need to sort by more than one field, create a query on which to base the form. The form inherits the sort order you set up in the query. You can, of course, place the fields anywhere you want on the form design and the records will still be sorted correctly.

I'm having trouble sorting on lookup and memo fields

Source of the problem

Lookup fields can be deceiving. For one thing, they display a value that is not the same as the value stored in the table that the lookup field refers to. This means that sorting on a lookup field can have unsettling results. When you design a query to retrieve records and set the sort order for a lookup field in the query design grid, you sort on the stored value, not on the value that's displayed. If that isn't confusing enough, when you sort the records by the lookup field in the query results datasheet, you're sorting by the displayed value, not the stored value.

Sorting on memo fields can also present problems. You won't run into many situations where you'll want or need to sort records on the basis of what is usually miscellaneous text, and Microsoft probably didn't think anyone would want to so they didn't provide sorting for memo fields in all situations. If you set the Order By property for a form to the name of a memo field, it is ignored. In report design, a memo field name isn't included in the Sorting And Grouping dialog box. But in datasheets and form views, you can sort on a column or control for a memo field.

The following steps show you how to solve these problems.

Tip

The same sorting problem happens when you try to filter records in a query based on the value in a lookup field. To achieve the correct results, you must use the stored value in the filter expression instead of the displayed value in the Criteria cell of the query grid or in the advanced filter/sort window.

How to fix it

If you're trying to sort on a lookup field, follow these steps:

1. In the database window, select the query with the lookup field you want to sort by and click Open. Review the order of the returned records. ▶

2. Click in the lookup field's column in the query result datasheet.

LookTable Query : Select Query

TransID	Shippers	Date of Shipment	Paid
1	Speedy Express	7/23/2000	☑
4	Speedy Express	6/30/2000	☑
7	Speedy Express	10/23/2000	☐
2	United Package	9/13/2000	☐
5	United Package	6/30/2000	☑
9	United Package	8/19/2000	☐
3	Federal Shipping	8/31/2000	☑
6	Federal Shipping	5/25/2000	☑
8	Federal Shipping	9/18/2000	☐
(AutoNumber)			

Record: 1 of 9

Field:	TransID	ShipperID	Date of Shipment	Paid
Table:	LookTable	LookTable	LookTable	LookTable
Sort:		Ascending		
Show:	☑	☑	☑	☑
Criteria:				
or:				

3. On the toolbar, click one of the Sort buttons to sort by displayed values. ▶

4. Close the datasheet and respond Yes to save the sort order with the query result.

To sort on a memo field in a report, follow these steps:

1. In the database window, select the report and then click Design.

2. On the View menu, click Sorting And Grouping.

3. In the Field/Expression box, type the name of the memo field. (As you can see, the memo field name doesn't appear in the drop-down list.) ▶

4. In the Sort Order box, select the sort order you want, close the Sorting And Group dialog box, and then run the report.

Other tricky sorts

You can never sort on an OLE Object field, no matter where it is or how hard you try. You can, however, sort on the displayed value of a hyperlink field—the address, a file name, or other text—in a datasheet or form. If you want to sort on a hyperlink field, be sure to press Tab to reach the field rather than click in the field, which jumps to the hyperlink address.

You can sort on a hyperlink field in a report if you type the field name in the Field/Expression box in the Sorting And Grouping dialog box. Like a memo field, a hyperlink field is not included in the drop-down list in the box.

Tip

If you use a query that's sorted by a lookup field as the basis for a form, you encounter the same sorting problem. Click in the lookup field when the form is open in Form view and then click the Sort Ascending or Sort Descending button to fix the problem.

I can't sort a text field in numeric order

Source of the problem

Everyone has to mix apples and oranges once in a while. Sorting numeric data in a text field might sound unusual, but at times it's important to do so. For example, let's say you created a database to manage projects and the individual tasks within each project. To identify tasks, you use a field named ProjectItem, which is composed of a series of numbers followed by no more than one letter. In this field you have entries such as 101A, 25A, 25B, 59A, 632B, 250C, 1001C, and 5000.

When you sort a text field, the values are sorted from left to right in alphabetical order. When you sort a field with the Number data type, the values are sorted in numeric order. With a field such as ProjectItem, which includes both numbers and letters, you need to split the value into the numeric portion and the alphabetic portion to be able to sort the field numerically. You need to maintain a certain field value structure, however, to sort in this way. Notice that the sample ProjectItem values limit the number of trailing alphabetic characters to one. The normal sorting order for this field yields the results shown in the figure. ▶

The following steps show you how to solve the problem of sorting text fields in numeric order.

How to fix it

1. In the database window, click Queries and then click New. In the New Query dialog box, click Design View and then OK.

2. In the Show Table dialog box, select the table that includes the field with both numbers and letters. Click Add, and then click Close.

3. Drag the fields you want to the query grid, including the field with text and numbers. You probably want at least the primary key field in the query results.

4. In the Field row of a blank column in the query grid, type an expression such as **NBR: Val([ProjectItem])** to retrieve the number portion of the field value. NBR is the name of the expression. Val is a function that returns the numeric value of a field. (See "About the functions used in this solution" on the next page for a more detailed explanation.)

5. In another new column, add an expression such as **LTR: IIf(Val(Right$([ProjectItem],1)) =0, Right$([ProjectItem],1), "")**. The LTR expression isolates the alphabetic portion of the field value. It uses the IIf function to test the rightmost character in the field with numbers and letters. If the value of that character is 0, the character is alphabetic and is included in the sort process. Otherwise, it is ignored. ▶

6. Run the query to see the results of the new expressions. ▶

7. Return to the query design and in the Sort row for each of the new columns, select Ascending.

8. Clear the Show box in both columns.

9. Run the query again. ▶

About the functions used in this solution

The Val function returns the numeric value of the field and ignores any alphabetic characters. It actually stops reading the numbers as soon as it encounters the first non-numeric character. The IIf function returns one value if the condition specified in the function is true and another value if it is false. In our example, this function tests the rightmost character to see whether it is alphabetic (value = 0). If the character is alphabetic, Access adds the character to the value of the expression. If it is not, the function ignores that character completely. The Right$ function returns a string of characters containing a specified number of characters (1 in this case) from the right end of a string.

Tip

When you close a table after sorting the records in it, you're asked whether you want to save the changes you made, including the sort order. Click Yes to save the sort order. The next time you open the table, the records appear in the same order. If you click No, the records revert to their original primary key order.

Tip

Another way to sort numbers numerically in a text field is to add zeros to the start of the field to fill any spaces. The numbers will all be the same length and will sort in correct numeric order. If you know there will never be alphabetic characters in the field, simply change the data type of the field to Number.

I can't sort grouped records in a report the way I want

Source of the problem

You created an innovative report that clearly demonstrates an upward trend in your business. The report groups records by the values in one of the fields, but when you preview the report the records in the Detail section don't appear in the order you want. They're no longer in the order you established in the table or query you used as the basis for the report.

This problem happens because when you group records in a report, the sort order the report inherits from the table or query the report is based on is overridden by the settings you make in the Sorting And Grouping dialog box.

In this example, records were sorted by product within a product category, but after the records are grouped in the report, the sort order is disrupted. ▶

The following steps show how you can overcome this problem.

How to fix it

If the records in the Detail section of your report are not in the right sort order, do the following:

1. In the database window, select the report and then click Design.

2. On the View menu, click Sorting And Grouping.

3. In the first empty row below the row that sets the grouping, select the field you want to sort the records by from the drop-down list. ▶

4. Leave Group Header and Group Footer properties for this field set to No.

5. Click the View button on the toolbar to preview the report. ▶

More about inherited sort orders

If you haven't grouped records in a report but you still want to change the sort order the report inherits from its underlying table or query, open the report in Design view, click the

Properties button on the toolbar, and then set the Order By On property to Yes. Then type the field name you want to sort by in the Order By property box. If the field name contains a space, be sure to enclose it in brackets. If you want descending order instead of the default ascending order, type **DESC** after the field name. You can sort on more than one field by typing the field names separated by commas. You can also mix and match ascending and descending sort orders this way. For example, to sort the records by CategoryName in ascending order first and then by ProductName in descending order within each category, type **CategoryName, ProductName DESC** in the Order By property box. ▶

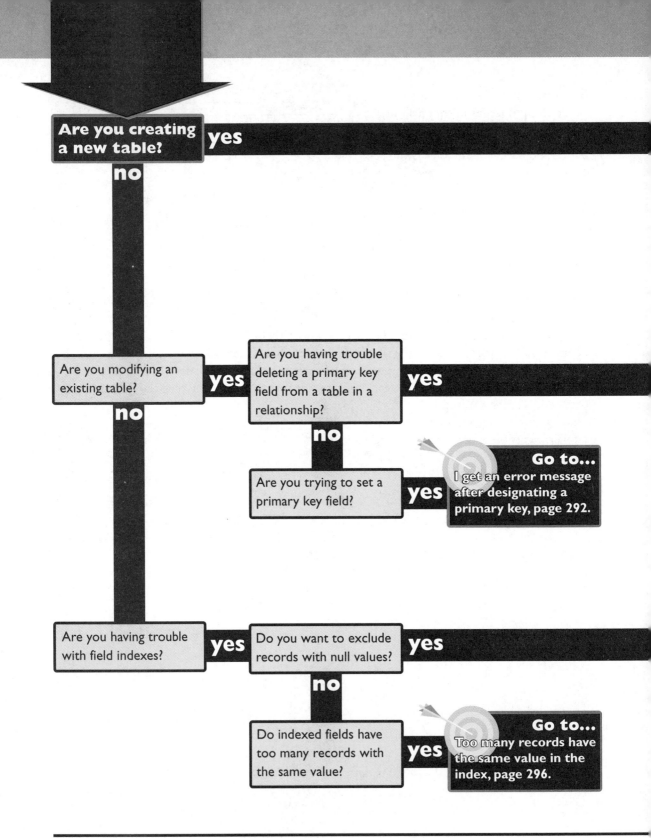

Are you creating a new table?

yes

no

Are you modifying an existing table?

yes → **Are you having trouble deleting a primary key field from a table in a relationship?** **yes**

no

no → **Are you trying to set a primary key field?** **yes** → **Go to...** I get an error message after designating a primary key, page 292.

Are you having trouble with field indexes? **yes** → **Do you want to exclude records with null values?** **yes**

no

Do indexed fields have too many records with the same value? **yes** → **Go to...** Too many records have the same value in the index, page 296.

Table design

Are you having trouble deciding which data types to use?

yes

Go to...
I don't know which data types and properties to choose in a new table, page 298.

no

Do you want to prevent data entry errors?

yes

Go to...
I need to control errors in my data, page 294.

Quick fix

Deleting a primary key First delete the relationship between the field and other tables.

1. On the Tools menu, click Relationships.
2. Right-click the relationship line from the primary key field to the table it's related to.
3. Click Delete on the shortcut menu.
4. Return to the table design and delete the primary key field.

Quick fix

Excluding null values from tables You need to set the field's Ignore Nulls property.

1. Open the table in Design view.
2. Click the Indexes button on the toolbar.
3. Select the name of the index from which you want to exclude null values.
4. If the index doesn't have a name, re-create and name the index.
5. Set the Ignore Nulls property to Yes.

If your solution isn't here, check these related chapters:

- Data, setting field properties, page 42
- Queries, action, page 192

Or see the general trouble-shooting tips on page xv.

I get an error message after designating a primary key

Source of the problem

Primary keys are the essential key (no pun intended) to relational databases. They ensure that you don't enter duplicate records, and they provide a means to relate information in different tables. Because the rules governing primary keys are strict, it's easy to encounter problems.

If you don't designate a primary key field before you save a new table design, Microsoft Access reminds you of this and asks whether you want to add one. You can click No to save the table without a primary key, but by clicking Yes, you have Access add an AutoNumber field named ID to the table and set it as the primary key. ▶

If you have entered records into a table before you designate a primary key field and then save the table, you might see a message indicating some trouble. For example, you might have entered duplicate values in the field you want to designate as the primary key—but values in the primary key field need to be unique. Or the primary key field in one or more records might be blank. You can't leave a blank (or null) value in a primary key field. ▶

The following solutions show how to get around these problems.

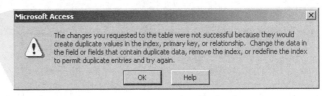

How to fix it

If you're trying to set a primary key and get a message about duplicate values, follow these steps:

1. Click OK to close the message box.

2. Select the primary key field and then click the Primary Key button on the toolbar to remove the primary key designation from the field.

3. Save changes to the table design and then click the View button to switch to Datasheet view.

4. Click in the column for the field you want to use as the primary key, and then click the Sort Ascending button to sort the records in that field.

> ### Tip
> You can also create a primary key using two fields instead of just one. With two fields, you might not have any duplicates in the combination. Simply select both fields in the table design and click the Primary Key button.

5. Locate the duplicate values and edit them so they're no longer the same.

6. Click the View button to switch to Design view.

7. Select the field you want to use as the primary key, and then click the Primary Key button. ▶

8. Click the Save button.

If you see a message indicating that a record contains a null value in the primary key field, follow these steps:

1. Click the Primary Key button to remove the primary key designation.

2. Click the Save button to save changes to the table design and then click the View button to switch to Datasheet view.

3. Click in the column for the field you want to use for the primary key and then click the Sort Ascending button on the toolbar to display the blank records at the top of the column.

4. Enter data in the records where the field is blank.

5. Click the View button to switch to Design view.

6. Select the field you want to use as the primary key and then click the Primary Key button.

7. Click the Save button.

> **Tip**
> An additional advantage to having a primary key field in the table is that the records in the datasheet appear sorted by the primary key value by default. Of course, you can still sort the records any way you want.

Do I need a primary key?

No, you don't have to choose a primary key for every new table. But Access tries to help by re-minding you when you haven't chosen one, and it even offers to create one for you. Although primary keys are not required, they are recommended. If you plan to use a table in a relationship with other tables, you need to specify a primary key field or at least a unique index.

Letting Access create a primary key field by adding a field to the table with the AutoNumber data type ensures that no two records will be the same, an important feature in a relational database. If you specify as the primary key one of the fields you added to the table to contain data, it's up to you to make sure you don't enter duplicate values in it.

I need to control errors in my data

Source of the problem

Humans, being what they are, make mistakes when entering data. Working with Access, you can try to prevent errors from being stored along with valid data in your database. After incorrect or invalid data is in place, it's hard to find and correct. It's a lot more productive to keep it out of your database in the first place.

What can you do ahead of time to help ensure data accuracy? If a field's values must lie within a range of values or must be one of a few specific items in a list of values, you can apply a validation rule that limits the values entered in the field. The rule is enforced when you enter or edit data in that field, whether in Datasheet view, in a form, or with an append or update query. You can also display a message to indicate that invalid data has been entered.

Each table also has a validation rule property you can use to compare field values and set restrictions. A record validation rule is enforced when you move to another record. A table can have only one record validation rule so if you need more than one criterion, combine them in a single expression with *And* and *Or* operators.

How to fix it

To set up a field validation rule, follow these steps:

1. In the database window, select the table and then click Design.

2. In the table design window, on the General tab, select the field you want to apply the rule to and then click the Validation Rule property box.

3. Enter an expression that controls the values the field can contain. For example, if the value in a date field must be less than one year from today, type the expression **<Date()+365**. If the value in a number field must be greater than 0, type **>0**. The rule can also limit the field to a short list of values—for example, "Small" OR "Medium" OR "Large". Be sure to enclose any text in double quotation marks in the Validation Rule property box. ▶

4. Click in the Validation Text property box.

5. Type a message that explains what's wrong with a value when an incorrect value is entered. ▶

To set up a record validation rule for a table, do the following:

1. In the Database window, select the table and then click Design.

2. Click the Properties button on the toolbar.

3. In the Validation Rule property box on the General tab, enter the record validation rule expression. For example, you can type an expression that compares two amounts, such as **[SalesPrice]>[UnitPrice]**.

4. In the Validation Text property box, type explanatory text about the rule. ▶

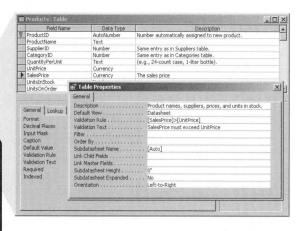

> ### Tip
>
> If you need help with an expression you want to use as a validation rule, click the Build (...) button next to the Validation Rule property box. The Expression Builder will help you.

More about data validation

If you add a field validation rule after data has been entered, Access offers to test the existing data against the rule. If you click No in response to the offer, you can still test the data later by switching to Table Design view and clicking Test Validation Rules on the Edit menu. ▶

If users are entering data in a form, you can spare them the anxiety of reading an error message by placing a label control next to the text box control that explains the requirements of the field data. This can save time and also create a user-friendly atmosphere for those who enter data.

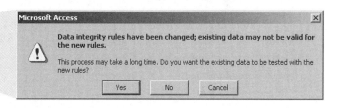

Too many records have the same value in the index

Source of the problem

You create indexes for tables in a database for the same reason authors create indexes for their books—so you can find things in a hurry. If one index entry in a book refers you to 100 different pages, it's not much help. The same goes for table indexes, which are used to help speed up queries, sorts, and searches. Table indexes build a list of values that is shorter than the number of records in the table and point to records with the specified values. If the field you set as an index for the table contains a lot of records with the same value, the index won't speed up your queries or other operations very much.

If this is the case, you probably need to modify the index to add another field. Multiple-field indexes help distinguish between records that have the same value in the first indexed field. By adding a second index field, you create smaller groups of records with the same combined-field index values. You can have up to 10 fields in a single index. If you don't want more than one record with the same value in the index, you can set either a field property or an index property to prevent duplicates.

The following steps show how to solve your indexing problems.

How to fix it

To add another field to an existing index, do the following:

1. Open the table in Design view.

2. On the toolbar, click the Indexes button.

3. In the Field Name drop-down list, select the name of the field you want to index first (ShipVia, in this example).

4. In the Index Name column, change the name of the new index from the field name to a more descriptive name (Route, in this example).

5. Click in the next empty row in the Field Name column and then select the second index field from the list (ShipRegion, in this example). ▶

6. Leave the Index Name row blank for the second field.

7. In the Index Properties area, set the Unique property to Yes if you want to prevent duplicate combined values.

8. Set the Ignore Nulls property to Yes if you want to keep records with null values in the index. ▶

Indexes: Orders		
Index Name	Field Name	Sort Order
EmployeeID	EmployeeID	Ascending
OrderDate	OrderDate	Ascending
PrimaryKey	OrderID	Ascending
ShippedDate	ShippedDate	Ascending
ShipPostalCode	ShipPostalCode	Ascending
Route	ShipVia	Ascending
	ShipRegion	Ascending

Index Properties

Primary	No
Unique	Yes
Ignore Nulls	Yes

If Yes, records with a Null value excluded from the index.

Timesaving hint

You can save time by creating fields that Access will index for you. All you have to do is give the field a name that ends with the characters *ID, key, code,* or *num*—and presto! The Indexed property for the field is automatically set to Yes (Duplicates OK).

For example, you can add a field named CompanyCode, and it will be automatically indexed. If you want to add other trailing characters to the list of auto-indexes, click Options on the Tools menu and then click the Tables/Queries tab. In the Table Design area, look at the list in the AutoIndex On Import/Create box. To further personalize your database design, you can add other character combinations to the list, separated by a semicolon. ▶

Tip

In the example, the index named Route will find order records shipped by each shipper and, within each shipper, by ShipRegion. Notice that the ShipVia Indexed property was changed to No in the table design window when the second field was added to the index.

Options

View	General	Edit/Find	Keyboard	Datasheet	Forms/Reports
Pages	Advanced	International	Spelling	Tables/Queries

Table design

Default field sizes
- Text: 50
- Number: Long Integer

Default field type: Text

AutoIndex on Import/Create: ID;key;code;num

Query design
- ☑ Show table names
- ☐ Output all fields
- ☑ Enable AutoJoin

Run permissions
- ○ Owner's
- ● User's

SQL Server Compatible Syntax (ANSI 92)
- ☐ This database
- ☐ Default for new databases

OK   Cancel   Apply

Tip

Although the Indexed Property topic in Access online help advises that you can't index memo, hyperlink, or OLE object fields, memo and hyperlink fields have an Indexed property and their names appear in the Field Name list in the Indexes dialog box.

I don't know which data types and properties to choose in a new table

Source of the problem

You carefully split your data into several tables for your new database, but the problem of choosing field data types and setting field and table properties still faces you. You need to consider several issues if you want to end up with an efficient, easy-to-use database. Proper selection of field data types and appropriate table and field properties is essential for smooth data management.

For example, should you index a field? When you index a table by a field, Access creates a list of values from the field along with pointers to their locations in the table. Indexes speed up searching and sorting significantly if there aren't too many different values. A table's primary key field is automatically indexed, but you can create additional indexes on one or more fields.

The following solution describes what data types to select for the fields in your tables and which fields to use in an index.

How to fix it

To decide what data type to choose for a field, keep the following in mind:

Choose this data type...	...for this type of data
Text	Values containing both letters and numbers. If you plan to store only numbers but don't expect to do any calculating, using the Text data type is often the best choice.
Memo	Variable-length text values. Memo fields can store more text than a Text field but are not very useful in sorting and filtering. You should use Memo fields sparingly.
Number	Numeric values you plan to sort on or use in calculations.

Choose this data type...	...for this type of data
Currency	Fields that will contain monetary values. In calculations, the Currency data type rounds off the results to two decimal places, which can help prevent errors resulting from the way Number fields truncate values.
AutoNumber	To create a primary key field that contains none of your actual data but will guarantee a unique value in every record. It's a good idea to place an AutoNumber field at the top of the field list in the table design.
Date/Time	Date and time values you plan to sort on or use to perform date arithmetic, such as computing the time between two dates.
Yes/No	If you simply want the equivalent of a check mark in the field.

Table properties and how to set them

To set table properties, open the table in Design view and then click the Properties button on the toolbar. The text you type in the Description property is displayed in the database window when you select the Details view. The Filter property sets the selection criteria that's saved with the table when you choose to save changes you made in the datasheet. The Order By property specifies the sort order that's saved with the table. ▶

Which fields to use for indexing

Here are some criteria for choosing which fields to index:

- Fields you expect to search in for specific values.

- Fields you expect to sort by.

- Fields you expect to use in a relationship with another table. This can speed up processing if the field is indexed.

> **Tip**
>
> Data-related field properties are discussed in "Data, setting field properties." The Indexed property is discussed in more detail earlier this chapter.

If you don't want duplicate values in the field, choose Yes (No Duplicates) in the Indexed property box in the table design window; otherwise, choose Yes (Duplicates OK). When you set a field's Indexed property to Yes, it's added to the list in the Indexes dialog box. Remember, if you expect the field to contain the same value in a lot of records, indexing won't help much.

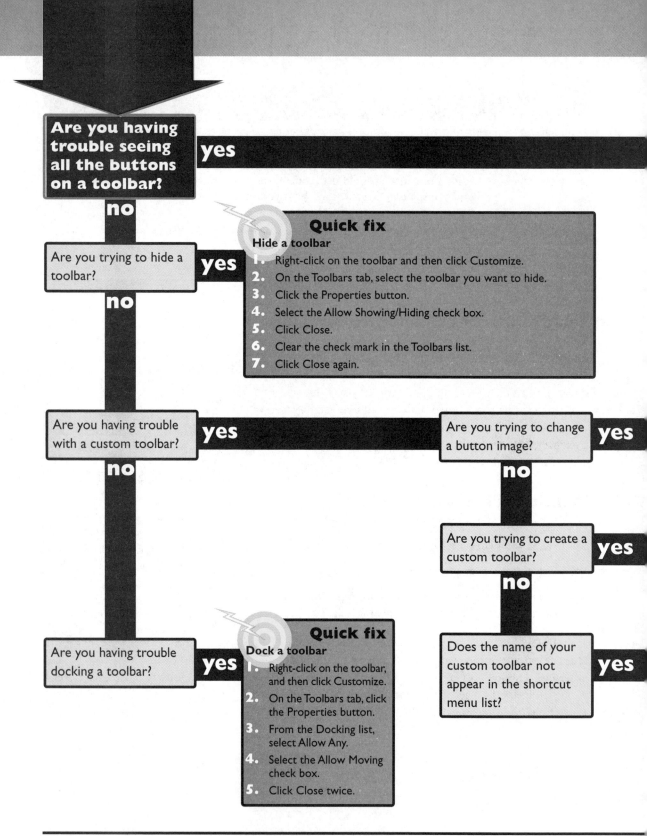

Are you having trouble seeing all the buttons on a toolbar?

yes

no

Are you trying to hide a toolbar?

yes

no

Quick fix

Hide a toolbar
1. Right-click on the toolbar and then click Customize.
2. On the Toolbars tab, select the toolbar you want to hide.
3. Click the Properties button.
4. Select the Allow Showing/Hiding check box.
5. Click Close.
6. Clear the check mark in the Toolbars list.
7. Click Close again.

Are you having trouble with a custom toolbar?

yes

no

Are you trying to change a button image?

yes

no

Are you trying to create a custom toolbar?

yes

no

Are you having trouble docking a toolbar?

yes

Quick fix

Dock a toolbar
1. Right-click on the toolbar, and then click Customize.
2. On the Toolbars tab, click the Properties button.
3. From the Docking list, select Allow Any.
4. Select the Allow Moving check box.
5. Click Close twice.

Does the name of your custom toolbar not appear in the shortcut menu list?

yes

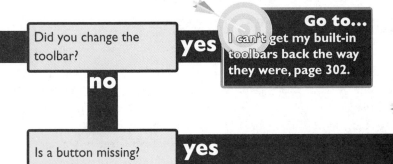

Did you change the toolbar?

yes — Go to... **I can't get my built-in toolbars back the way they were, page 302.**

no

Is a button missing?

yes — Go to... **Some of the built-in buttons aren't displayed, page 304.**

Go to... **When I paste an image on a button, it doesn't look right, page 308.**

Go to... **I can't create the custom toolbar I need, page 306.**

Quick fix

Toolbar name not in list If you don't see the name of your custom toolbar on the shortcut menu that appears when you right-click on a visible toolbar the Show On Toolbars Menu option might not be selected.

1. Right-click on an empty spot on a visible toolbar, and then click Customize on the shortcut menu.
2. Click the Toolbars tab.
3. In the list of toolbars, select your custom toolbar.
4. Click the Properties button.
5. Click the Show On Toolbars Menu option and then click the Close button.

If your solution isn't here, check this related chapter:

● Menus, page 170

Or see the general troubleshooting tips on page xv.

I can't get my built-in toolbars back the way they were

Source of the problem

Toolbars look so sturdy, it hardly seems possible that they can be drastically changed. But buttons can be removed or rearranged, and the icon on a button can be different from the one you remember and have grown accustomed to. You might even see only one toolbar where you used to see two, or a button might trigger an action you don't expect. Maybe you used a new icon, or perhaps you replaced an icon image with text. Now you want all those buttons back the way they were.

If you or someone else changed a toolbar, you have three paths of reclamation to consider:

- Resetting the entire original toolbar, including all its buttons. When you reset the entire toolbar, all the buttons revert to their original behavior so that they perform the same action when you click them as they did when Microsoft Access was first installed. The buttons appear in their original positions on the toolbar and display their original icons.

- Resetting individual buttons that are on a toolbar or that appear in a drop-down list similar to a shortcut menu.

- Restoring the default toolbar settings that were in effect when you first installed Access, including settings such as allowing docking, moving, resizing, and showing/hiding. Restoration is not available for custom toolbars because they have no original properties, only the ones you created.

The following steps show you some ways to fix these problems.

How to fix it

To reset a toolbar to its original structure and behavior, follow these steps:

1. On the View menu, point to Toolbars and then click Customize.

2. Click the Toolbars tab, and select the name of the toolbar you want to reset.

3. Click Reset and then click OK to confirm the change. ▶

4. Click Close or keep the Customize box open to reset more toolbars.

> **Microsoft Access** ✕
>
> ⚠ Are you sure you want to reset the changes made to the 'Form Design' toolbar?
>
> OK   Cancel

To reset individual buttons on a built-in toolbar, follow the steps 1 and 2 above and then do the following:

1. To reset all aspects of the button, right-click the button on the toolbar and then click Reset on the shortcut menu. ▶

2. If you just want to restore the button image, right-click the button and then click Reset Button Image on the shortcut menu.

3. Click Close in the Customize dialog box.

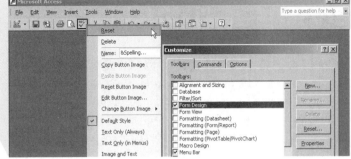

To reset a button that is part of a drop-down list, do the following:

1. On the View menu, point to Toolbars and then click Customize.

2. Click the Toolbars tab and then select the toolbar from the Toolbars list.

3. Click the down arrow next to the button on the toolbar that contains the button you want to reset.

4. Right-click the button, and then click Reset or Reset Button Image on the shortcut menu. ▶

5. In the Customize dialog box, click Close.

If you want to restore the default properties and options of a toolbar, do the following:

1. On the View menu, point to Toolbars and then click Customize. In the Customize dialog box, click the Properties button.

2. From the Selected Toolbar list, select the name of the toolbar whose properties you want to restore. ▶

3. Click the Restore Defaults button and then click Yes to confirm the action.

4. If you want to restore other toolbars, select each one from the list and click Restore Defaults again.

5. Click Close in the Toolbar Properties dialog box and then click Close in the Customize dialog box.

Some of the built-in buttons aren't displayed

Source of the problem

One of your friendly old toolbars suddenly looks shorter than it used to. Some of its buttons are missing or maybe it's gone altogether. It might be that you or someone else changed the startup settings to keep the toolbars from appearing. Or it could be that this was one of those times when Access tried to help you save display space by placing two toolbars together in the same row at the top of the window. There might not be room for all the buttons on the combined toolbars to be shown on your screen. You'll see the Toolbar Options button (>> with a down arrow) at the right end of the toolbar if this is the case. You will also see the Toolbar Options button if there's not enough room to display all the buttons on a single toolbar. Perhaps you added buttons to the toolbar or resized the Access window to a narrower width. A button might also be missing because it's been removed or moved to another toolbar. You can easily move it back or add a copy of the button to the original toolbar.

The following steps show how to deal with each of these possibilities.

> **Tip**
>
> If you're reluctant to change the startup options but still want to see all the built-in toolbars, hold down the Shift key when you open the database.

How to fix it

To change your startup settings so that toolbars appear, follow these steps:

1. On the Tools menu, click Startup.

2. Select the Allow Built-in Toolbars check box to restore a complete set of built-in toolbars. Click OK. ▶

3. Close and reopen the database to activate the changes.

If some of your buttons are missing, choose the appropriate action from this list:

1. If you see the Toolbar Options button, click the down arrow to have access to the missing buttons. ▶

---

2. If you have two toolbars in the same row, click the vertical bar at the left end of the second toolbar (the bar will appear between the toolbars sharing the row) and drag the toolbar down to its own row.

3. If the Access window is too narrow, widen it or use the Toolbar Options button to see the other buttons.

4. If the toolbar is floating (that is, it is not tucked against one edge of the window), you can drag one of the edges to resize it so all the buttons are visible.

If you want to add a missing button back to a built-in toolbar, follow these steps:

1. Click the Toolbar Options down arrow, and point to Add Or Remove Buttons.

2. Point to the name of the toolbar to display a list of all the built-in buttons that belong on that toolbar. ▶

3. Check each of the buttons you want to restore to the toolbar. You can also use this list to remove buttons from the toolbar.

4. Click anywhere outside the button list to return to your database object.

Keeping buttons the way you want

After you struggle to get your built-in toolbars customized just the way you want them, you might not want anyone else adding more buttons or even restoring the toolbar to its original plain vanilla style. To prevent changes to a toolbar after you restore or customize it to your requirements, click Toolbars on the View menu and then click Customize. In the Customize dialog box, select the built-in toolbar on the Toolbars tab and then click the Properties button. Clear the Allow Customizing check box and then click Close in the dialog boxes.

Tip

If you can't move or resize a toolbar, one of the Allow check boxes in the Toolbar Properties dialog box might be cleared. Click the Properties button on the Toolbars tab of the Customize dialog box, and check the properties you need.

Tip

You can also use the Customize dialog box to drag commands to your toolbars. But when using the Customize dialog box, keep in mind that not all buttons are found in the most logical category. For example, the Spelling button falls under Records rather than Edit. Often a button is related to the menu where a corresponding menu command can be found—but not with Spelling, which is found on the Tools menu.

I can't create the custom toolbar I need

Source of the problem

You have some really great ideas about creating a friendly and useful customized workplace for your database. You especially want some customized toolbars containing just the buttons you need, looking just the way they should. But something gets in the way, and you can't get the toolbar the way you want. You can run into problems trying to customize a toolbar for a couple of reasons:

- In the Startup dialog box, the Allow Toolbar/Menu Changes check box isn't selected. That means you aren't allowed to change any toolbar, menu bar, or shortcut menu, whether it's a built-in one or a custom one you created earlier. In fact, if this check box is cleared, the Customize dialog box isn't even available to you.

- The Allow Customizing check box for the specific toolbar you want to work on is cleared. This means you can't make any changes to the toolbar even if you created it in the first place.

How to fix it

To set the startup options so you can customize toolbars in a database, follow these steps:

1. Open the database you're working with.

2. On the Tools menu, click Startup.

3. In the Startup dialog box, select the Allow Toolbar/Menu Changes check box and then click OK. ▶

4. Close and reopen the database to apply the change.

To make sure you can customize an individual toolbar, follow these steps:

1. With the toolbar displayed, right-click the toolbar and then click Customize on the shortcut menu.

2. On the Toolbars tab, click Properties.

3. From the Selected Toolbars list, select the name of the toolbar you want to customize.

4. Select the Allow Customizing check box. ▶

5. Click Close in the Toolbar Properties dialog box and again in the Customize dialog box.

Tip

Even if the Allow Toolbar/Menu Changes check box is cleared, you can still move, size, and dock the toolbar unless you have forbidden these actions with the individual toolbar's Allow Moving, Allow Resizing, and Docking property settings.

Tip

After you make changes to the toolbar, you might want to clear the Allow Customizing check box again to keep others from making more changes.

Why doesn't the toolbar go away?

When you display a toolbar that doesn't usually appear during your current activity, it remains on the screen until you manually remove it. This goes for built-in toolbars as well as your own custom toolbars. If you haven't attached the toolbar to a form, report, or other database object and you open it by selecting it from the Toolbars shortcut menu, you must get rid of it yourself. Right-click the toolbar, and then clear the check box next to the toolbar name in the shortcut menu.

It works the other way, too. If you close a toolbar in a window where it normally appears, it doesn't show up when you restart the associated activity. To see the toolbar, you have to select it from the list of toolbars that you want to display.

Forming a toolbar

If you created a custom toolbar that contains just the activities you need for working in a specific form, you can set a form property that replaces the default toolbar with your own. To display a custom toolbar when a form opens, open the form in Design view, click the Properties button on the toolbar, and then click the Other tab. Click the down arrow next to the Toolbar property box and then select the custom toolbar name from the list. The selected toolbar replaces the default built-in toolbar that normally appears when you open a form in Form view. ▶

When I paste an image on a button, it doesn't look right

Source of the problem

The image you place on a custom toolbar button is supposed to give you a clue about what will happen when you click the button. Unfortunately, when you're working with a special picture file that you want to show on the button, you can often run into problems getting the button to look the way you want. If you imported an image from another source, such as clip art or a scanned drawing, the graphic image might be a different size than the built-in images that fit perfectly on the standard buttons. Be sure to adjust the scale of the image before importing it to the toolbar button. Enlarging or reducing an imported image after placing it on the button can produce blurred results.

The images that come with Access are all sized properly at 16x16 pixels. If you start with one of them and use the Button Editor to create a custom image, the image should work just fine. Here are some solutions for making custom toolbar buttons appear the way you want.

How to fix it

To replace a button image with one of the other images that comes with Access, do the following:

1. Right-click on the toolbar, and then click Customize on the shortcut menu.

2. Right-click the button you want to change and then point to Change Button Image on the shortcut menu. ▶

3. In the image palette, click the new image you want to use and then click Close in the Customize dialog box.

Tip

If you used a built-in command such as Print as the basis for the custom button, when you paste the new image on this copy of the button, the image will appear on the button in all the toolbars that include that button. All your Print buttons will show the new image.

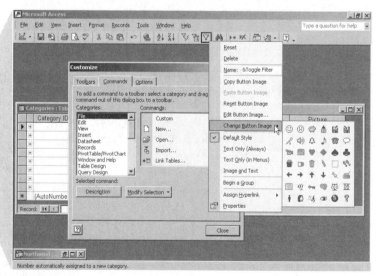

To edit one of the toolbar button images that comes with Access, use the Button Editor:

1. Right-click the toolbar that contains the button you want to edit, and then click Customize.

2. Right-click the button with the image you want to change and then click Edit Button Image.

3. In the Button Editor, click the color you want in the color palette.

4. Use the pointer to click a pixel you want to recolor and drag over other pixels to change their color as well. Click and drag over the pixels again to remove the color if you change your mind. The preview pane shows what the button will look like on the toolbar. ▶

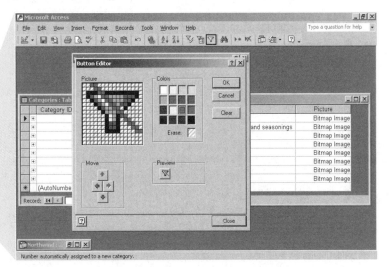

5. To erase pixels, click the Erase box and then click and drag the mouse pointer over all the pixels you want to get rid of. Click a color to turn erasing off.

6. Click Clear to start over, or click OK to keep the changes and return to the Customize dialog box. Click Cancel to leave the button with its original image.

If you want to use your own bitmap image, do the following:

1. Use a graphics program such as Microsoft Paint to adjust the size of the button to 16x16 pixels before importing it.

2. After editing the image, save the file in the graphics program and then copy the image to the Clipboard.

3. Return to Access, right-click the toolbar, and click Customize on the shortcut menu.

4. Right-click the button on the toolbar that you want to add the image to and then click Paste Button Image.

> **Tip**
>
> Don't forget that the button's style property must be set to allow the image to be displayed. Right-click the button and select either Default Style or Image And Text to show an image on the button.

Glossary

action query A type of query that copies or changes the values in your data. Action queries include append and make-table queries, which copy existing data, and update and delete queries, which change or delete existing data.

ActiveX control An object similar to a built-in Access control that you can add to a form for user interaction with the application.

add-ins Tools included with Access that make repetitive tasks easier, help automate processes, or add other features. Wizards, builders, and menus are examples of add-ins provided by Access.

append The process of adding records after the existing records in a table.

AutoForm A form that displays all the fields and records in the underlying table or query. You have a choice of five AutoForm layouts.

AutoNumber field A field in a table that uniquely numbers each record automatically as it is added to the table.

AutoReport A report that contains all the fields and records in the underlying table or query. You have a choice of two AutoReport layouts.

backward compatibility The ability of a newer version of an application to support features from earlier versions.

bitmap file A frequently used image file format. Bitmap files are usually saved with the file extension .bmp.

bound control A control that displays the values from a specific field in the table or query that a form or report is based on.

byte A numeric data type used to hold small positive integers ranging from 0 to 255.

calculated field A field defined in a query that displays the result of calculations on your data. Access updates the value in the calculated field whenever a value in the calculation changes.

cascade delete In table relationships with referential integrity enforced, the cascade delete option deletes all related records in the child table or tables when a record in the primary table is deleted.

cascade update In table relationships with referential integrity enforced, the cascade update option automatically changes related records in the child table or tables when the primary key field in a record in the primary table is changed.

case-sensitive The distinction between uppercase and lowercase letters. A case-sensitive search, for example, finds only text that is an exact match of uppercase and lowercase letters.

child table The table on the "many" side of a one-to-many relationship.

class module Class modules contain event procedures, which can be used to control how a form or report behaves. Class modules are associated with a particular form or report.

combo box A control that acts like a list box and a text box combined. You can click the arrow and select a value from the drop-down list, and usually you can type a field value in the box.

concatenation The act of merging two values together, for example "FirstName" & "LastName". The concatenation operator is the ampersand (&).

conditional formatting Formatting that's applied according to the value in a field or through a comparison of the values in other fields in a record.

Continuous Form view A view of data in a form in which the form displays as many records as will fit on the screen. Single form view displays data from only one record.

control A graphical object (such as a text box, list box, or label) that you place on a form or report in order to display data, enhance the appearance of the form or report, or provide user interaction.

Control Source The property that specifies what data appears in a control. The value of the property can be a field name or an expression.

criteria Used in a query or filter, criteria are a set of conditions that limit the results of the query or filter to a specific set of records.

Criteria row The row in the query design grid in which you enter record selection criteria for each field or expression.

crosstab query A type of query that calculates summary totals of values in rows and columns and displays the results down the right side and across the bottom of the datasheet.

data type The designation of what type of data will be entered and stored in a field. Examples of data types are text, number, currency, and date/time.

datasheet An arrangement of data in a tabular view, with records displayed in rows and fields displayed in columns. You can view the data in a table, form, or query in datasheet view.

docking Repositioning a menu bar, a toolbar, or the toolbox to the top, bottom, or side of the Access window.

dynamic link library (DLL) A program containing functions and other program elements that are used by an application such as Access while it runs (that is, dynamically).

embed To insert a copy of an object (such as an image file) that was created in a different application in a form or report. Embedded objects are not updated in the form or report when they are changed in their original application.
See also **link (objects)**.

event   An action that is recognized by an object (such as a form). You can define a response to an event (such as a user clicking a button) by setting an event property that will run a macro, for example.

expression   An expression can be used to set properties, to specify criteria or define calculated fields in queries, or to set conditions in macros. Expressions contain a combination of operators, literal values, and functions, together with the names of the fields, controls, and properties that the expression will affect.

field   An element in a table that contains a specific item of information. Fields in a table about employees might include FirstName, LastName, and Address; in a table about products, fields might include Size, Color, and Price.

filter   A set of conditions (criteria) that is used to select specific records or to sort records.

format   A setting that specifies how text, number, and date/time values are displayed and printed.

function   A built-in or user-defined procedure used in an expression or a program to return a value. For example, the Date function returns the current system date.

grouping   A means of organizing data in a query or report in order to summarize the data and perform calculations. The data might be organized by field values, a range of values, or by category.

hyperlink   Text or an image that "jumps" to other information when clicked. The information can be in the current or in another database, a location on your computer, or a site or page on the Internet or an intranet.

import   The process of copying data such as a text file, spreadsheet, or database table from an external source into an Access table and saving it in Access format.

index   A feature that speeds up searching and sorting in a table. Indexes are stored and maintained in smaller files for quick data retrieval.

inner join   A join that selects records from two tables only if the joined fields have matching values. This is the default join type in Access.

join   The association that specifies how the data in a field in one table or query is related to a field of the same data type in another table or query. In Access, the default join is an inner join, which returns records when the joined fields have matching values. An outer join returns all records from one table and matching records from another.

join line   The line drawn between related tables in a query or in the Relationships window that indicates the existence and type of relationship.

keyboard shortcut   A key or key combination that, when pressed, provides quick access to frequently used commands or actions.

Layout Preview   A report preview window that provides a complete view of the basic layout of a report but may not include all the data in the report. Layout Preview is available only from the report Design view.

legend A box in a chart that identifies the table data used as the series in the chart. The legend usually shows the column headings from the underlying table or query.

link (objects) A dynamic connection between an object (such as an image or a spreadsheet) created in one application and used in another application. When the linked object is updated or changed in its original application, those changes are reflected in the application using it.

list box A control used on a form or report that provides a list of values from which users can choose. A list box can be used in a form or datasheet to enter field values or in a dialog box to make choices.

literal value A number, text string, or date value that Access uses exactly as it appears.

lookup field A field in one table that displays data from a different table or query or from a fixed set of values. When you select a value from the list, it is stored in the lookup field.

macro An action or set of actions that you can use to automate tasks with a single command, such as clicking a button on a form.

module A set of program elements (declarations, statements, and procedures) stored together as one named unit.

moving handle The black square in the upper-left corner of a control border that you can use to drag the control to a different position in the form or report design.

Name AutoCorrect A feature that automatically updates references to a control, field, query, table, form, or report when the control, field, query, or other object is renamed.

navigation buttons The buttons displayed in a row at the bottom of a form that are used to move between records. The current record number is also displayed with the buttons.

null The lack of a value in a field because the value is either missing or unknown. A null state can be used as a criterion to find records with missing data. *See also* **zero-length string.**

object In an Access database, objects include tables, queries, forms, reports, data access pages, macros, and modules. A chart, drawing, or spreadsheet created in another application is often also referred to as an object.

OLE (object linking and embedding) A feature through which an object such as a chart, graph, or spreadsheet that is created in one Windows application can be used (linked or embedded) in another application.

OLE object A spreadsheet, document, image, or other object type that is embedded in or linked to an Access table.

option button A control that give users a choice among different selections. An option button is often used as part of an option group. It can also be used for fields with the Yes/No data type.

option group A control that contains a set of check boxes, option buttons, or toggle buttons representing a set of mutually exclusive options. An option group may be bound to a field to provide the values for the controls it contains.

outer join   A type of join in which all records from one table are included in the query results even if no matching values are found in the other table. Records from the second table are included only if the join field matches the value in the first table.

parameter prompt   A dialog box that appears when you run a parameter query. A user enters information (for example, a date) in the dialog box, and this information is used to select specific records.

parameter query   A type of select query for which the user is required to enter criteria before the query is run.

parent table   The table on the "one" side of a one-to-many relationship.

primary key   One or more fields whose value or combined values uniquely identify each record in a table.

property   A named characteristic of a control, field, or database object that defines its appearance (such as size , color, or screen location) or an aspect of its behavior (such as whether it can be reached by clicking the Tab key).

query   A database object used to select or otherwise work with a specific set of records. A query can be used as the source of data for a form or report.

record   A collection of data about a particular item, such as a person, place, or thing.

Record Source   A property that specifies the table or query that includes the data used in a form, report, or data access page.

referential integrity   Rules that preserve the relationships defined between tables. When referential integrity is enforced, you cannot add records to a related table when the primary table contains no associated record or change values in the primary table that would create orphan records in the related table. You also cannot delete records from the primary table when a related table still contains matching records.

report snapshot   A file (named with the .snp extension) containing a high-fidelity copy of each page of a report. A report snapshot preserves the report's layout, graphics, and other embedded objects and is suitable for sending via e-mail.

reset   In relation to menus and toolbars, the process of returning a built-in menu or toolbar to its original property settings, including size, screen location, and hiding or showing.

restore   In relation to menus and toolbars, the process of returning a built-in menu or toolbar to its original condition, with all the commands and buttons.

Row Source   A property that specifies which table or query provides the values for a control. This property applies to lookup table fields, combo boxes, list boxes, unbound objects frames, and chart controls.

self-join   A type of join in which records from the same table are combined if the joined fields contain matching values. For example, a self-join can match employees with their managers in a table that contains all the employees for a company or organization.

shortcut key   A function key or a key combination—such as F5 (which opens the

File menu) or Ctrl+A (Select All)—that carries out a menu command.

shortcut menu   A menu that appears when you right-click an object.

sizing handle   One of the small squares displayed around the edge of a control when the control is selected. You can click and drag a handle to resize the control.

SQL (Structured Query Language)   A set of commands that can be used in queries. Details of the query operation are specified by using SQL commands such as SELECT, UPDATE, or DELETE, and clauses such as WHERE and ORDER BY.

subdatasheet   A means of viewing related data in Datasheet view in a table, query, form, or subform.

subform   A form contained within another form or a report. A subform is often used to display data from related tables in a single form or report.

subreport   A report contained within another report. A subreport is often used to display data from related tables in a single report.

tab control   A form control that displays multiple tabbed pages on which you can place other controls. A tab control is often used to group related information or options.

tab order   The sequence in which the cursor moves from one field or control in a form to another when you press the Tab key.

toolbox   The toolbar that contains buttons you use in Design view to place controls on a form, report, or data access page. The toolbox includes buttons for all types of controls (text boxes, list boxes, and so on) and the Control Wizards button.

Total row   The row in a query design grid in which you can select an aggregate function that you want to use to perform a calculation on a field or expression.

unbound control   A control that is not tied to a field in the underlying record source.

validation rule   A rule that specifies limits or conditions on the values that can be entered in one or more fields. You can set a validation rule for a single field or for a record.

Visual Basic   The Microsoft programming language that you can use to automate and carry out actions in your Access databases.

wildcard character   Special characters that represent one or more characters in a search string or filter.

zero-length string   A text field value containing no characters. A zero-length string is used to indicate that the field has no value. A zero-length string is entered by pressing the space bar or by typing two double quotation marks with no space between (""). *See also* **null.**

Zoom box   A window in which you can enter or view an expression or text that is too long to view easily in the space available in a control's property dialog box, for example. Press Shift+F2 to open the Zoom box.

Glossary

Quick fix index

Quick fix index

Index

& (ampersand) symbol, 47, 100
* (asterisk) symbol
  append queries and, 196–97
  date searches, 228
  grouped record fields, 205
  overview of, 229
  sorting with, 280
  text/memo fields, 47
  too many columns and, 242–43
@ (at) sign, 46–47, 162–63
\ (backslash) symbol, 47
" "(double quotation marks), 77, 100
= (equal) sign
  expressions and, 163
  queries and, 228–29
  wildcards/operators and, 225
#Error message, 26–27
! (exclamation mark) symbol, 47, 101, 229
> (Greater Than) operator, 29, 47
- (hyphen) wildcard, 229
∞ (infinity) sign, 253
< (Less Than) operator
  date searches, 228
  formatting and, 29
  overview of, 47
#Name? message, 33
+ (Plus) operator, 206–7
# (pound) sign
  date calculation, 100, 104–5
  overview of, 229
  tables, exporting, 93

[ ] (square brackets)
  controls and, 29
  field names and, 101
  queries and, 229
  wildcards/operators and, 73, 225
? (question mark) symbol, 229

"abc" symbol, 47
Access
  exporting data to Excel, 92–94
  Picture Builder, 18–19
  publishing reports, 90–91
Add Colon property, 32
address lists, 102–3
Advanced Filter/Sort command
  filters, saving as queries, 122–23
  operators for, 118–19
  overview of, 119
  records, returned by, 114–15
After Update property, 164–65
Alignment and Sizing toolbar, 60–61
ambiguous outer joins, 250–51
ampersand (&) symbol, 47, 100
And operator
  filtering and, 118–19
  query selection criteria, 227, 231, 232–33
  validation rules and, 294–95

Keep Together properties, 268

Label X property, 133
Label Y property, 133
labels
  data validation with, 295
  designing, 130, 133
  printing, 272–73, 276–77
  textboxes without, 32–33
Layout Wizard, 58–59
left outer joins, 251
legend labels, 6–7
legends, chart, 9
Less Than (<) **operator**
  date searches, 228
  formatting and, 29
  overview of, 47
libraries. See **DLLs (dynamic link libraries)**
Like, 226
Limit to List property, 142–43
Link Child Fields property boxes, 81, 148–49
Link Master Fields property boxes, 11, 81, 148–49
linking, 150–53. See also **tables, linked**
  defined, 189
  images, 184–85
  overview of, 150–51
  records, 151
  spreadsheets, 150
list boxes
  controls, formatting/placing, 61
  data entry, 142–43
  display, speeding up, 33
  rows, reordering, 24–25
Locate Web Page dialog box, 54–55

lookup fields
  filtering, 121
  sorting on, 246–47, 284–85
lookup lists, 247
LTrim function, labels, 273

macros, 160–69
  AutoKeys, 161
  "Can't find the macro" error message, 164–65
  converted, 168–69
  documenting, 160
  grouped, 165
  missing messages, 171
  MsgBox multiline messages and, 162–63
  overview of, 160–61
  SendKeys, 161
  SetValue, 166–67
  turning off warnings, 160
Mail Merge feature, blank labels, 272–73
Mail Merge Wizard dialog box, 97
make-table query
  error messages, 202–3
  linked table copies, 152–53
many-to-many relationships, 212–13
margins, report, 35
Medium Date format, 71
Memo data type, 298
memo fields
  sorting problems, 284–85
  table relationships, 255
  tables, exporting, 94
  zooming in on text, 75
memory, 40–41
Menu Bar property box, 176–77
menu bars
  hiding, 170
  menus or commands, missing, 174–75
  restoring defaults, 172–73

About the authors

Virginia Andersen saw her first computer in 1951, and she has been infatuated with them ever since. Grace Hopper, the inventor of the compiler concept, told her that there was a future to be found for women in "high-speed digital computers."

Virginia didn't start writing computer books until after she retired from her job as a computer systems analyst and programmer for the defense industry. During her years in that profession, she used computers for interesting projects, such as mapping the surface of the moon in preparation for the Apollo landing, detecting enemy submarines with computerized undersea surveillance, weapon system simulation, and a lot of system reliability mathematical modeling. During those years, she also taught mathematics, systems analysis, and computer science at several universities in southern California.

Becoming an author was a great step forward: she didn't have to wear power suits and nylons to the office anymore. Virginia has authored and contributed to more than 30 books about PC-based applications, mostly database management systems such as Microsoft Access, dBASE, and Paradox.

These days, Virginia and her husband, Jack, enjoy their home in southern California. Each summer, they load the computer and the cats into their trailer and head for the High Sierra. In between book assignments, they find time to hike, bird-watch, and fish for the famous Eagle Lake trout.

John Pierce has worked with Microsoft Access since version 1.0, when he helped convert the product's printed documentation to Windows Help files and built a simple database to track human resource information. John is a senior editor for Microsoft Press and has worked on books about Windows and Office, Microsoft Exchange, the Microsoft .NET Framework, and other Microsoft software and technologies. He lives in Seattle and Indianola, Washington.

The manuscript for this book was prepared and galleyed using Microsoft Word 2000 and Microsoft Word 2002. Pages were composed using Adobe PageMaker 6.52 for Windows, with text in ACaslon Regular and display type in Gill Sans. Composed pages were delivered to the printer as electronic prepress files.

Cover designer

Landor Associates

Interior graphic designer

James D. Kramer

Production services

nSight, Inc.

Project manager

Tempe Goodhue

Technical editor

Christopher M. Russo

Copy editor

Bernadette Murphy Bentley

Principal compositor

Patty Fagan

Proofreaders

Janice O'Leary, Rebecca Merz

Indexer

Jack Lewis

Target your problem and
fix it yourself—
fast!

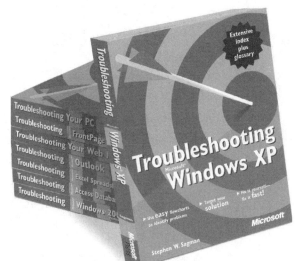

When you're stuck with a computer problem, you need answers right now. *Troubleshooting* books can help. They'll guide you to the source of the problem and show you how to solve it right away. Get ready solutions with clear, step-by-step instructions. Go to quick-access charts with *Top 20 Problems* and *Prevention Tips*. Find even more solutions with *Quick Fixes* and handy *Tips*. Walk through the remedy with plenty of screen shots. Find what you need with the extensive, easy-reference index. Get the answers you need to get back to business fast with *Troubleshooting* books.

Work smarter—
conquer your
software *from the inside out!*

Hey, you know your way around a desktop. Now dig into Office XP applications and the Windows XP operating system and *really* put your PC to work! These supremely organized software reference titles pack hundreds of timesaving solutions, troubleshooting tips and tricks, and handy workarounds in a concise, fast-answer format. They're all muscle and no fluff. All this comprehensive information goes deep into the nooks and crannies of each Office application and Windows XP feature. And every *Inside Out* includes a CD-ROM full of handy tools and utilities, sample files, links to related sites, and other help. Discover the best and fastest ways to perform everyday tasks, and challenge yourself to new levels of software mastery!

MICROSOFT WINDOWS® XP INSIDE OUT
ISBN 0-7356-1382-6

MICROSOFT® OFFICE XP INSIDE OUT
ISBN 0-7356-1277-3

MICROSOFT WORD VERSION 2002 INSIDE OUT
ISBN 0-7356-1278-1

MICROSOFT EXCEL VERSION 2002 INSIDE OUT
ISBN 0-7356-1281-1

MICROSOFT OUTLOOK® VERSION 2002 INSIDE OUT
ISBN 0-7356-1282-X

MICROSOFT ACCESS VERSION 2002 INSIDE OUT
ISBN 0-7356-1283-8

MICROSOFT FRONTPAGE® VERSION 2002 INSIDE OUT
ISBN 0-7356-1284-6

MICROSOFT VISIO® VERSION 2002 INSIDE OUT
ISBN 0-7356-1285-4

Microsoft Press® products are available worldwide wherever quality computer books are sold. For more information, contact your book or computer retailer, software reseller, or local Microsoft® Sales Office, or visit our Web site at microsoft.com/mspress. To locate your nearest source for Microsoft Press products, or to order directly, call 1-800-MSPRESS in the United States (in Canada, call 1-800-268-2222).

Prices and availability dates are subject to change.

Microsoft
microsoft.com/mspress

Self-paced
training that works
as hard as you do!

Information-packed STEP BY STEP courses are the most effective way to teach yourself how to complete tasks with the Microsoft® Windows® XP operating system and Microsoft® Office XP applications. Numbered steps and scenario-based lessons with practice files on CD-ROM make it easy to find your way while learning tasks and procedures. Work through every lesson or choose your own starting point—with STEP BY STEP'S modular design and straightforward writing style, *you* drive the instruction. And the books are constructed with lay-flat binding so you can follow the text with both hands at the keyboard. Select STEP BY STEP titles also provide complete, cost-effective preparation for the Microsoft Office User Specialist (MOUS) credential. It's an excellent way for you or your organization to take a giant step toward workplace productivity.

- **Microsoft Windows XP Step by Step**
  ISBN 0-7356-1383-4

- **Microsoft Office XP Step by Step**
  ISBN 0-7356-1294-3

- **Microsoft Word Version 2002 Step by Step**
  ISBN 0-7356-1295-1

- **Microsoft Excel Version 2002 Step by Step**
  ISBN 0-7356-1296-X

- **Microsoft PowerPoint® Version 2002 Step by Step**
  ISBN 0-7356-1297-8

- **Microsoft Outlook® Version 2002 Step by Step**
  ISBN 0-7356-1298-6

- **Microsoft FrontPage® Version 2002 Step by Step**
  ISBN 0-7356-1300-1

- **Microsoft Access Version 2002 Step by Step**
  ISBN 0-7356-1299-4

- **Microsoft Visio® Version 2002 Step by Step**
  ISBN 0-7356-1302-8

Microsoft

microsoft.com/mspress

Work anywhere, anytime

with the Microsoft guide to

mobile technology

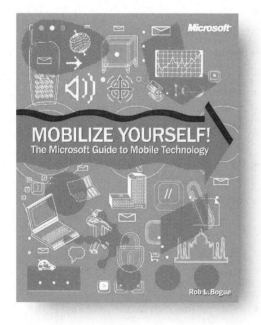

Okay. You're at the airport but your flight has been delayed. For four hours. No worries—you've got your laptop so you're ready to work. Or are you? Can you connect to the Internet? What about reliable battery power? Here's the answer: MOBILIZE YOURSELF! THE MICROSOFT GUIDE TO MOBILE TECHNOLOGY. This comprehensive guide explains how to maximize the mobility of the technology you have today. And it provides smart answers about the mobile technologies and services you might be considering. From PDAs to the wireless Web, this book packs the insights and solutions that keep you—and your technology—up and running when you're out and about.

microsoft.com/mspress

Work smarter,
add value,
and get results!

U.S.A. **$39.99**
Canada $57.99
ISBN: 0-7356-1434-2

For every business professional swamped with e-mail, drowning in paper, and wading through data, here are real-world solutions for turning all that information into business results! TAMING THE INFORMATION TSUNAMI demonstrates simple ways to change how you think about and use everyday technologies such as Microsoft® Office and Microsoft Internet Explorer—helping you match the right tool to the task, the right solution for your situation. Apply the skills, principles, and habits that empower you to work smarter and faster—and get out from under the deluge of too much work, too little time! Learn best practices for turning information into knowledge. Use Microsoft Office XP and other software to take control of your worklife. Work even smarter using the tools and eBook included on the CD-ROM!

microsoft.com/mspress

Get a **Free**
e-mail newsletter, updates,
special offers, links to related books,
and more when you
register on line!

Register your Microsoft Press® title on our Web site and you'll get a FREE subscription to our e-mail newsletter, *Microsoft Press Book Connections.* You'll find out about newly released and upcoming books and learning tools, online events, software downloads, special offers and coupons for Microsoft Press customers, and information about major Microsoft® product releases. You can also read useful additional information about all the titles we publish, such as detailed book descriptions, tables of contents and indexes, sample chapters, links to related books and book series, author biographies, and reviews by other customers.

Registration is easy. Just visit this Web page and fill in your information:

http://www.microsoft.com/mspress/register

Microsoft

- -